—THE—
WESTERN
TRADITION

Study Guide

THE
WESTERN
TRADITION

Study Guide, Semester II

Jay Boggis

 The Annenberg/CPB Project

MACMILLAN PUBLISHING COMPANY
NEW YORK

NOTE TO THE READER: Every attempt to avoid sexist language has been made. Nevertheless, terms such as "statesman," "clergyman," or the "rights of Man" have been retained to draw attention to sexual discrimination in the past or to avoid anachronism. In some cases, the use of neutral language might lead the reader to believe that women were participants in certain activities when, in fact, they were not.

Macmillan Publishing Company
866 Third Avenue, New York, New York 10022

Collier Macmillan Canada, Inc.

LIBRARY OF CONGRESS CATALOGING-IN-PUBLICATION DATA

WGBH Educational Foundation.
   The Western tradition : study guide, semester II.

   1. Civilization, Occidental — Study and teaching (Higher)   2. Europe — Civilization — Study and teaching (Higher)   I. Boggis, Jay.   II. Title.
CB245.W488   1989   909'.09821   87-34973
ISBN 0-02-426600-0

Printing: 4 5 6 7   Year: 2 3 4 5

This text has been developed for general use as the Semester II Study Guide for "The Western Tradition" television course. The television course consists of fifty-two half-hour public television programs, this Study Guide for Semester II, a Study Guide for Semester I, a Faculty Guide for each semester, and a choice of existing textbooks. The series was produced by WGBH-TV, Boston, Massachusetts and funded by the Annenberg/CPB Project.

For further information about available television courses, licenses, and off-air taping contact

> PBS Adult Learning Service
> 1320 Braddock Place
> Alexandria, VA 22314 – 1698
> 1-800-ALS-ALS-8

For information about purchasing videocassettes, off-air taping, and print materials contact

> Annenberg/CPB Project
> 2040 Alameda Padre Serra
> P.O. Box 4069
> Santa Barbara, CA 93140 – 4397
> 1 (800) – LEARNER

Film Credits

Thomas Agnew and Sons, Ltd.; Kenneth M. Newman, The Old Print Shop, NY; American Numismatic Society, NY; Soprintendenza Archeologica di Etruria Meridionale, Rome; Museo Archeologico, Foligno, Perugia; Museo Archeologico Nazionale/ Fotografia Foglia, Naples; Artothek/Bayerische Hypotheken-und Wechsel-Bank; Art Institute of Chicago; Musée d'Art et d'Histoire, Geneve/Art Resource, NY; Alinari/Art Resource; Borromeo/Art Resource; Breitenbach/Art Resource; Bridgeman/Art Resource; Giraudon/Art Resource; Haeseler/Art Resource; Kavaler/Art Resource; Marburg/Art Resource; Minca/Art Resource; Nimattalah/Art Resource; Sandak/Art Resource; Saskia/ Art Resource; Scala/Art Resource; SEF/Art Resource; Snark/Art Resource; Tzavores/Art Resource; Arxiu Mas, Barcelona; Ashmolean Museum, Oxford; Lucy Barber; Basketball Hall of Fame, Springfield, MA; Bayerische Nationalmuseum, Munich; Bayer, Staatsbibliothek, Munich; Musée des Beaux Arts de Dijon; Beth Hatefutsoth, the Nahum Goldmann Museum of the Jewish Diaspora; Biblioteca Ambrosiana, Milan; Bibliotheque Municipale, Dijon; Biblioteca Nacional, Madrid; Service Photographique Bibliotheque Nationale, Paris; Bodleian Library, Oxford; Lee Bolton Picture Library; Werner Braun, Jerusalem; Penny Brewer; British Library, London; Trustees of the British Museum, London; Brooklyn Museum, NY; Brown Brothers; Anne S. K. Brown Military Collection, Brown University Library; Professor Giorgio Buccellati, UCLA; Leslie Bussis; California State Library; Musée Calvet, Avignon; British Crown copyright reserved/Cambridge University, Department of Aerial Photography, Cambridge University Library; Museo Capitolino/Arte Fotografica, Rome; Cincinnati Art Museum; Musées Royaux d'Art et d'Histoire, Brussels; Langdon Clay; Cleveland Museum of Art; William L. Clements Library, University of Michigan, Ann Arbor; Abby Aldrich Rockefeller Folk Art Center, Williamsburg, VA; Civica Galleria d'Art Moderna, Milano; Library of Congress; Corning Museum of Glass, Corning, NY; Courtauld Institute Galleries, London (Courtauld Collection); Jane Crow; Culver Pictures, Inc.; Dean and Chapter Library, Durham; Jerrilynn Dodds/Charles Gifford; Andrew Dolkart; Donaldson, Lufkin & Jenrette, Collection of Americana; Dumbarton Oaks, Washington, DC; Dr. Louis Dupree, Duke University; Phil Eagleburger; Edinburgh University Library; Egyptian Tourist Authority; Ente Regionale di Sviluppo Agricolo, Avezzano; Mary Evans Picture Library, London; Field Museum of Natural History, Chicago; Fitzwilliam Museum, Cambridge; Harvard University Art Museums (Fogg Art Museum); Frans Halsmuseum, Haarlem; J. R. Freeman and Co., London; Freer Gallery of Art, Smithsonian Institute, Washington, DC; French Government Tourist Office; Robert Frerck, Odyssey Productions; Frick Collection, NY; Gascoyne Cecil Estates, Hatfield, England; Paula Gerson; Rijksmuseum Meermanno-Westreenianum, The Hague; Hamburg Kunsthalle/Fotostudios-Fotofachlabore, Hamburg; Harlan Hatcher Graduate Library, University of Michigan, Ann Arbor; Abraham Hay; University of Heidelberg; Andre Held CH – 1024 Ecublens; Herzog Anton Ulrich-Museum, Braunschweig; Hirmer-Verlag, Munich; Michael Holford, Essex; Hoxie; Israel Museum, Jerusalem; Italian Government Travel Office; Jerry Jacka, Phoenix/The Paul Dycke Research Foundation Collection; Roxby Publications Ltd., *The Making of Civilization*, p. 142/University of Jena; Joselyn Art Museum, Omaha, NE; Lichtbildwerkstatte, "Alpenland"/Kunsthistorischen Museum, Wein; Robert Llewellyn; Musée du Louvre, Paris; Jeremy Maas, London; Magyar Nemzeti Museum, Budapest; Mansell Collection, London; Musée d'Art et d'Histoire, Metz; The Metropolitan Museum of Art/Robert Lehman Collection, NY; Modern Museum of Art; Pierpont Morgan Library; Marion & Tony Morrison, Suffolk; Ann Munchow, Aachen; Westfälisches Landesmuseum fur Kunst und Kultergeschichte, Munster, W. Germany, Leihgabe des Westfälischen Kunstvereins; Museo Archeologico Nazionale, Cividale; National Gallery of Art, Washington, DC; Trustees, The National Gallery, London; The National Gallery of Canada, Ottowa; Scottish National Portrait Gallery, National Gallery of Scotland, Edinburgh; National Portrait Gallery, London; Reunion des Musées Nationaux, Paris; American Museum of Natural History, Department of Library Services, NY; New Brunswick Museum; Historic New Orleans Collection, Louisiana; Ny Carlsberg Glyptotek, Copenhagen; New York State Historical Association, Cooperstown; Olivetti, Milan; Oronoz, Madrid; Osterreichische Nationalbibliothek, Wein; Historical Society of Pennsylvania; University Museum, University of Pennsylvania; Portland Art Museum, Oregon; Princeton University, Department of Art and Archeology; Oliver Radford; University of Reading, England; Rheinisches Landesmuseum, Bonn; Fordererkreis des Rheinisches Landesmuseum, Trier; Rijksmuscum – Stichting, Amsterdam; Romisches – Germanisches, Museum der Stadt Koln; Royal Academy of Arts, London; Bibliotheque Royal Albert 1er, Brussels; Windsor Castle, Royal Library, © Her Majesty Queen Elizabeth II; Royal Ontario Museum, Toronto; Down House and Royal College of Surgeons of England; Harvard University Art Museums (Arthur M. Sackler Museum); Saskia Ltd./Glyptotech, Munich; Saint Louis Art Museum; Schlossmuseum, Gotha, E. Germany; Schweizerische Radio Und Ferngehgesellschaft, Bern; Schweiz-Landes Museum, Zurich; Annie Shaver-Crandall; Sherbourne Castle Estates; Ancient Art & Architecture Collection; Sovfoto, NY; Staatliche Museum, Berlin; Stadelsches Kunstinstitut und Stadtische Galerie, Frankfurt; Stadtbibliothek, Trier; Statens Historiska Museum, Stockholm; Stiftsbibliothek, St. Gall, Switzerland; Musée de la Ville de Strasbourg; Master and Fellows of Trinity College, Cambridge; Trinity College of the University of Dublin, Ireland/Green Studio; Bibliothek Trivulziana/Foto Saporeti, Milan; Office of Culture and Tourism of the Turkish Government; United States Naval Academy Museum; Vassar College Art Gallery; Biblioteca Apostolica, The Vatican Museums; Monumenti Musée e Gallerie Pontificie, The Vatican Museums; Museum of Virginia; Walters Art Gallery, Baltimore; Washington University Gallery of Art, St. Louis; Henry Francis du Pont Winterthur Museum; Jacquelyn Wong; Worcester Art Museum; *The Western Tradition;* Wurtembergisches Landesmuseum, Stuttgart; Yale Center for British Art, Paul Mellon Collection; Yale University Art Gallery

Acknowledgments

We would like to thank the Annenberg/CPB Project, whose support made this telecourse possible. We wish also to acknowledge Dr. Eugen Weber whose lectures were the foundation of the curriculum design for "The Western Tradition," and the invaluable assistance of the members of our advisory committee who directed the development of the print materials:

Eugene Brucker
University of California/Berkeley

Evelyn Edison
Piedmont Virginia Community College

Lon Gault
College of DuPage

Raymond Grew
University of Michigan

Donald Kagan
Yale University

Richard Means
Mountain View College

Theodore Rabb
Princeton University

Dr. Raymond Grew deserves special thanks for the many hours he spent making sure that our work reflected the goals of the course.

A special note of thanks goes to the producers and WGBH staff whose cooperation helped us meet deadlines: Leah Osterman, Jeanne Hartnett, Lisa Mirowitz, Tom Friedman, Fred Barzyk, Art Cohen, Scot Osterweil, Robin Gilbert, Susan Dreier, Lois d'Annunzio, Karen Silverstein, Andy Jablon, and Harlan Reiniger.

Jay Boggis
Author
Ann Strunk
Director of Print Projects
Carol Greenwald
Project Director
WGBH Educational Foundation
Boston, MA

Introduction

"The Western Tradition" is a public television series and a college-level television course based on the presentations of Eugen Weber, Joan Palevsky Professor of History at the University of California at Los Angeles, whose lectures span the range of western history from the ancient world to the present.

Through his writing and lectures, Professor Weber has earned the reputation of one who has successfully synthesized various approaches to the telling of history by focusing on political as well as social events. In fifty-two half-hour lectures Professor Weber integrates such diverse disciplines as religion, demography, government, and economics. He describes the leaders who shaped their worlds, as well as the larger forces that shaped them and their subjects. He relates the story of the unending struggle to create societies that provide order and justice, protection and fulfillment.

Professor Weber explains, in a broad historical sweep, how Europeans shaped and developed their environment to an extent greater than previous civilizations, and how, as a consequence, their influence spread beyond Europe's borders. His lectures illustrate (1) the relation between ideas, on the one hand, and conditions and experience on the other; (2) the link between social order and productive or military structures; (3) the effects of current interests and ideas on arts and architecture; and (4) the profound differences, subsisting into the twentieth century, between the values and living conditions of the elite and popular masses.

"The Western Tradition" is a two-semester telecourse consisting of fifty-two half-hour television programs, two student study guides and two faculty guides (Semesters I and II), and a choice of three currently available textbooks (*The Western Heritage,* Second Edition; *The Western Experience,* Fourth Edition; and *Western Civilizations,* Tenth Edition). This is the Study Guide for Semester II. A second Study Guide is available for Semester I.

"The Western Tradition" is produced by WGBH-TV, in Boston, Massachusetts, and is close-captioned for the hearing impaired.

Contents

The Telecourse

"The Western Tradition" is a two-semester television course consisting of the following components:

- Fifty-two half-hour television programs:
    Semester I — Programs 1–26
    Semester II— Programs 27–52
- Two student study guides (Semesters I and II)
- A textbook (assigned by the instructor)
- Two faculty guides (Semesters I and II)

THE TELEVISION PROGRAMS

The fifty-two television programs of "The Western Tradition" are grouped into twenty-six units with two programs per unit. Each week students are assigned one unit, or two programs, to view. The twenty-six televised units that comprise the series include the following topics of study.

Semester I

- Unit One
    Program 1: The Dawn of History
    Program 2: The Ancient Egyptians

Professor Weber traces the evolution of the human race, describes the origins of agriculture, and concludes with a discussion of one of the earliest civilizations.

- Unit Two
    Program 3: Mesopotamia
    Program 4: From Bronze to Iron

Professor Weber describes the Mesopotamian culture and argues that, in many respects, western Europe owes even more to ancient Mesopotamia than to Egypt.

- Unit Three
    Program 5: The Rise of Greek Civilization
    Program 6: Greek Thought

This unit examines the growth of Greek civilization and stresses the deep connection between Greek philosophy and Greek political institutions.

- Unit Four
    Program 7: Alexander the Great
    Program 8: The Hellenistic Age

Greek culture establishes itself throughout the eastern Mediterranean world as the successors of Alexander the Great establish empires of their own.

- Unit Five
    Program 9: The Rise of Rome
    Program 10: The Roman Empire

Rome rises from the obscurity of a small city in Italy to establish an empire that becomes one of the great shaping forces of the western tradition.

- Unit Six
    Program 11: Early Christianity
    Program 12: The Rise of the Church

Professor Weber examines the growth of Christianity and the early influence of the church in the midst of a hostile empire.

- Unit Seven
    Program 13: The Decline of Rome
    Program 14: The Fall of Rome

The Roman Empire is battered from without by a series of barbarian invasions and from within by moral decay. With the fall of Rome, the church and the barbarian kingdoms become heir to the Western Empire.

- Unit Eight
    Program 15: The Byzantine Empire
    Program 16: The Fall of Byzantium

Following the fall of Rome, the Byzantine Empire, based in Constantinople, becomes the stronghold of culture from Egypt, Greece, and Rome. The empire preserves and enriches the heritage of the ancient world throughout the eastern Mediterranean.

- Unit Nine
    Program 17: The Dark Ages
    Program 18: The Age of Charlemagne

A new political and economic order forms in the centuries after the fall of the Western Empire.

- Unit Ten
    Program 19: The Middle Ages
    Program 20: The Feudal Order

By the year 1000 Europe stands firm against outside invaders. Professor Weber describes what society was like in the early Middle Ages and the feudal power structure of the aristocracy, peasants, and clergy.

- Unit Eleven
    Program 21: Common Life in the Middle Ages
    Program 22: Cities and Cathedrals

Professor Weber explores the often harsh realities of daily life in the Middle Ages. However, this is also an age when city life revives and European culture blossoms. The period is characterized by the growth of trade and the building of great churches.

- Unit Twelve
    Program 23: The Late Middle Ages
    Program 24: The National Monarchies

By the late fifteenth century the rulers of many states are centralizing power within their own domains. Professor Weber describes important religious and political thought at the time and the expansion of great states.

- Unit Thirteen
    Program 25: The Renaissance and the Age of Discovery
    Program 26: The Renaissance and the New World

Professor Weber argues that the great European explorers shared the Renaissance spirit that appeared in the works of artists, scholars, and writers of the period.

Semester II

- Unit Fourteen
    Program 27: The Reformation
    Program 28: The Rise of the Middle Class

The Protestant Reformation arises as many Europeans, particularly in cities, look for new forms of piety and worship.

- Unit Fifteen
    Program 29: The Wars of Religion
    Program 30: The Rise of Trading Cities

Trade begins to transform European politics and economics. At the same time much of Europe is devastated by wars between Protestants and Catholics.

- Unit Sixteen
    Program 31: The Age of Absolutism
    Program 32: Absolutism and the Social Contract

Some rulers, especially in France, claim they are answerable to no earthly authority. At the same time, in England, some political theorists argue that authority depends on the consent of the governed.

- Unit Seventeen
    Program 33: The Enlightened Despots
    Program 34: The Enlightenment

In western Europe philosophers argue that the dignity of man can best be raised through practical knowledge and reforms.

- Unit Eighteen
    Program 35: The Enlightenment and Society
    Program 36: The Modern Philosophers

At this time many writers think of themselves as social reformers, actively working to change society.

- Unit Nineteen
    Program 37: The American Revolution
    Program 38: The American Republic

The American Revolution is examined as a test case of Enlightenment ideals.

- Unit Twenty
    Program 39: The Death of the Old Regime
    Program 40: The French Revolution

As the kingdom of France collapses, the new revolutionary state becomes an ideal for some Europeans and a terror for others.

- Unit Twenty-One
    Program 41: The Industrial Revolution
    Program 42: The Industrial World

New sources of power and techniques of production begin the age of industrial expansion.

- Unit Twenty-Two
    Program 43: Revolution and the Romantics
    Program 44: The Age of the Nation-States

By the early nineteenth century many subject peoples in the empires of central and eastern Europe aspire to establish independent countries.

- Unit Twenty-Three
    Program 45: A New Public
    Program 46: Fin de Siècle

By the late nineteenth century the productivity of the Industrial Revolution is raising standards of living throughout Europe and North America. Development of mass communication and culture becomes an important force in modern society.

- Unit Twenty-Four
    Program 47: The First World War and the Rise of Fascism
    Program 48: The Second World War

Wars and revolution arise from the unresolved conflicts of the previous century: class struggle, commercial and colonial rivalries, and struggles for national sovereignty.

- Unit Twenty-Five
    Program 49: The Cold War
    Program 50: Europe and the Third World

The United States and the Soviet Union, the two great victors of the Second World War, now dominate Europe. In the Third World poor countries try to develop in the midst of superpower rivalries and competition from industrialized nations.

- Unit Twenty-Six
    Program 51: The Technological Revolution
    Program 52: Toward the Future

The last unit emphasizes the speed with which modern life has changed and considers the future of Western civilization.

STUDENT STUDY GUIDES

The student study guides—Semesters I and II—are designed to help identify and achieve objectives on a weekly basis, to integrate the television programs with textbook reading assignments, and to identify and follow the themes of the course.

The Semester II Study Guide contains the lessons for Units Fourteen through Twenty-six and comprises the second part of the course. The Semester I Study Guide contains the lessons for Units One through Thirteen, the units in the first semester of the course.

Each unit in the Study Guide corresponds to two, half-hour television programs per week. For example, during the first week of Semester II students view Programs 27 and 28—"The Reformation" and "The Rise of the Middle Class"—and complete the corresponding activities for Unit Fourteen in the Study Guide. The textbook reading assignments for each unit are also given in the Study Guide.

Further, each unit in the Study Guide contains the following sections:

- *Learning Objectives:* Listed are the essential issues students should understand after finishing the unit. The objectives also synthesize the goals of the textbook readings and television programs.
- *Overview:* The overview outlines each television program, emphasizing Professor Weber's special lines of argument.
- *Key to the Images:* Additional information about the images that appear in each program is given here.
- *Focus Questions:* The focus questions highlight themes that students should watch for in each television program. They point out issues about which students should take notes.
- *In Context:* The in-context section sets each unit *in context* by raising related issues in earlier or later units.
- *Textbook Assignment:* The student's instructor assigns one of the three textbooks listed in this section. The textbook assignments are an essential part of the course. The exercises in each unit require students to draw information from both the textbook and the programs.
- *Issues for Clarification:* Some issues in the programs or readings may require additional explanation. This section amplifies points that might otherwise be misleading or difficult to understand.
- *Glossary:* The glossary provides short explanations of specialized terms in each unit. Students may wish to use the glossaries in conjunction with a dictionary or encyclopedia.
- *Timeline:* The timeline exercise asks students to visualize and place events and dates in a chronological manner.
- *Map Exercise:* Each unit contains a map on which students are asked to mark important locations. To prepare for the exercise students should view the map in each program and refer to the maps in the textbook. In some cases students are asked to search for relevant maps in the textbook or, if necessary, to consult a historical atlas. Answers are provided for

only some of the map exercises. *There will be no answers for questions requiring nothing more than a location.*

• *Self-Test:* Part I of the self-test asks questions about important factual issues. Part II tests students' understanding of Professor Weber's interpretations. If students find they disagree with Professor Weber's views, they should be prepared to defend their own interpretations.

• *Optional Activities:* Although these activities are not required unless assigned by the instructor, students are encouraged to read them. The activities contain interesting material on literature, art, and film, some of which students may wish to investigate on their own.

• *Review Questions:* The review questions require students to interpret important issues discussed in each unit. In some cases students may disagree with the interpretations of Professor Weber or the textbook; in such instances students must be prepared to explain how they arrived at their own interpretations.

• *Further Reading:* Listed here are additional readings, many of them primary sources, that explore in depth the various issues presented in each unit.

• *Answer Key:* An answer key to the self-test, timeline, and map exercise appears at the end of each unit.

THE TEXTBOOK

In addition to corresponding directly to the television programs, each Study Guide unit is cross-referenced to three currently available textbooks:

1. *The Western Heritage,* Fourth Edition (Macmillan, 1991), by Donald Kagan, Steven Ozment, and Frank M. Turner.
2. *The Western Experience,* Fifth Edition (McGraw-Hill, 1991), by Mortimer Chambers, Raymond Grew, David Herlihy, Theodore K. Rabb, and Isser Woloch.
3. *Western Civilizations,* Eleventh Edition (Norton, 1988), by Edward McNall Burns, Robert E. Lerner, and Standish Meacham.

Students should contact their instructor to find out which textbook is required for the course.

The textbook is an essential part of "The Western Tradition" course — students cannot complete the exercises for each unit without it. Further, the textbook helps students to take notes more efficiently. That is, if students generally understand the topics in each assigned chapter, they can avoid unnecessary notetaking as they view the programs and can give full attention to Professor Weber's presentations.

The textbook is also an important source of maps and images. After Professor Weber comments on the images that appear in the programs, students can turn to the textbook for similar images and study them more closely.

Finally, the textbook provides interpretations that students can compare with Professor Weber's. Sometimes the program and the assigned reading emphasize different aspects of the same issue; other times they present the same conclusions but follow different lines of argument; and at still other times they disagree altogether. The most important goal of "The Western Tradition" course may be to teach students to ask an essential question: How do people know what they claim to know?

FACULTY GUIDES

Similar to the study guides, the faculty guides have been developed for Semesters I and II of "The Western Tradition." The faculty guides are for use by instructors only, and are designed to help in teaching the course in the most effective manner. Semester I and II faculty guides contain all of the information found in the student study guides, as well as additional classroom activities and reading material.

Taking "The Western Tradition" Telecourse

Following registration in the course, students must find out:

- Which textbook is required.
- If and when an orientation session has been scheduled.
- When "The Western Tradition" will be broadcast.
- When examinations are scheduled for the course and mark the dates on a calendar.
- If any additional on-campus meetings have been scheduled and plan to attend as many review sessions, seminars, and other meetings as possible.

To learn the most from each unit, students are encouraged to use the various components of the course in the following order:

1. *Read the Study Guide unit* that corresponds to the programs so to become familiar with the events, people, and vocabulary of the period.
2. *View the film,* keeping in mind the information and questions in the Study Guide.
3. *Read the textbook chapter* that corresponds to the film so to gain a better understanding of the events and issues of the time.
4. *Reread the Study Guide unit,* attempt to answer the focus questions, and prepare the assignment given by the instructor.

VIEWING THE PROGRAMS

Schedule

If students' viewing areas have more than one public television station, several opportunities to watch the programs may be available. Further, many public television stations repeat the program at least once during the week it is first shown. The films may also be available on videocassettes at

xxi

universities. Students must determine at what time they will watch each film and adhere to their schedule.

Preparation

It is easier for students to follow the films if they first review the Study Guide sections that correspond directly to the programs. These include the Overview, Key to the Images, and Focus Questions sections. However, it is also recommended that students read the other sections in the Study Guide in preparation for viewing the films.

Be an Active Viewer

To learn as much as possible from the television programs students must pay careful attention to the films. Watching television for a telecourse requires much more concentration than watching television for entertainment.

Notetaking

Some students may find notetaking while viewing the television programs helpful; others may find it distracting and may prefer to make audio- or videotapes of the programs for later review. It is of course helpful to view the programs twice whenever possible.

COURSE ASSIGNMENTS

Keep Up with Weekly Course Assignments

Each unit of the Study Guide builds on the knowledge gained from previous units. Therefore, it is imperative that students stay current with the films, readings, and assignments. Some students may find that by entering study activities in a study log they can better focus on the assignments that require special attention. A study log is also a good place to note questions for the course instructor and to judge the best order of study and review.

Keep in Touch with Your Instructor

Students should make a note of their instructor's mailing address, telephone number, and call-hours. Students do not need to wait until they have a problem to contact their instructor. Rather, the instructor wants to know how students are doing in the course. Students should contact their instructor whenever a need to discuss the content of the course or to obtain clarification of course content arises.

THE
WESTERN
TRADITION

Study Guide

- CHRISTO · SACRVM ·

ILLe · Dei · VERBO · MAGNA · PIETATE · FAVEBAT ·
· PERPETVA · DIGNVS · POSTERITATE · COLI ·

D · FRIDR · DVCI · SAXON · S · R · IMP ·
· ARCHIM · ELECTORI ·
ALBERTVS · DVRER · NVR · FACIEBAT ·
· B · M · F · V · V ·
· M · D · XXIIII ·

Albrecht Dürer's Engraving of Frederick the Wise, Elector of Saxony, the Patron and Protector of Martin Luther (1524) The Latin phrase says that through his great piety, Frederick promoted the word of God and therefore deserved to be honored for all time. (Clarence Buckingham Collection, 1945.42. © 1987 The Art Institute of Chicago. All rights reserved.)

UNIT FOURTEEN

Program 27: The Reformation

Program 28: The Rise of the Middle Class

LEARNING OBJECTIVES

After completing Unit Fourteen students should understand the following issues:

- The means by which rulers centralized power in the fifteenth and sixteenth centuries. Use your textbook to trace the strategies followed in different European states.
- The financial and economic bases of the new states.
- The changing economy of the sixteenth century. Does your textbook support or rebut Professor Weber's argument about the link between economic development and the Reformation?
- The ways in which Protestant reformers reacted to the popular and institutional piety of the Catholic church. Use your textbook to distinguish the reforms carried out by Protestants in different countries.
- The ways in which Protestantism was suited to the urban bourgeoisie. On the basis of your textbook, why do you think that many European cities remained unaffected by the Reformation?
- The ways in which different painters portrayed the relationship between everyday life and the sacred.
- The countermeasures taken by the Catholic church during the Counter-Reformation.

TV INSTRUCTION

OVERVIEW
PROGRAM 27: THE REFORMATION

I. By the end of the fifteenth century monarchs were creating powerful centralized governments.
   A. Some of the centralizing monarchs had recently pacified or unified their countries.
      1. Louis XI of France.
      2. Ferdinand and Isabella of Spain.
      3. Henry VII of England.
   B. The monarchs tried to refocus patriotism from the local to the national level. French kings, for instance, hoped that their subjects would think of themselves as Frenchmen rather than as Normans or Bretons.
   C. The monarchs needed to dominate religious life.
      1. In some countries rulers broke with Rome and established national churches of their own.
      2. Monarchs who remained Catholic used the church to buttress their own power.
   D. To maintain law and order and to neutralize challenges to their power, the new monarchs tried to gain the monopoly of force within their kingdoms.
      1. Roman law, which exalted the rights of a ruler over his subjects, was a useful tool for many of the new rulers.
      2. New military technology also worked to the advantage of the central monarchy because even the greatest of their subjects could rarely afford trains of artillery or many of the other new weapons.

II. The great task of these rulers was to find ways to pay for their new powers.
   A. Some of their other goals also brought economic benefits.
      1. Law and order often led to economic growth.
      2. The monarchy's monopoly of force made it easier to collect taxes.
   B. Parliaments or assemblies also made it possible for the central power to collect taxes with the consent of the governed.
      1. Because the monarchies, like those of ancient Greece, were too large to permit assemblies in which all adult male citizens could participate, the medieval notion of representation became increasingly important.
      2. Parliaments, however, could become centers of opposition when the government was weak or unpopular.
      3. These parliaments also fostered a sense of national unity, as men from many scattered areas of a country came together to do business.

   C. A ruler's power now depended on his ability to raise money to pay for the new instruments of state. Charles V, for instance, was the first emperor to be able to maintain a standing army from
     1. Taxes.
     2. The wealth of his other possessions.
     3. Dealings with the great bankers such as the Fuggers.

III. Many other features of government that we take for granted became common at this time.
   A. Large permanent bureaucracies developed, especially in
     1. France.
     2. Spain.
   B. Many countries began to maintain permanent embassies in foreign countries.
   C. International law became increasingly complex.

IV. Professor Weber argues that, with the growth of national states, the empire and the papacy declined in power.
   A. The pope was one Italian ruler among many, although he could take advantage of his ecclesiastical powers.
     1. He could grant dispensations from church law.
       a. For instance, he could annul marriages.
       b. He could pardon sins, often for a price.
     2. He could sell indulgences, often at a great price, which could shorten a person's time in purgatory after death.
   B. The emperor had now become the highest bidder in the imperial auction.
     1. In 1519 the kings of England, France, and Spain all bid to become emperor.
     2. Although Charles V, the candidate of the House of Habsburg, became emperor, his real source of power was not his imperial title but his hereditary possessions in Europe and America.

V. Perhaps the most striking of these rulers was Philip II of Spain (1527–1598), whose empire stretched to Asia and America and included some of the richest parts of Europe.
   A. The Spanish ruled their empire by elaborate bureaucratic methods.
     1. As early as 1538 a university was founded at Santo Domingo to train officials.
     2. Other universities were soon founded in
       a. Mexico.
       b. Peru.
   B. The wealth of the Americas made Spain the most powerful European nation of the sixteenth century.

   VI. Professor Weber argues that the rise of the new monarchies upset the economic balance that endured throughout most of the Middle Ages.

     A. The medieval economy had not been highly productive but it had been fairly stable.

     B. In the fifteenth and sixteenth centuries, however, a series of economic problems developed that were not much different from those of modern times.

       1. As the value of money fluctuated, unemployment became increasingly common.

       2. Many other workers became impoverished as their wages failed to keep up with rising prices.

       3. Cities became overcrowded.

     C. Professor Weber argues that economic problems often created open revolt.

       1. Revolts broke out in some trading cities.

       2. Peasants sometimes revolted in the countryside.

       3. Even landowners agitated, as they suffered from inflation.

  VII. Professor Weber argues that social discontent took the form of religious revolt, especially in Germany and the Netherlands, where the concentration of capital was especially high.

     A. On October 31, 1517, Martin Luther proposed ninety-five theses on the power of the church as subjects of debate. Among them:

       1. That the entire life of the believer should be one of repentance (number 1).

       2. That repentance meant something more than the sacrament of penance administered by the clergy (number 2).

       3. That the pope could not remit any penalties except those that he imposed himself (number 5).

       4. That the sellers of indulgences were mistaken in claiming that indulgences could absolve every penalty (number 21).

     B. Conflicts between Catholics and Protestants broke out all over Europe.

       1. Germany was torn by religious wars until the 1550s.

       2. France and the Netherlands suffered throughout the second half of the century.

 VIII. Professor Weber argues that religious conflicts do not break out in irreligious societies.

     A. Luther himself was tormented by fears that he could not win salvation.

       1. He finally argued that faith in God was the only requirement for salvation.

       2. Salvation was not won by practicing rituals or doing pious works.

B. The age just before the Reformation was a time of flamboyant piety.
   1. The cult of the Virgin Mary was especially strong:
      a. The devotion of the Rosary.
      b. The doctrine of the Immaculate Conception.
   2. In art, images of a suffering, human Christ were especially common.
   3. The cult of the Sacred Heart developed.
   4. Fraternities of the Passion grew.
C. Pilgrimages were common.
   1. The Venetians specialized in taking pilgrims to the Holy Land.
   2. New pilgrimage sites sprang up, such as the shrine of Our Lady of Loreto, at Ancona.
D. Holy relics were widely worshiped.
   1. In 1485 the Venetians stole the remains of San Rocco from Montpellier.
   2. Luther's patron, the Elector of Saxony, had an extensive collection of relics.
E. Pious works were widely produced in art and literature.
   1. Flemish domestic scenes provide evidence of religious practices in the home.
   2. Popular religious books were widely distributed.
F. The piety of the age tried to bring religion closer to daily life.
   1. Earlier art often concentrated on the splendor of God.
   2. Christ and the Virgin were now portrayed to emphasize their human characteristics.
G. At the same time, however, new forms of piety and worship were developing.

Key to the Images

Martin Luther: One of the most intriguing images of Program 27 shows the reformer Martin Luther with Duke Johann Friedrich of Saxony and the ducal family. In the background is the city of Wittenberg, where Luther first presented his controversial theses. This is not a purely contemporary scene, however, for Luther and the others are watching the Baptism of Christ.

As in many other works that have appeared in the series, the artist has not hesitated to put together figures from widely separated periods of history. In this picture, however, the juxtaposition is especially important because Luther and other Protestant reformers argued that they were trying to reform the church to its original state of purity. The picture suggests that Luther wanted to make the reformed church as pure as it was in Christ's own time.

The fact that Luther and the Duke of Saxony appear together is also important. The Protestant Reformation was not carried out by churchmen alone. Laypeople, especially layrulers, also played an enormously important role.

The Crucifixion: Matthias Gruenewald's crucifixion scene from the Isenheim altarpiece illustrates one of Professor Weber's most important theses about the religious atmosphere in which the Reformation took place.

Depictions of Christ are always important clues about Christian religious attitudes. From the late Middle Ages onward, Professor Weber argues that Christians were seeking a more personal, more human vision of Christ. In Gruenewald's crucifixion Christ is portrayed in such strongly human terms that his agony looks like a scene of a modern atrocity.

Focus Questions

1. What were the tasks of the rulers who created the modern state?
2. What doctrines and institutions were useful to the state-builders?
3. What role did representative institutions play in the centralization of power?
4. How did financiers help build the new states?
5. What groups of people benefitted from the changing economy of the early modern period? What groups were hurt by it?
6. Which were the most controversial of Luther's theses?
7. What were the most prominent features of popular piety in the years before the Reformation?

OVERVIEW
PROGRAM 28: THE RISE OF THE MIDDLE CLASS

The Protestant Reformation was not confined to the cities, nor did all the cities of Europe embrace the new religion. Nevertheless, Professor Weber argues that the Reformation drew much of its strength from the urban middle classes, who wanted a more direct relationship with God. They wanted to understand religion for themselves. By the middle of the sixteenth century the Roman Catholic church had begun its counteroffensive: the Counter-Reformation.

I. Professor Weber argues that the urban middle classes were developing new habits of thought that called for a new kind of piety.
    A. Their habits of dealing with money and materials led them to look for practical solutions. They respected

1. Precision.
2. Exactness.
B. They were often travelers and traders or accustomed to dealing with such people.
   1. They were used to comparing customs and places.
   2. They had a sense of the relativity of values.
C. The middle classes wanted a religion that was
   1. Clear.
   2. Reasonable.
   3. Understandable to ordinary intelligent people.

II. Professor Weber argues that the educated middle classes were not well served by the Catholic church.
   A. The church often catered to simple people who were impressed by
      1. Miracles.
      2. Saints.
      3. Hellfire.
   B. When educated people looked for a more intellectual understanding of religion
      1. They often found clerics who were
         a. Perfunctory.
         b. Formalistic.
      2. Or theologians who wrote in a language that could be understood only by other theologians.
   C. Professor Weber argues that the Catholic church was unreceptive to these intellectual needs.
      1. The church taught that dogma was beyond the grasp of reason.
      2. Clergymen taught that people should simply accept the teachings of the church without trying to understand them.
      3. The faithful should practice certain rites simply because they were told to.
   D. Protestants revolted against the church on several levels.
      1. They hated its dryness of spirit, as they saw it.
      2. They believed that much Catholic doctrine was superstition.

III. The Roman Catholic church did not respond quickly enough to these new needs.
   A. Even apart from the middle classes, there was also strong discontent among the
      1. Nobility.
      2. Peasantry.
   B. The gap between the church and the middle classes grew greater,
      1. Partly because the clergy lived too much apart from the rest of society,
      2. And, therefore, was largely concerned with its own problems rather than with the troubles of the laity.

C. In the past the church destroyed or absorbed heretics but now the reformers were out of control.

IV. Some members of the Catholic hierarchy believed that matters could be mended simply by better educating the clergy and improving the administration of the church.
    A. Professor Weber argues, however, that the reformers actually had an altogether different view of authority.
        1. The reformers did not simply want the authorities to be better informed.
        2. The reformers wanted to make up their minds for themselves.
    B. The church did not respond to the issues most important to the reformers.
        1. Translations of the Bible into the vernacular languages.
        2. The doctrine of justification by faith alone.
            a. This is the idea that faith alone saves the believer.
            b. Therefore, the rituals of the church are not necessary for salvation.
    C. These beliefs had been in the air long before they were set down by such reformers as
        1. Martin Luther, who published his ninety-five theses in 1517.
        2. John Calvin, who was banished from Paris in 1528 for his Protestant teachings.

V. Study of the Bible lay at the center of Protestantism.
    A. The Bible was now translated into most of the vernacular languages of Europe.
    B. The vernacular Bible met two important needs:
        1. An image of a living, human God.
        2. A transformation of the notion of priesthood.
    C. Protestants wanted a more direct relationship to God.
        1. Now they could read His word in their own language.
        2. They did not need a priest to explain religion to them.
        3. Nor did they need to rely exclusively on the rituals of the church.
    D. Professor Weber argues that this view of religion was especially congenial to people who were used to relying on their own efforts.
        1. Protestants were still deferential to their spiritual and social betters.
        2. But they had a new sense of pride and responsibility for their own beliefs.

VI. The Reformation took place at a time when many rulers were centralizing the power of their states.
    A. Centralization was promoted by the growth of the urban economy.
    B. The king himself became the symbol and incarnation of centralization.

C. In religious terms Christ Himself was seen as a kind of king.
  1. According to Professor Weber, Christ Himself was a symbol of centralization.
  2. Christ was seen as the leader of a fighting faith.

VII. During this period the middle classes also created a new respect for manual labor.
  A. For centuries the ideal man had not worked but rather
    1. Fought.
    2. Prayed.
  B. In the sixteenth century Protestants and Catholics alike began to think that only people who worked deserved to eat.
    1. Protestants like Calvin.
    2. Catholics like Rabelais.
    3. They looked on monks as parasites.

VIII. Professor Weber finds a subversive logic in the Protestant emphasis on the Bible.
  A. Luther preached that "every Christian is a priest; every believer is his own priest."
  B. The doctrine of Justification by Faith Alone was a great psychological comfort.
    1. Believers were relieved of such practices as
      a. Personal mortification.
      b. Punishment of the body.
      c. Rejection of the active life.
    2. People no longer lived in dread of dying before their sins had been forgiven through the rituals of the church.

IX. Such beliefs profoundly altered the structure of the church in Protestant countries.
  A. The cult of the dead disappeared.
    1. There were no longer endowed masses for the souls of the dead.
    2. Wealth that had once been spent on these practices was now turned to other purposes.
  B. Protestant churches tended to be plainer and more sober.
    1. Because Protestantism was a religion of the book, images were less important than in the Roman Catholic church.
    2. Art in Protestant countries sometimes moved away from religious subjects to
      a. Secular affairs.
      b. Landscapes.
      c. Portraits.

X. Changes in the visual arts can be seen clearly by comparing the careers of Hieronymous Bosch (1450–1516) and Pieter Brueghel (1525–1569).
  A. Professor Weber argues that Bosch's works are often grotesque nightmares of

1. Temptation.
2. The Fall.
3. Punishment in the next world.
- B. Bosch had little interest in ordinary untroubled people.
- C. Most of Brueghel's works, however, deal with mundane matters.
  1. Landscapes.
  2. Scenes of peasant life.
- D. Brueghel was influenced by Bosch but
  1. Brueghel was also influenced by the humanists.
  2. Where Bosch was catastrophic Brueghel was satirical.
  3. Brueghel's religious ideas were
     a. Commonsensical.
     b. Rational.
     c. Ethical.
- E. Professor Weber argues that Brueghel's interest in ordinary people made him the first modern painter.
  1. Brueghel's works, however, were not appreciated solely by Protestants.
  2. His major patron was a Catholic cardinal.

XI. In 1545, with the opening of the Council of Trent, the Roman Catholics began a sweeping counteroffensive against Protestantism.
- A. The church strengthened the powers of the Inquisition to investigate heresy.
- B. In 1559 the first Index of Prohibited Books appeared.
- C. The church compiled a catechism that outlined the principles of belief for all Catholics.
- D. Ignatius Loyola (1491–1556) founded the Society of Jesus.
  1. The Jesuits were disciplined, highly educated, and subjected to strong central authority.
  2. They prepared for battle on many fronts:
     a. Education.
     b. Missionary work.
     c. Preaching.

XII. Professor Weber argues that by the middle of the sixteenth century three essential items of modern civilization were in place:
- A. Printing.
- B. Gunpowder.
- C. The Protestant religion.

Key to the Images

The Sacraments: Professor Weber emphasizes that the nature of the sacraments was a key issue in the Protestant Reformation. Rogier van der Weyden's *Seven Sacraments* gives a sense of how people in the late Middle Ages conceived of them. The detail presented in Program 28 shows the sacraments of baptism and penance.

The fact that the two sacraments are presented in the same picture stresses their interdependence. In the sacrament of baptism a person is cleansed from the burden of original sin through Christ's sacrifice. The sacrament of penance allows a person to atone for new sins committed throughout one's life.

The Lutheran belief had in Justification by Faith Alone rocked a view of the sacraments that developed over many centuries.

The Vernacular Bible: The printing press was essential to the Protestant Reformation, especially for printing translations of the Bible. In Program 28 we study the title page of Luther's 1534 translation. A German phrase appears as a motto for the translation: *Gottes wort bleibt ewig,* or "God's word remains eternal."

The intention of the phrase is intriguing. Luther, of course, believed that God's word was eternally true and therefore needed to be made available to all people in a language they could understand. It is interesting to speculate whether this motto also meant that by translating the Bible into a vernacular language Luther had not corrupted the word of God.

Pieter Brueghel: Program 28 includes a number of Brueghel's most important paintings: "The Wedding Dance," "The Harvesters," and "The Parable of the Blind." Like other northern painters, especially those who followed him, Brueghel was fascinated by scenes of everyday life.

His religious and moral parables grew quite naturally out of the same vision. "The Parable of the Blind," for instance, has none of the surreal intensity of Bosch's paintings. Instead, Brueghel painted the blind men as though they could step out of one of his paintings of ordinary peasant life.

Focus Questions

1. What were some of the moral and intellectual qualities of the bourgeoisie?
2. In what ways did the Protestant Reformation object to the powers of the clergy?
3. What reforms did Protestants demand?
4. What was the attitude of the middle classes toward physical labor?
5. What were some of the psychological forces at work in Protestantism and Catholicism?
6. In what ways was the printing press essential to the Reformation?
7. In what different ways did Hieronymous Bosch and Pieter Brueghel portray the relationship between the human and the divine?
8. In what ways did the Catholic church counterattack the Protestant Reformation?

ASSIGNMENTS AND ACTIVITIES

IN CONTEXT

Themes and issues that set Unit Fourteen in context with other units include the following:

- In Unit Fourteen Professor Weber shows that representative institutions played a role in the centralization of the state. Remember from earlier units in Semester I that in most European countries parliaments had roots far back in the Middle Ages. In earlier times, however, parliaments, at least in theory, only met to raise funds for unusual situations. As the expenses of the modern state increased, these parliaments or estates met with increasing frequency. In later units watch for ways in which representative institutions could become focuses of discontent. The English Civil War and the American and French revolutions are of special importance.

- Earlier units in Semester I stress that religious observances were deeply woven into the fabric of medieval life. In Unit Fourteen ask yourself why Protestants should have objected so strongly to the cult of the saints, the veneration of relics, and many other practices that had long been part of European life. This desire to make a radical break with the past appears with increasing frequency in later units. Look especially closely at the early days of the French Revolution.

- Although economic activity increased through much of this period, the European economy had lost much of its earlier stability. The feudal relations studied in Unit Twenty of Semester I often showed a tenacity that allowed them to endure for several centuries. In the units that follow watch for ways in which economic instability contributed to revolutionary movements. Look closely at the disturbances behind the Fronde in seventeenth-century France. Pay special attention to the years immediately preceding the French Revolution.

- The Protestant Reformation could not have occurred without the printing press or the textual scholarship of the Renaissance. The Bible was one of the first books to enjoy mass circulation. In later units look for the changes that developed in intellectual life now that books were not confined to a small class of literate people. Pay special attention to the role of the *philosophes* in the years before the French Revolution.

Textbook Assignment

Read the following pages in your assigned textbook:

Text: *Western Civilizations* (Eleventh Edition, 1988)
Read: Chapter 15, "Europe Expands and Divides: Overseas Conquests and the Protestant Reformation," pp. 455–500.

Text: *The Western Experience* (Fifth Edition, 1991)
Read: From Chapter 13, "Overseas Expansion and a New Politics
        1415–1560," pp. 509–534; and Chapter 14, "Reformations in
        Religion 1500–1570," pp. 535–568.

Text: *The Western Heritage* (Fourth Edition, 1991)
Read: Chapter 11, "The Age of the Reformation," pp. 385–425.

Issues for Clarification

The King Shall Live of His Own

In most European countries parliaments or other sorts of representative
assemblies began to meet in the thirteenth and fourteenth centuries. In the
Middle Ages, however, meetings were called only on extraordinary occasions. In normal times it was expected that "the king shall live of his own."
This doctrine meant that the king was supposed to pay for the daily
expenses of government from the revenues of the crown lands and from
other customary sources, such as the profits the king derived from the law
courts.

Parliaments granted extra taxes only when the king's ordinary revenues
were insufficient, during a war, for instance, or some other national emer-
gency. By the sixteenth century, however, the expenses of government had
increased so much that very few rulers could "live of their own." Parliamentary taxes were becoming routine.

Patriotism

Up until this period patriotism was usually a local matter. People might
feel attached to their city or province, but attachment to a nation as a
whole was just beginning. The Hundred Years' War, in which the French
drove the English from the continent, was one of the first great examples
to demonstrate the power of national patriotism.

Penance

Penance was one of the most important sacraments of the Catholic church.
It was believed that anyone who died in a state of mortal sin would be
eternally damned. The church's method of cleansing sin was to have the
sinner make a full and sincere confession to a priest, who would then grant
absolution and impose a penance or punishment for the sins. Penances
might consist of prayers, a pilgrimage to a holy shrine, fasting, or some
other bodily mortification. It was also believed that after death the souls of
most people would have to do additional penances in purgatory.

Protestants and the Clergy

Protestant attacks on the Catholic clergy were so strong that it would be
easy to assume that Protestants simply abolished the clergy in their own
churches. This is not true, however. Although Protestant laypeople often

assumed important roles in the government of their churches, the Protestant clergy was an honored and respected class. Protestant clergy, however, were looked on as moral and spiritual teachers, not as special intercessors with God. They continued to perform religious rituals but the rituals were not in themselves supposed to be necessary to salvation.

Glossary

Indulgence: In the Catholic church a remission of punishment either in this world or in purgatory. Indulgences applied only after the sin itself had been forgiven in the sacrament of penance. Indulgences could be bought for a price and in Luther's time were often used to raise money.

Intercessor: A mediator; a person who pleads on behalf of another. In Catholic doctrine the saints and the Virgin Mary were thought to help the faithful by acting as intercessors with God.

Justification by Faith Alone: The Protestant belief that salvation depends only on personal faith, not on the rituals of the church.

Remission of Sins: The forgiveness or pardon of sins. Catholic doctrine declared that salvation came only through the rituals of the church.

Timeline

Place each of the following events on the timeline. In some cases you may have to specify a roughly defined period of time rather than a precise date.

1. Kings of England, France, and Spain bid to become Holy Roman emperor.
2. Life of Philip II.
3. Founding of the first university in the Western Hemisphere.
4. Luther proposes his ninety-five Theses.
5. Period of German religious wars in the sixteenth century.
6. Theft of the remains of San Rocco.
7. Calvin is banished from Paris.
8. Lifetime of Hieronymus Bosch.
9. Lifetime of Pieter Brueghel.
10. Opening of the Council of Trent.

1400   1600
├──┤

Map Exercise

Find the following locations on the map. You may have to do extensive cross-referencing in your textbook. If you do not find all these places on the maps associated with the current chapter, look at the maps in earlier or later chapters.

1. Shrine of Our Lady of Loreto.
2. Native country of Ignatius Loyola.
3. Homeland of Bosch and Brueghel.
4. Kingdom ruled by Henry VIII.
5. City where Luther proposed his ninety-five Theses.
6. Site of remains of San Rocco before theft by Venetians.
7. Native country of John Calvin.
8. Kingdom that sponsored Columbus.

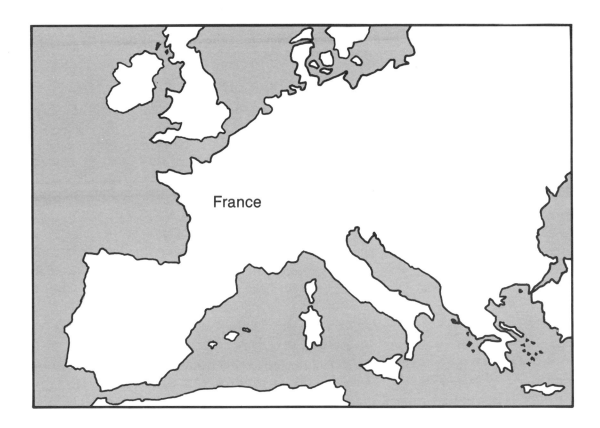

Self-Test

Part I of the self-test asks about important factual material. Part II is interpretive. The answers in Part II are keyed to Professor Weber's interpretations. If you disagree with an answer, be prepared to defend your own understanding of the material. Check your answers at the end of Unit One.

Part I

1. Which of the following was *not* part of the domains of Philip II?
   a. France.
   b. Spain.
   c. Portugal.
   d. Mexico.

2. Which of the following was *not* one of Lüther's ninety-five theses?
   a. "When our Lord and Master Jesus Christ said, 'Repent,' he willed the entire life of believers to be one of repentance."
   b. "This word [repentance] refers to the sacrament of penance, that is confession and satisfaction, as administered by the clergy."
   c. "The pope neither desires nor is able to remit any penalties except those imposed by his own authority or that of the canons."
   d. "Thus those indulgent preachers are in error who say that a man is absolved from every penalty and saved by papal indulgences."

3. Which of the following was *not* one of the expressions of Catholic popular religion in the century before the Reformation?
   a. Veneration of relics.
   b. The priesthood of all believers.
   c. The cult of the Virgin Mary.
   d. Pilgrimages.

4. Which of the following was *not* one of the responses of the Catholic church to the Protestant Reformation?
   a. To abandon the cult of saints.
   b. To draw up the Index of Prohibited Books.
   c. To found the Society of Jesus.
   d. To give new powers to the Inquisition.

5. In 1519 the kings of _____England_____, _____France_____, and Spain all bid to become Holy Roman emperor.

Part II

1. Mark the false choice. The Protestant doctrine of Justification by Faith Alone
   a. undermined the cult of the dead.
   b. relieved the fear of dying without the sacrament of penance.
   c. required the clergy to act as intermediaries with God.
   d. attacked Roman Catholic practices such as Mortification of the Flesh.

2. According to Professor Weber, which of the following was *not* one of the goals of the statebuilders of the fifteenth and sixteenth centuries?
   a. To gain the monopoly of force within the state.
   b. To control economic life.

c. To create a patriotic identity at the national level.

d. To encourage religious diversity.

3. Mark the false choice. Roman law was a useful tool to statebuilders because
    a. it included the idea of an absolute ruler.
    b. it was easy to reconcile with the common or traditional law of most countries.
    c. it generally favored the monarch over his feudal vassals.
    d. a great body of commentary had grown up around it.

4. Mark the false choice. Representative institutions
    a. were popular assemblies, like those of the Greek city-states, consisting of all citizens.
    b. were used by rulers to obtain their subjects' consent to greater taxation.
    c. could create a sense of unity over disparate territories.
    d. could become centers of opposition to the ruler.

5. Mark the false choice. The new alliance between capital and the state
    a. gave governments access to greater sources of money.
    b. made possible the financing of expanded armies.
    c. created a stabler economic system than that of the Middle Ages.
    d. led to agitation by nobles who suffered from inflation.

Optional Activity

Although the following activity is not required for the course unless assigned by the instructor, students are encouraged to use it as a source of interesting topics for further study.

Patriotism in Shakespeare

Shakespeare's *Henry V* is one of the most important patriotic works written during this period. King Henry himself was one of the most successful English warriors during the Hundred Years' War and the play celebrates his great victory at Agincourt.

Write a paper of 3–5 pages on one of the following topics:

• What qualities, as seen in the play, made Henry V a great king? How would you describe him as a hero and as a national leader? Is the play similar to the kinds of nationalist propaganda that Professor Weber discusses in Unit Fourteen?

• Use the Signet Classics' edition of *Henry V* for this topic. After you read the play itself look at the historical documents in the appendix. How did Shakespeare shape the historical record to suit his purposes? For additional insight, read the sections on Henry V in Edouard Perroy's *Hundred Years' War*. (See the Further Reading section for Unit Thirteen.)

- During the Second World War Laurence Olivier made an important film of *Henry V,* which is now available on videocassette. Does the film live up to your expectations of the play? How did the patriotism of the 1940s influence Olivier's vision of the play?

Films

You may wish to view some of the following films, which deal with matters discussed in this unit.

- *Luther,* a film made by a group of Protestant churches, is available from many Lutheran churches.
- *A Man for All Seasons,* starring Paul Scofield, tells the story of Thomas More, a Catholic martyr who died under Henry VIII.
- *Anne of a Thousand Days* tells the story of Anne Boleyn, the woman for whom Henry VIII divorced his first wife.
- *The Private Life of Henry VIII* is worth seeing, simply because Charles Laughton is its star.

Review Questions

The following questions are designed to help you think critically and to construct explanations from factual knowledge. Remember that whenever you learn a new piece of information you should always ask yourself "so what?" questions.

Keep in mind that historians continually disagree on emphases, interpretations, and even on simple matters of fact. Many of the following questions emphasize Professor Weber's particular point of view and ask you to compare it to what you find in your textbook. When you find important disagreements, you should remember that historians are always struggling with each other; this struggle is one that you can enter yourself.

1. What were some of the ways in which monarchs tried to centralize power in their states? What role did finance play in this process? In what ways did Roman law contribute to the centralization of power?
2. How did representative institutions such as parliament strengthen or weaken the financial powers of the state? In what ways did the institutions foster a sense of national unity? In what ways could the institutions be dangerous to a ruler?
3. Hieronymus Bosch and Pieter Brueghel were two of the most important painters of the Low Countries. What were some of the ways in which they expressed their religious visions? How were they similar or different in the ways in which they portrayed daily life? Compare their treatments of daily life to that of Jan Van Eyck, whose work is discussed in Unit Thirteen of Semester I.
4. What were some of the most important expressions of popular piety

around 1500? In what ways do many of them emphasize the performance of sacred or worthy acts that were supposed to accrue merit?

5. What were the most important consequences of Luther's doctrine of the Priesthood of all Believers? What practices or institutions were attacked by the doctrine? To what classes of people did the doctrine most strongly appeal?

Further Reading

Primary Sources

Loyola, Ignatius. *The Spiritual Exercises.* (1964). The manual used on religious retreats. Reveals a great deal about Jesuit education and spiritual discipline.

Luther, Martin. *Martin Luther: Selections from His Writings.* (1961). A large selection of the most important writings.

Strauss, Gerald, ed. and trans. *Manifestations of Discontent in Germany on the Eve of the Reformation.* (1971). A collection of sources on discontent in both cities and countryside.

Weber, Eugen. *The Western Tradition,* 2nd ed. (1965). "Reformation and Counter-Reformation," pp. 325–363.

Ziegler, D. J. *Great Debates of the Reformation.* (1969).

Secondary Sources

Chadwick, Owen. *The Reformation.* (1964). A good survey. Especially good on theology and issues within the church.

Dickens, A. G. *The Counter-Reformation.* (1969). A good brief survey. Illustrated.

De Lamar, Jensen. *Reformation Europe, Age of Reform and Revolution.* (1981). One of the best modern surveys. Discusses both political and religious issues.

Mitchell, David J. *The Jesuits, a History.* (1980).

Osborne, John. *Luther.* (1966). A modern play about Luther's personal crisis.

Ozment, Steven. *The Age of Reform 1250–1550: An Intellectual and Religious History of Late Medieval and Reformation Europe.* (1980). Very good. Traces the origins of the Reformation far back into the Middle Ages.

Skinner, Quentin. *The Foundations of Modern Political Thought II: The Age of Reformation.* (1978). Extremely comprehensive. Especially good on Lutheran political thought.

Answer Key

Timeline

1. 1519.
2. 1527–1598.
3. 1538.
4. 1517.
5. 1520s–1550s.
6. 1485.
7. 1528.
8. 1450–1516.
9. 1525–1569.
10. 1545.

Map Exercise

1. Ancona, Italy.
2. Spain.
3. Low Countries (in what is now Belgium).
4. England.
5. Wittenberg, Germany.
6. Montpellier, France.
7. France.
8. Spain.

Self-Test

Part I

1. (a) France.
2. (b) "This word [repentance] refers to the sacrament of penance, that is confession and satisfaction, as administered by the clergy."
3. (b) The priesthood of all believers.
4. (a) To abandon the cult of saints.
5. England; France.

Part II

1. (c) required the clergy to act as intermediaries with God.
2. (d) To encourage religious diversity.
3. (b) it was easy to reconcile with the common or traditional law of most countries.
4. (a) were popular assemblies, like those of the Greek city-states, consisting of all citizens.
5. (c) created a stabler economic system than that of the Middle Ages.

PARIS

German Representation of the Massacre of Saint Bartholomew on August 23–24, 1572 The slaughter killed many of the Protestant nobility who had come to Paris for the wedding of Henry of Navarre, the future Henry IV, to the sister of the French king. Although real newspapers did not yet exist, pamphlets and prints spread the news throughout Europe. (GIRAUDON/Art Resource, NY.)

UNIT FIFTEEN

Program 29: The Wars of Religion

Program 30: The Rise of Trading Cities

LEARNING OBJECTIVES

After completing Unit Fifteen students should understand the following issues:

- The causes and results of the religious civil wars in the sixteenth and seventeenth centuries. From your textbook, try to understand why the Reformation brought civil war to some countries, whereas other countries reformed their churches with relatively little bloodshed.
- The ways in which international politics complicated the religious civil wars.
- The varying patterns of religious toleration that appeared by the middle of the seventeenth century. From your textbook, determine which countries allowed a degree of toleration. How broad was this toleration?
- The importance of the *politiques* as statesmen.
- The most important cities and trade routes in the European economy.
- The special qualities of the art produced in trading cities. Compare the art of the Netherlands and of Northern Italy to art being produced in other areas during this period.
- The development of the Dutch Republic into a new kind of state.
- The major scientific discoveries of the period.

————————— *TV INSTRUCTION* —————————

OVERVIEW
PROGRAM 29: THE WARS OF RELIGION

After the beginning of the Protestant Reformation, Europe endured more than a century of religious wars. In many cases religion simply aggravated conflicts that were already under way. By the middle of the seventeenth century some countries were experimenting with religious toleration, not so much for its own sake, but because it seemed the best way to keep the peace. In the midst of this turmoil arose the Dutch Republic, which soon became an important state in its own right and a precursor of republican government throughout the world.

I. By the middle of the sixteenth century most parts of Western Europe had been embroiled in conflicts between Protestants and Catholics.
   A. In the 1530s the cantons of Switzerland fought a bloody civil war that resulted in a division between Protestants and Catholics that still endures.
   B. In 1555 the Peace of Augsburg ended a generation of civil war in Germany.
      1. The peace lasted for another fifty years.
      2. The treaty provided a formula, *cuius regio eius religio,* which meant that the ruler of each German state would determine the religion of his subjects.
   C. The model of the universal Christian church had broken down.
      1. Religious unity was part of the unity of the state.
      2. Instead of there being a universal church, each ruler demanded that his subjects belong to the church he ordained.
   D. In the 1530s Henry VIII of England became the first sovereign prince to leave the church of Rome and establish his own national church.
      1. Henry first broke with Rome not for religious reasons but because he wanted to divorce his wife, who had not given him a male heir.
      2. He confiscated much of the church's wealth and used it to support the crown and reward his followers.
   E. After 1558 Queen Elizabeth I stabilized the religious situation in England by permitting a sort of *de facto* toleration.
      1. Elizabeth and her advisors did not trust Catholics.
         a. Partly for religious reasons.
         b. Partly because English Catholics were suspected of aiding foreign Catholic powers.
      2. Much of the time, however, Elizabeth was not interested in hunting Catholics out.
      3. They were often left alone if they
         a. Worshiped only in private.
         b. Remained loyal to the crown.

    4. Nevertheless, Catholics could be heavily fined for not attending Protestant services.

II. In the second half of the sixteenth century, France and the Netherlands were torn by civil war.
    A. Foreign powers often intervened on behalf of one side or the other.
        1. England intervened on the side of Protestants in both France and the Netherlands.
        2. Spain gave much more decisive help to Catholics.
    B. Catholic rulers had been persecuting French Protestants since the 1520s.
        1. A substantial part of the nobility were now Protestants, however.
        2. The nobles found Protestantism a strong force to use against the centralizing monarchy.
    C. Catholicism was popular with the majority of the French, however, and the series of civil wars lasted until the end of the century.
        1. In August 1572 Catholics massacred thousands of Protestants on Saint Bartholomew's Night.
        2. Eventually, a Protestant prince, Henry IV, inherited the throne.
        3. In 1594, however, he became a Catholic and prepared the end of the war.
    D. Under the leadership of William of Orange, the Protestants of the Netherlands began a revolt against their Spanish rulers.
        1. Ultimately, the area that is now Belgium remained Catholic.
        2. In the north, however, Protestants set up a new state, known as the United Provinces, or Holland.
    E. By 1598 Henry IV had unified most of France and had made peace with the Spanish, who had intervened on the Catholic side.
        1. As a basis of religious peace Henry issued the Edict of Nantes.
        2. This document left Catholicism the dominant religion in France.
        3. But it did give Protestants many important rights.

III. Out of the turmoil of religious war a new political attitude toward religion now emerged.
    A. In France, a group of statesmen known as the *politiques,* now emerged.
        1. They argued that unity in the state was more important than religious unity.
        2. They favored a limited amount of religious toleration,
           a. Not so much for its own sake,
           b. But to spare the state of the agony of civil war.
        3. If people remained loyal subjects, they could enjoy a certain measure of toleration.
        4. Professor Weber argues that the *politiques* wanted to make religion a private matter rather than the public matter it had always been.

     B. This attitude was also found in a few other European countries:
       1. To a limited extent in England.
       2. In the Netherlands.

IV. Professor Weber argues that arguments in favor of toleration introduced new ways of thinking.
     A. The first Protestant Reformers had not been in favor of toleration:
       1. Martin Luther.
       2. John Calvin.
     B. People who believed in toleration could not maintain that truth was indivisible.
     C. For *politiques* like Henry IV toleration was an instrument of state.
     D. Professor Weber contrasts this attitude to that of the Spanish Inquisition, established in 1479.
       1. The Inquisition believed that heresy or dissent could not be tolerated but had to be destroyed.
       2. The heretic was a danger to society.
       3. Further, the Inquisition wanted to save the heretic's soul by forcing him to repent.

V. The Thirty Years' War (1618–1648) was the greatest of the religious wars.
     A. Although Germany was the center of the fighting, nearly every European power became involved:
       1. Sweden.
       2. Denmark.
       3. Bohemia.
       4. Spain.
       5. France.
     B. In 1617 Ferdinand of Bohemia became Holy Roman emperor and decided to withdraw the rights of Protestants in his realm.
       1. In 1618 the Protestants of Bohemia revolted.
       2. Within a few years the whole of Europe was involved.
     C. The fighting lasted, with few interruptions, until 1648. Only the plague had caused greater devastation.
     D. The Treaty of Westphalia, which ended the fighting, had a number of paradoxical results:
       1. It confirmed the territorial sovereignty of Germany's many principalities.
       2. Therefore, it perpetuated Germany's weakness and division.
       3. It confirmed France as a great power.
       4. It marked the decline of Spain.
     E. Religion was now ceasing to be a focus of international politics.
       1. The war had started with Protestants against Catholics.
       2. By the end, however, the two major enemies were both Catholic:
         a. France.
         b. Spain.

    F. The geographical divisions between Protestant and Catholics in many places follow the boundary lines of the old Roman Empire.
        a. Countries within the old empire tend to be Catholic.
        b. Countries outside these boundaries tend to be Protestant.
    G. It also became clear that most people were ready to obey the religious laws of their rulers.

  VI. During this same period the United Provinces, or Holland, became established as a sovereign country.
    A. Holland now became one of the few republics in Europe.
    B. Holland served as a model for other republics:
      1. For the short-lived English republic in the seventeenth century.
      2. For the United States in the eighteenth century.

Key to the Images

Saint Bartholomew's Massacre: The massacre of French Protestants on August 23–24, 1572, was the great atrocity story of the sixteenth century. European Protestants thought of it as we think of the Holocaust. As you look at the images of the massacre that appear in Program 29, remember that the sixteenth century had no mass media. Newspapers had not yet been invented.

It was at about this time, however, that something like modern journalism began to appear. Although there were no regular publications, pamphleteers would immediately set to work to report newsworthy events. The massacre was one of the great news stories of the time.

The Catholic League: The other side in the religious wars had its own occasions to celebrate or deplore. Program 29 shows a procession by the Catholic League to celebrate their defense of Paris against Henry IV.

Images of the news: Artists often portrayed newsworthy events in something like our sense of the word. One image in Program 29 shows Spanish troops leaving Paris in 1594, after Henry IV had converted to Catholicism and entered the city. This is the sort of image that might appear in a modern newsreel.

Focus Questions

1. Which countries suffered from religious wars during the sixteenth and seventeenth centuries?
2. Which countries intervened in the religious civil wars of other states?
3. What were the goals of the *politiques*?
4. What were the earliest motives for allowing religious toleration?

5. What were some of the ways in which the religious wars were settled?
6. What were the original causes of the Thirty Years' War? What complications prolonged the war?
7. What were the results of the Thirty Years' War?
8. What were the new or innovative features of the Dutch commonwealth?

OVERVIEW
PROGRAM 30: THE RISE OF TRADING CITIES

Professor Weber defines the economic spine of Europe as running from northern Italy through the Netherlands. During this period, commerce was expanding rapidly and many of today's commercial practices and institutions were developed. On the whole, the trading cities were more tolerant and cosmopolitan than the rest of Europe.

I. The economic spine of Europe, which Professor Weber calls Lotharingia, has rarely been united under a single power, but it contains many of Europe's commercial centers.
   A. It runs from the North Sea to the Mediterranean.
   B. It includes major cities and the lines of communication between them:
      1. The Rhine.
      2. The Alpine passes.
   C. Lotharingia includes areas of such modern states as
      1. Belgium.
      2. The Netherlands.
      3. Luxembourg.
      4. The Rhineland.
      5. Switzerland.
      6. Italy.

II. Outside the area of Lotharingia, other trading networks grew up.
   A. In the North a league of German cities included
      1. Riga.
      2. Danzig.
      3. Lubeck.
   B. Most of the Hanseatic cities lay on the Baltic and maintained trade routes among
      1. Scandinavia.
      2. Poland.
      3. Russia.

III. Trading centers also grew up at spots where traders from the North and South could meet.
   A. At the fairs of Champagne.
   B. At Lyon, where connections could be made between

      1. The Rhone.

      2. The Alps.

    C. At Augsburg, which linked

      1. The Danube.

      2. The Rhine.

IV. During the Middle Ages the greatest commercial wealth was concentrated at the gateways to Lotharingia.

    A. Venice dominated Mediterranean trade.

      1. In the fifteenth and sixteenth centuries, however, the Turks crippled Venice's spice trade.

      2. Other European traders developed trade routes that bypassed the Turks and the Venetians.

    B. Bruges focused the trade of the North Sea and the Baltic.

      1. The harbor silted up at Bruges.

      2. Trade then moved to Antwerp.

      3. Antwerp was crippled in the religious wars.

      4. Amsterdam became the great trading center.

V. The cities were becoming vital to rulers.

    A. The cities controlled

      1. Industrial production.

      2. Exchange.

      3. Capital.

      4. Credit.

    B. Without credit from the cities, rulers found it increasingly difficult to wage war.

VI. Many modern business practices were developed.

    A. In the fourteenth century Venetians formed one of the first business districts in a European city by concentrating many sorts of businesses near the Rialto bridge:

      1. Merchants.

      2. Bankers.

      3. Moneychangers.

    B. Many sorts of transactions could be conducted on the Rialto:

      1. Fixing commodity prices.

      2. Fixing interest rates on loans.

      3. Fixing premiums on marine insurance.

    C. Many modern business practices were becoming standard:

      1. Payments made by bookkeeping rather than by cash.

      2. Overdrafts.

      3. Credit notes.

      4. A form of stock exchange.

    D. The locations of early stock exchanges trace the spread of commercial activity.

      1. Barcelona had one by 1393.

      2. London and Paris did not have stock exchanges until the sixteenth century.

      3. New York built its exchange in the eighteenth century.

VII. The trading cities were generally cosmopolitan and tolerant.
  A. Even during the religious wars, both Protestants and Catholics traded at
  1. Antwerp.
  2. Amsterdam.
  B. Many of the cities tried to avoid the religious turmoil of the times.
  1. Venice did not allow the Inquisition.
  2. In Amsterdam, despite the religious authorities, the city council was generally tolerant of
  a. Catholics.
  b. Jews.
  C. The cities took great care to impose security and order.
  1. They formed guard companies of citizen volunteers.
  2. Brawls and public disturbances were better controlled than in the capitals of many kingdoms.
  D. The cities organized their own charities.
  1. Orphanages.
  2. Almshouses.
  3. Distribution of food and fuel.

VIII. Joint stock companies and public banks were set up around the beginning of the seventeenth century.
  A. Although many people could own shares, the companies traded as a single unit.
  B. Profits were divided among stockholders.
  C. Shares were bought and sold on the exchanges.
  D. The Bank of Amsterdam, the first public bank, was set up in 1610.
  1. It attracted great numbers of depositors and investors.
  2. Through the bank the Dutch were able to borrow at lower interest rates than their competitors.

IX. Public display was often magnificent in the great cities.
  A. Public buildings.
  B. Art collections, many of which were open to the public.
  C. Promenades.
  D. Public streets.
  E. Public gardens.
  F. Even Rome, which was not one of the trading cities, showed some of their tolerance and cosmopolitanism.
  1. Rome was the center for tourists and pilgrims.
  2. Even Protestants were usually safe there.

X. Amsterdam, one of the most important trading cities, was unlike most other great cities in Europe.
  A. It lacked many of the features that distinguished other European cities:
  1. No monasteries.
  2. No castle.

       3. No cathedral.

       4. No university.

       5. Even the churches were rather subdued.

    B. The houses of the rich were built for comfort rather than for show.

  XI. Seventeenth-century art was divided between the baroque and the quiet realism of the Dutch painters.

    A. Baroque art, which prevailed in Catholic countries, was highly theatrical.

       1. Full of movement.

       2. Highly emotional.

       3. In architecture it often engaged in enormous productions.

       4. Professor Weber argues that the baroque created dazzling effects for political purposes:

         a. Bernini in sculpture.

         b. Rubens in painting.

    B. Many of the best Dutch painters, on the other hand, concentrated on domestic scenes:

       1. Paul Potter.

       2. Vermeer.

  XII. The seventeenth century was also the age of the Scientific Revolution.

    A. Many of the great scientists came from modest backgrounds.

       1. Galileo was the son of a musician.

       2. Newton was the son of a yeoman farmer.

    B. Galileo extended the bounds of the visible universe through

       1. Observations with the telescope.

       2. Mathematical calculations.

       3. Eventually, he demonstrated that heavenly and earthly bodies are all governed by the same laws of mechanics.

    C. Newton carried Galileo's work even farther by demonstrating that all bodies are subject to the law of gravity.

    D. The Scientific Revolution went on in both Protestant and Catholic countries.

       1. Copernicus had been a canon of his cathedral.

       2. Kepler was a Protestant, even though he did much of his work for the Catholic Emperor Rudolph.

       3. Even Galileo, whose theories were eventually condemned by the church, tried to be a loyal Catholic.

       4. Pope Gregory XIII improved the calendar in 1582, although many countries were slow to adopt it.

         a. The English used the old calendar until 1752.

         b. The Russians did not adopt the Gregorian calendar until 1918.

  XIII. Holland harbored some of the most radical thinkers of the seventeenth century.

    A. Although Descartes was a French Catholic who tried to avoid religious controversy, he spent much of his career in Protestant Holland.

    1. His thorough-going rationalism was not meant to oppose religious truth.

    2. He still found it convenient to live outside the authority of the church.

B. Baruch Spinoza, who grew up in Amsterdam, was condemned by Jewish authorities for heresy.

    1. He wanted to purge religion of

        a. Miracles.

        b. Prophecies.

        c. Superstition.

    2. He also wanted to demonstrate the natural foundations of the state.

        a. Religion and politics had to be purged of fear and hatred.

        b. He believed that people were the natural-born protectors of their rights.

        c. He opposed religious and political compulsion.

Key to the Images

Domestic interiors: In earlier programs Professor Weber mentions that in Protestant countries painters often concentrated on portraits, landscapes, and scenes of domestic life. In Program 30 especially strong examples appear in the work of Vermeer and Paul Potter.

The Dutch were also pioneers in domestic architecture. The design of the modern home owes much to their example. In particular, they were among the first to divide up living space in the ways we do today.

The Baroque: The term *baroque* derives from a Portuguese word meaning irregular. Instead of concentrating on harmony or symmetry, baroque artists and architects strove for energy and drama. Baroque buildings sometimes appear ready to burst with their own energy. Painters like Rubens and sculptors like Bernini tried to capture highly charged moments, as in Bernini's "Ecstasy of Saint Teresa." Painters often organized their compositions along a diagonal rather than a vertical or horizontal line. The resulting energy often seems to make the paintings spill out of their frames.

Painters of light: Professor Weber argues that in painting this was an age of light. Many of the greatest painters made light itself one of their principal subjects. Georges de la Tour, for instance, a great religious painter, created scenes where all the light emanated from a single source, often a solitary candle. The effect is of light swimming in darkness. Vermeer concentrated on domestic scenes but his luminosity invested even the most ordinary scene with a glow that seems to come from another world. Rembrandt was perhaps the greatest painter of light. The passion of his greatest paintings often comes across most clearly in the contrasts between dark and light.

Focus Questions

1. What was "Lotharingia"? What was its economic importance during this period?
2. What were the important trading cities of Europe in the late Middle Ages and in the sixteenth century?
3. What were some of the commercial institutions that were founded during this period?
4. Why did the governments of the trading cities tend to be more tolerant than those of the dynastic states?
5. Why did trading cities promote public display?
6. How did Dutch painters differ from the baroque painters who were their contemporaries?
7. What were the major scientific achievements of this period?
8. In what ways did the Dutch Republic protect personal freedom and freedom of thought?

——— ASSIGNMENTS AND ACTIVITIES ———

IN CONTEXT

Themes and issues that set Unit Fifteen in context with other units include the following:

• Professor Weber raises the issue of religious toleration in Unit Fifteen. Remember that the Christian parts of Western Europe had never been very tolerant. When Charlemagne, for instance, conquered pagan tribes, his victims usually had to choose between baptism and death. Earlier units show the vigor with which the Catholic church persecuted heresy. The Jews were the most substantial body of non-Christians in Western Europe, and they lived under many legal disabilities, subject to enormous persecution.

• This persecution was the result of more than simple, bloody mindedness. Most Christians sincerely believed that anyone not of their faith was doomed to eternal damnation. Therefore, all false doctrine had to be stopped before it could poison other souls. The church considered that it was being merciful when it persecuted heresy, for the heretic's only chance of salvation was to repent. In later units look especially closely at the area in which religious toleration was first permitted. In some places the authorities decided that they would rather permit diversity of worship rather than destroy the state in an effort to enforce uniformity.

- This was an age of great scientific discovery. In the units that follow we learn that a certain amount of scientific knowledge became part of the intellectual baggage of every educated person. Voltaire and Diderot were men of letters, not scientists; but they both wrote popularized articles on science for a wide audience. Watch for ways in which scientific attitudes began to influence religious belief.
- Professor Weber emphasizes that the Dutch trading cities were especially tolerant during this period. Part of this tolerance was a matter of necessity. The rulers of the cities were Protestant, but Holland contained a substantial Catholic minority. Because foreign Catholic powers were all too ready to intervene in Dutch affairs, the Protestant rulers decided on a relatively tolerant policy.

Textbook Assignment

Read the following pages in your assigned textbook:

Text: *Western Civilizations* (Eleventh Edition, 1988)
Read: Chapter 16, "A Century of Crisis for Early-Modern Europe (c. 1560–c. 1660)," pp. 501–542; and Chapter 17, "The Economy and Society of Early-Modern Europe," pp. 543–586.

Text: *The Western Experience* (Fifth Edition, 1991)
Read: Chapter 15, "A Century of War and Revolt," pp. 569–616; and Chapter 16, "Culture and Society in the Age of the Scientific Revolution," pp. 617–662.

Text: *The Western Heritage* (Fourth Edition, 1991)
Read: Chapter 12, "The Age of Religious Wars," pp. 427–463; and Chapter 14, "New Directions in Science and Thought in the Sixteenth and Seventeenth Centuries," pp. 495–521.

Issues for Clarification

Edict of Nantes

Although the Edict of Nantes (1598) did provide a foundation for a religious peace, it did not create true toleration nor did its provisions survive the seventeenth century.

Certain of the nobility were allowed to worship as Protestants, and Protestants were allowed to hold public offices. In addition, the Protestants of certain cities and towns were allowed to worship publicly. Protestants also obtained a number of fortified towns, which they maintained with their own troops.

During the seventeenth century, the French kings attacked these privileges because it seemed to them that the Protestants were setting up their own state inside France. The fortified towns were recaptured by royal troops and in 1685 the Edict was revoked altogether.

Lotharingia

Lotharingia was an area of Europe that included Belgium, Holland, Luxembourg, the Rhineland, Switzerland, and Northern Italy. The name comes from the Emperor Lothar, or Lothair, who was one of the few rulers to hold this area in a consolidated state. The area is useful to consider as a unit because it has often formed an important network of industrial and commercial powers.

Toleration in Return for Payment

When Professor Weber says that Catholics in Elizabethan England could obtain toleration in return for payment, you should not imagine that they could buy a kind of license that allowed them to practice their religion.

The number of people who remained loyal to the Catholic church seems to have been rather small, perhaps a few hundred thousand. For the most part, Elizabeth and her successors did not want to launch a major effort to search them out. If Catholics remained quiet and practiced their religion in private, they were often left unmolested.

It should also be remembered that England, like most European countries of the time, had no professional police force. Law enforcement was left in the hands of justices of the peace, who were prominent local gentlemen serving in their spare time. If a Catholic family got along with their neighbors, they might very well be left alone.

There was a law, however, that required everyone to attend church. Because the Pope had forbidden the faithful to attend Protestant services, many Catholics felt obliged to stay away. The payments Professor Weber mentions were principally fines for nonattendance.

The surviving records show that many people were fined, sometimes quite heavily, but it is not clear that the fines were always collected. Nor do we know if a careful count was taken at most church services.

These laws were not aimed exclusively at Catholics, for many dissenters —Protestants who refused to participate in the Church of England—were also fined for staying away from church.

Glossary

Bourse: A stock exchange.

Cantons: The major political divisions of Switzerland. During this period Switzerland was a loose confederation of almost independent cantons. The religious war of the 1530s left the Swiss Confederation even more disunited than before.

Cuius reqio eius reliqio: The principle that each ruler should determine the religion of the state.

Huguenots: French Protestants. Most Huguenots were Calvinists.

Timeline

Place each of the following events on the timeline. In some cases you may have to specify a roughly defined period of time rather than a precise date.

1. Religious civil war in Switzerland.
2. Peace of Augsburg.
3. Henry VIII breaks with Rome.
4. Beginning of the religious wars in France and the Netherlands.
5. Saint Bartholomew's Day Massacre.
6. Henry IV becomes a Roman Catholic and enters Paris.
7. Edict of Nantes.
8. Founding of Spanish Inquisition.
9. Beginning and end of Thirty Years' War.
10. Gregory XIII reforms the calendar.

1400   1700

Map Exercise

Find the following locations on the map.

1. Lotharingia.
2. Amsterdam.
3. Lyons.
4. Country that intervened in French religious wars on side of Catholics.
5. Area where Thirty Years' War began.
6. Rhone River.
7. Venice.
8. First sovereign state whose ruler broke with Rome.
9. Area of the Low Countries that remained Catholic.
10. One area where the English aided local Protestants.
11. Bohemia.
12. Holland.

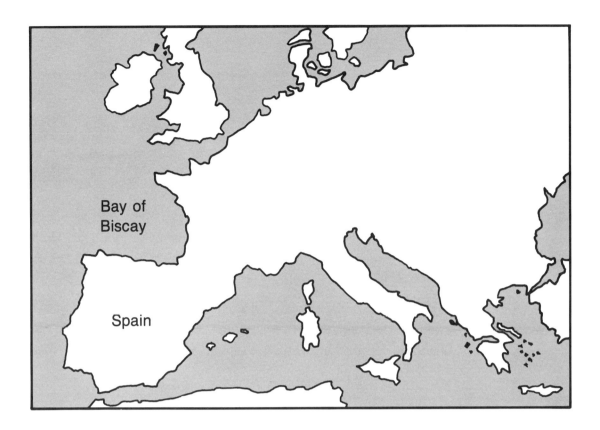

Self-Test

Part I of the self-test asks about important factual material. Part II is interpretive. The answers in Part II are keyed to Professor Weber's interpretations. If you disagree with an answer, be prepared to defend your own understanding of the material. Check your answers at the end of Unit One.

Part I

1. The _____Hanseatic_____ was a league of German trading cities, mostly along the Baltic Sea, including Riga, Danzig, and Lubeck.

2. Augsburg lay in a good position for a trading city because it was close to the Alps, between the _____Rhine_____ and the _____Danube_____ rivers.

3. Until its harbor silted up, Bruges was a focus of trade with the Baltic and the North seas. Shipping then shifted to the city of _____Antwerp_____, and then, after that city was ruined in the wars of religion, to _____Ghent_____.

4. The city of _____A_____ was a pioneer in the development of such commercial institutions as the stock exchange.
   a. Venice
   b. London
   c. Paris
   d. Rome

5. _____Capernos_____ was the Polish astronomer who argued that the earth turns on its own axis and follows an orbit around the sun. The astronomer _____Kepler_____ made an important modification of this theory when he discovered that the earth and other planets actually follow elliptical orbits.

Part II

1. Mark the false choice. Great trading cities such as Antwerp and Amsterdam
   a. sheltered a cosmopolitan population.
   b. maintained order with guard companies composed of their own citizens.
   c. were too interested in commerce to patronize the arts.
   d. tried to permit some degree of religious toleration.

2. Mark the false choice. The *politiques*
   a. were more interested in effective government than in ideal government.
   b. believed that only a strong state could bring order and stability.
   c. believed that only religious uniformity could make the state strong.
   d. tried to create national unity.

3. Which of the following leaders was an advocate of religious toleration?
   a. Martin Luther.
   b. John Calvin.
   c. Philip II of Spain.
   d. Henry IV of France.

4. Mark the false choice. The Treaty of Westphalia
   a. finally established religious toleration in the Holy Roman Empire.
   b. confirmed the territorial sovereignty of Germany's many principalities.
   c. brought an end to the Thirty Years' War.
   d. confirmed France as a great European power.

5. Mark the false choice. In the course of winning independence from Spain, the Dutch
   a. established a republican form of government.
   b. became one of the greatest trading nations in Europe.
   c. drove Catholics out of their realm.
   d. made Amsterdam one of the great trading cities of Europe.

Optional Activity

Although the following activity is not required for the course unless assigned by the instructor, students are encouraged to use it as a source of interesting topics for further study.

Brecht and the Thirty Years' War

Bertolt Brecht was one of the greatest playwrights of the twentieth century. *Mother Courage and Her Children,* which has also been made into a film, is a lengthy play about the Thirty Years' War.

The play's principal character, Mother Courage, travels around Germany with her wagon, supplying goods to the soldiers. In the course of the play it becomes clear that no one really knows what the war is about, and Mother Courage is perfectly willing to do business with both Protestants and Catholics.

Write a paper of 3–5 pages in which you discuss the antiwar themes of the play. Confine your discussion to one or two short scenes. Also remember that Brecht was a communist and that he intended his play to be an indictment of capitalism. Here are some issues to consider. Your paper should confine itself to only one or two of these questions:

- In what sense does the play present the struggle as a specifically capitalist war?
- Or does the play really seem to be about war in general, whatever Brecht may have intended?
- Does Mother Courage herself seem to be a villainess, a heroine, or simply another victim?

Review Questions

The following questions are designed to help you think critically and to construct explanations from factual knowledge. Remember that whenever you learn a new piece of information you should always ask yourself "so what?" questions.

Keep in mind that historians continually disagree on emphases, interpretations, and even on simple matters of fact. Many of the following questions emphasize Professor Weber's particular point of view and ask you to compare it to what you find in your textbook. When you find important disagreements, you should remember that historians are always struggling with each other; this struggle is one that you can enter yourself.

1. Professor Weber discusses Europe's economic "spine," running from Northern Italy to the Low Countries. What were the important cities at either end of the "spine"? With what areas of the world did they trade? What were the important cities in the middle of the "spine"? What natural features, such as mountain passes, rivers, or other bodies of water, made them important?

2. In discussing religious toleration Professor Weber emphasizes a body of politicians called the *politiques,* statesmen such as Henry IV and theorists such as Jean Bodin. What were their principal goals in political life? Why did they adopt their attitude toward religious toleration? The word *politique* is French. In what ways were the *politiques* responding to the special problems of France?

3. What European countries were hurt severely by religious wars? In which of these wars did foreign powers play important roles? Explain in detail. How were these conflicts finally resolved? What countries were spared such wars? Why?

4. In discussing the art of the seventeenth century Professor Weber contrasts Rubens and Vermeer. What are the most important differences between the two in style and subject matter? How do these differences reflect the different classes for whom they worked? Who were Rubens's principal patrons? Who were Vermeer's?

5. What were some of the financial and commercial activities that promoted the growth of a capitalist society? In what cities did they begin? To what cities did they spread?

Further Reading

Sources

Weber, Eugen. *The Western Tradition,* 2nd ed. (1965). "Political and Economic Changes," pp. 364–391.

Studies

Dunn, Richard. *The Age of Religious Wars, 1559–1689.* (1979). One of the best surveys. Especially good for comparative purposes.

Elliott, J. H. *Imperial Spain, 1469–1716.* (1964). An excellent synthesis on the great power that dominated this age.

Mattingly, Garrett. *The Armada.* (1959). A beautifully written book on the Spanish attempt to invade England in 1588.

Parker, Geoffrey. *The Dutch Revolt.* (1977). Gives a good picture of Dutch society during this period.

Rabb, Theodore K. *The Struggle for Stability in Early Modern Europe.* (1975). A synthetic essay arguing that European politics achieved a degree of stability around 1660.

———, ed. *The Thirty Years' War.* (1972). A collection of essays on different aspects of the war.

Santillana, Giorgio di. *The Crime of Galileo.* (1955).

Answer Key

Timeline

1. 1530s.
2. 1555.
3. 1533.
4. 1560s.
5. 1572.
6. 1594.
7. 1598.
8. 1479.
9. 1618–1648.
10. 1582.

Map Exercise

4. Spain.
5. Bohemia (now part of western Czechoslovakia).
8. England.
9. Approximately the area of modern Belgium.
10. France or the Low Countries.

Self-Test

Part I

1. Hanseatic League or Hansa
2. Danube; Rhine
3. Antwerp; Ghent.
4. (a) Venice
5. Copernicus; Kepler

Part II

1. (c) were too interested in commerce to patronize the arts.
2. (c) believed that only religious uniformity could make the state strong.
3. (d) Henry IV of France.
4. (a) finally established religious toleration in the Holy Roman Empire.
5. (c) drove Catholics out of their realm.

Philippe de Champaigne's Portrayal of Louis XIV Conferring the Order of the Holy Spirit on the Duke of Anjou (1665) Royal ceremonies such as this became models for the rest of Europe. Louis XIV made a policy of drawing nobles to his court while reducing their real power in governing the kingdom. (GIRAUDON/Art Resource, NY.)

UNIT SIXTEEN

Program 31: The Age of Absolutism

Program 32: Absolutism and the Social Contract

LEARNING OBJECTIVES

After completing Unit Sixteen students should understand the following issues:

- The main features of political absolutism in the seventeenth century. The lectures concentrate on France. Use your textbook to examine absolutism in other countries.
- The causes of political weakness in France during the first sixty years of the seventeenth century. Professor Weber and your textbook discuss a number of important causes for the political troubles in France. Try to unify these different explanations.
- The attempts of French statesmen to end political disorder. How does your textbook supplement or rebut Professor Weber's arguments about the success or failure of various statesmen?
- The changing status of the French nobility during the seventeenth century.
- The ways in which art and architecture reflected political authority.
- The moral and political aspects of French tragedy in the seventeenth century. State your reasons for agreeing or disagreeing with Professor Weber's argument about the moral content of French tragedy.
- The outcome of the conflicts between parliament and the English crown.
- The ways in which Hobbes and Locke reflect the political events of their

times. Use your textbook to gain a sense of the differing political climates in which they wrote.

TV INSTRUCTION

OVERVIEW
PROGRAM 31: THE AGE OF ABSOLUTISM

Under Louis XIV, royal absolutism reached its height in France. Despite the often despotic qualities of their rule, many Europeans supported absolutist rulers, because it seemed that only a strong central government could suppress religious conflicts, feuding among the nobility, and the constant contending of special interests. Professor Weber argues that this desire for order at all costs carried over into most aspects of art and literature.

I. Apologists for royal absolutism argued that law and order could be achieved if all subjects obeyed a single will.
    A. Rulers claimed that God endowed them with the divine right of kings.
        1. Therefore, kings had absolute rights over their subjects.
        2. Kings also had strong *de facto* control over the church, even in Catholic countries.
    B. Without a strong central authority, countries seemed doomed to
        1. Civil war.
        2. Foreign war.
        3. Religious war.
        4. Social war.

II. France's political problems form the immediate background for much absolutist theory.
    A. Henry IV had been a strong, able king.
        1. Unfortunately, he was murdered in 1610.
        2. His heir, Louis XIII, was a boy of ten.
        3. The kingdom was ruled by the incompetent Queen Mother, Marie de Medicis.
    B. When he became an adult, Louis XIII appointed a brilliant first minister, Cardinal Richelieu, who
        1. Humbled the rebellious nobility.
        2. Restored civil order.
        3. Attacked the French Protestants.
    C. As one of their greatest tasks, Louis XIII and Richelieu tried to suppress violence and feuding.
        1. Duelling was severely punished, with some success.
        2. Private warfare was outlawed.
        3. Nobles were encouraged to serve in the royal army rather than fight one another in private quarrels.

D. By 1643, however, Louis XIII and Richelieu were dead and the throne was occupied by a five-year-old boy.
    1. His mother, Anne of Austria, was regent.
    2. Her minister, Cardinal Mazarin, was highly unpopular.
    3. In the 1650s a series of civil wars broke out, collectively known as the Fronde.
    4. Royal authority was attacked by
      a. The nobility.
      b. The great law court, the Parlement of Paris.

III. Once he came to rule in his own right, Louis XIV was determined never to see the crown humiliated as it had been when he was a boy.
A. As a boy, he had to flee the rioting of Paris.
    1. He never trusted the city.
    2. Eventually, he removed his court to Versailles.
B. Nor did he trust the great nobles.
    1. Many of his ministers were to come from the middle classes.
    2. He lured much of the nobility to Versailles to live lives of splendid harmlessness.

IV. The whole apparatus of royal propaganda created an image of hierarchy, order, and social discipline.
A. In architecture, the palace at Versailles was one of the greatest symbols of his rule.
    1. The facade and interior are splendid.
    2. Unlike baroque splendor, however, Louis's palace was disciplined and orderly.
    3. Even the formal gardens look like exercises in geometry or in close-order drill.
B. This disciplined splendor created a symbol of stable authority.
    1. Louis's art, architecture, and court life were copied by rulers all over Europe.
    2. This splendor gave authority an air of the marvelous, almost of myth.

V. Louis XIV was a great patron of French art but only of the kind of art that could be useful to him.
A. Early in the century French art had been diverse and lively:
    1. Jacques Callot, the etcher, whose great subject was the horror of war.
    2. The le Nain brothers, realistic painters of peasant life.
    3. Georges de la Tour, one of the great masters of light.
B. Much of this earlier work, however, fell into neglect during the reign of Louis XIV, a neglect that in some cases lasted centuries.
C. The king wanted a rigorous, reasonable, cool style.
    1. Nicolas Poussin.
    2. Rigaut.
    3. Nicolas Mansart, one of Louis's favorite architects.
D. Professor Weber argues that the style of Louis XIV was radically different from the other splendid styles of the times.

1. Bernini's baroque, for instance, had fantasy and warmth.
2. Many of Louis's buildings were constructed by gifted bureaucrats.

VI. Professor Weber argues that a counterpart to many of these trends can be found in the plays of Pierre Corneille (1605–1684).
   A. The theme of such a play as *The Cid* is that passions threaten such great interests as the family or the state.
      1. Professor Weber argues that this was a well-founded fear.
      2. Senseless quarreling had brought the country to civil war.
   B. In *The Cid* love has to be subordinated to honor and duty.
      1. Rodrigue and Chimene are about to be married.
      2. Honor, however, forces Rodrigue to kill Chimene's father in a duel.
      3. Chimene is then forced by her own sense of honor to ask the king that Rodrigue be executed.
      4. Significantly, Rodrigue is saved because the king needs him to fight against the Moors.
      5. Royal service seems to be the answer to otherwise insoluble problems.
   C. Professor Weber argues that Corneille was a profound moral thinker.
      1. The conflict here is not between right and wrong, but rather between two legitimate passions:
         a. Love.
         b. Honor.
      2. Professor Weber argues that although the Greeks had been able to conceive of a conflict between two just causes, most later moral codes were less flexible.
         a. Roman thinking was too legalistic.
         b. Christian thought was too simplistic.
   D. Corneille may have taught the nobility moral lessons they would otherwise not have accepted.
      1. He taught the virtues of self-discipline.
      2. He taught that following duty made a man great.
   E. Corneille was also an innovator as a dramatist.
      1. Earlier tragedy had lamented people's impotence before fate.
      2. Corneille exalted choice and free will.
      3. His characters were rational.
         a. They felt the same passions as other people.
         b. But they understood and continually explained those passions.

Key to the Images

Palaces of Louis XIV: The great baroque palaces, as well as those of Louis XIV, were meant to create structures of splendor and awe to house political authorities. In the baroque palaces, however, complexity and dynamic form can create a sense of drama, even fantasy. The palaces of Louis XIV, splendid though they are, are much more sober. They seem far more orderly and stable.

As you view the images in Program 31, look for how architects created these effects. For instance, the palace of Versailles is enormously complex, at least as complex as any baroque palace, but the main lines of the building and facade are clear. The eye is continually caught by ornament but the dominating forms are never in doubt.

This passion for order can best be seen in the great formal gardens at Versailles and the palaces that imitated it. There is no attempt to follow natural forms. Quite the opposite, ponds and hills were shaped artificially, and flower beds were laid out in great patches of color, like regiments on parade.

Portraits of Louis XIV: An age of great portraiture had begun long before this time but paintings rarely give a sense of Louis XIV as a human being. He is always a king, always on display. Paintings typically show him leading troops or conducting ceremonies at court.

Other sovereigns by this time occasionally allowed themselves to be portrayed in more private or more relaxed moments, but Louis seems never to have lived a moment when he was not on display.

Focus Questions

1. What were the arguments made in favor of political absolutism?
2. In what periods of the seventeenth century was the French crown especially weak?
3. What were the most important groups that opposed the centralization of power in the French crown?
4. In what ways were the French kings able to undermine these groups?
5. What were the most important features of the art and architecture patronized by Louis XIV?
6. What were some of the moral issues in the dramas of Corneille?
7. How are these moral issues related to the political problems of the seventeenth century?

OVERVIEW
PROGRAM 32: ABSOLUTISM AND THE SOCIAL CONTRACT

By the second half of the seventeenth century, England and France were the leading nations of two contrasting systems of government, economics, and political institutions. For the next century, much of Europe's history centered on this rivalry. Professor Weber argues that, because the French model emphasized stability and the status quo, the more dynamic English model eventually won out.

I. At first sight it might seem that the French were completely dominant in the eighteenth century.
   A. French culture ruled Europe.
      1. In some countries aristocrats preferred to speak French over their native language:
         a. Russian.
         b. German.
      2. Sometimes books written in English or Italian were published in French before coming out in the original language.
      3. Rulers all over Europe aped the French court:
         a. Germany.
         b. Russia.
         c. Poland.
   B. Life in the French court, however, was stiff and disciplined.
      1. Every courtier had an assigned role to play.
      2. Innovation and spontaneity were discouraged.
   C. Professor Weber argues that stability had become one of the dominant values of French culture.

II. Professor Weber argues that absolutism represented a special balance of forces.
   A. It reflected the triumph of secular values over spiritual ones.
   B. It meant the triumph of the centralized state over local interests.

III. Many absolute governments followed mercantilist economic policies to make their nations wealthy as well as strong.
   A. According to mercantilist theory, nations should try to maximize their stocks of gold and silver. Therefore,
      1. Nations should try to sell as much as possible abroad,
      2. And import as little as possible.
      3. National industries should be protected against foreign competition.
   B. The state often promoted or even ran industries of its own, such as trading and manufacturing companies in
      1. France.
      2. Italy.
      3. Central Europe.
   C. Mercantilist policies complicated relations between the government and the business community.
      1. Initially, businesspeople often welcomed government aid.
      2. As business prospered, however, businesspeople often came to resent government regulations.

IV. By the seventeenth century many thinkers were looking for the rules of human society in nature rather than in divine revelation.
   A. Natural law theorists such as Hugo Grotius argued that all people shared certain basic qualities:
      1. People are naturally sociable or gregarious.
      2. Therefore, people can develop a social consciousness.
      3. All people are capable of social responsibility.

       4. These qualities imply that all people possess certain natural rights.
   B. These assumptions were developed into the social contract theory of society.
       1. People naturally agree to obey certain rules for their common benefit:
         a. For instance, property will be defended against trespass.
         b. People agree to obey a common authority.
       2. Legitimate authority, therefore, derives not from some heavenly command but from the common interest of the governed.

V. In the course of the seventeenth century, English governments took a radically new direction.
   A. Charles I (reigned 1626–1649) tried to implement some of the absolutist policies of the continental monarchies:
       1. He tried to govern and raise taxes without parliament.
       2. He tried to unify and control the church.
   B. By the early 1640s a series of crises had brought the country to civil war:
       1. Religious troubles in Scotland.
       2. Colonial problems and revolt in Ireland.
       3. Political and religious problems in England.
   C. Finally, parliament refused to vote taxes for the king's army because parliamentarians feared that
       1. With a powerful army the king could force parliament to vote however he wanted.
       2. The king might be able to dispense with parliament altogether.
   D. After two civil wars, the king was defeated and finally executed in 1649, and England became a republic.
       1. The armies of Oliver Cromwell, the most powerful parliamentary general, went on to important victories in
         a. Scotland.
         b. Ireland.
       2. When parliament entertained a motion to disband these armies, Cromwell disbanded parliament.
         a. Cromwell ruled as Lord Protector until his death in 1658.
         b. After the failure to establish a stable republic, Charles II, son of the executed king, returned from exile in 1660.
   E. England had not yet reached political stability.
       1. In 1688 the Glorious Revolution deposed King James I.
       2. He was replaced by his daughter Mary and her husband William of Orange.
   F. From now on England would be ruled by both king and parliament; sometimes in harmony, sometimes not.

VI. Each of the English civil wars inspired a great work of political theory.
   A. In 1651 Thomas Hobbes published *Leviathan.*

      1. He upset the natural law theorists by arguing that
        a. Human beings are naturally selfish.
        b. The natural state of humanity is a savage chaos, a war of all against all.
      2. Therefore, only absolute power can preserve people from destroying one another.
        a. Government depends not on a contract but on force.
        b. Even arbitrary tyranny is better than the savagery of nature.
      3. Hobbes defended absolute rulers
        a. Not because they were appointed by God,
        b. But in the interest of ordinary people.
      4. His absolute rule was judged by his success.
  B. The other great English theorist was John Locke, who returned to England in 1688 with William of Orange.
      1. Locke argued that there were occasions when subjects could legitimately rebel against their rulers.
      2. Unlike Hobbes, he argued that the state of nature was not necessarily savage, only imperfect.
      3. Therefore, people band together for mutual benefit and agree to live together on certain terms.
      4. Anyone who breaks those rules should be punished, even the ruler.
  C. Professor Weber argues that Locke's assumptions about human decency form the basis of English legal and constitutional thought.
      1. These assumptions would influence reforming or revolutionary movements throughout the world.
      2. The assumption of human goodness was adopted by certain strains of Protestant thought.
        a. The idea of a human fall from grace became less powerful.
        b. Instead, some Protestants adopted the notion of human perfectibility.
  D. Natural law made the idea of divine right seem arbitrary and unjust.
      1. Political and legal theory became increasingly secular.
      2. People looked less and less for divine intervention in human affairs.

Key to the Images

Rembrandt (1606–1669):   There had been great portrait painters in the West long before the seventeenth century. Many of these painters possessed great psychological insight, but as you look at their work you see that they were often more concerned with their subject's social status than with an exploration of personality.

Rembrandt's portraits, especially the self-portraits and those of his son Titus, break new ground. The strong contrasts of light and dark oftentimes obscure the hints about social status that were so important to earlier portrait painters. The soul seems to shine like a light in the midst of darkness.

Hals (1580?–1666):   Frans Hals was a master of the group portrait. Many of his subjects were members of Dutch civic organizations, as in "The Banquet of the Officers of the Saint George Civic Guard Company." Group portraits, especially in modern photographs, often look stiff and cold, as though the people portrayed have no relationship to one another but only to the camera.

As a painter, however, Hals solved this problem by showing the tensions or interactions that exist within any group. His banqueting scenes are full of movement. Sometimes they seem to be little dramas, as though the painter caught a roomful of people in the midst of an especially lively moment. Even when the subjects are formally posed, however, Hals always gives a sense of them as individuals set down in the midst of a group.

Van Dyck (1599–1641):   Sir Anthony Van Dyck was one of the great portrait painters of the seventeenth century. He was especially famous for his paintings of people at the court of the English King Charles I.

A comparison of Van Dyck's portraits of Charles I to the various portraits of Louis XIV reveals a sharp contrast. Louis XIV is nearly always shown on a state occasion. Every painting declares that he is a great king. Charles I, on the other hand, is sometimes painted as though he was an ordinary gentleman—or an especially splendid gentleman—but the painter does not emphasize that Charles was a king.

Callot (1592–1635):   As an artist and engraver, Jacques Callot portrayed the ordinary life of the seventeenth century. The ordinary life of the seventeenth century being what it was, Callot was one of the first great realistic artists of warfare.

Many artists were fond of painting battles. In the next generation Louis XIV would often be portrayed as a victorious general, but Callot concentrated on the sordid details: the dead, the wounded, soldiers being executed. Callot's vision of brutality extended into other areas of life, as in his scenes of executions.

Focus Questions

1. How did the art and architecture in the palace at Versailles reflect the ideals of French absolutism? (Programs 31 and 32 in Unit Sixteen deal with this issue.)
2. In what ways were mercantile economic policies supposed to increase national strength?

3. Why did businesspeople oppose some aspects of mercantile policy?
4. How did theorists like Grotius and Locke describe the natural tendencies of humankind?
5. In what ways did the theories of Hobbes differ from those of Locke? How did Hobbes differ from French defenders of absolute power?
6. What were the sources of conflict between Charles I and his parliament?
7. What was the outcome of the Glorious Revolution of 1688?

——————— ASSIGNMENTS AND ACTIVITIES ———————

IN CONTEXT

Themes and issues that set Unit Sixteen in context with other units include the following:

- In Unit Sixteen Professor Weber discusses the theory and practice of absolutist rule in the reign of Louis XIV. Look back to earlier units to find reasons why so many of the French welcomed a strong central government. Invasion and civil war tore France apart in the fourteenth and fifteenth centuries. The second half of the sixteenth century was a time of religious warfare. The 1650s, during Louis's minority, witnessed the plotting and rioting of the Fronde. Many of the French believed that only a strong state could save them from civil war and anarchy.

- In Unit Sixteen Professor Weber discusses the natural law theories of Grotius and Locke. Natural law does not assume that people are faultless or innocent, but natural law theorists do argue that human beings are inherently reasonable and capable of pursuing rational goals. These theories go far back into the Middle Ages. In particular, look back to Professor Weber's discussion of the political theories of Thomas Aquinas. In later units watch for Professor Weber's discussion of utilitarianism.

- In earlier units Professor Weber discusses some of the ways in which representative institutions could promote the centralizing powers of the state. In Unit Sixteen the English civil wars of the 1640s and 1650s are a classic example of a parliament becoming a focus of national discontent. In the units that follow look for the parliamentary issues that arose in the early days of the American and French revolutions.

- In Unit Sixteen Professor Weber discusses the Glorious Revolution of 1688. In later units watch for the ways in which king and parliament learned to govern together. This gradual accommodation, which saw many stormy incidents, is one of the most important political developments of eighteenth-century England.

Textbook Assignment

Read the following pages in your assigned textbook:

Text: *Western Civilizations* (Eleventh Edition, 1988)
Read: From Chapter 18, "The Age of Absolutism (1660–1789)," pp. 587–606.

Text: *The Western Experience* (Fifth Edition, 1991)
Read: Chapter 17, "The Triumph of Aristocrats and Kings 1660–1715," pp. 663–704.

Text: *The Western Heritage* (Fourth Edition, 1991)
Read: Chapter 17, "Empire, War, and Colonial Rebellion," pp. 591–621; and Chapter 18, "The Age of Enlightenment: Eighteenth Century Thought," pp. 625–655.

Issues for Clarification

Absolutism

In his *Universal History,* Bishop Bossuet, at one time the tutor of Louis XIV, stated some of the basic principles of royal absolutism:

> The royal power is absolute. . . . The prince need render account of his acts to no one. . . . Without this absolute authority, the king could neither do good nor repress evil. It is necessary that his power be such that no one can hope to escape him, and finally the only protection of individuals against the public authority should be their innocence. [From "Politics Drawn from the Very Words of Holy Scripture," in James Harvey Robinson, ed., *Readings in European History,* vol. 2 (Boston: Ginn and Co., 1906), pp. 275–276.]

At first reading, this quotation sounds like a justification for a modern totalitarian state. Remember, however, that Louis XIV was not a seventeenth-century version of Hitler or Stalin. French kings did not enjoy the enormous armies and police forces needed to run a totalitarian state. Further, although all secular power was supposed to derive from the king, there were many practical limitations on his power.

Louis XIV did curtail the powers of the nobility but aristocrats remained influential. They no longer enjoyed a monopoly on the great positions in government but they staffed the officer corps of the army and the most important positions in the church. On the local level, aristocrats enjoyed important legal privileges in the government of their own estates.

Even within government, the king's powers were limited. Many official positions were up for sale and the men who bought them could not be easily removed. The king also claimed to be God's representative on earth, and the Catholic church generally preached obedience to secular authority. This alliance between church and state, however, meant that the church was too valuable an ally to be easily ignored. Louis XIV could quarrel with the church but he could not afford to do without it.

Law of Nature

In the seventeenth century many political theorists, notably Grotius and Locke, based their ideas on a conception of the law of nature. According to this law, people were naturally reasonable and would naturally act in their own interest if properly instructed. Further, people were naturally inclined to form societies for the protection of the rights they naturally enjoyed.

On this basis, Locke and Grotius erected elaborate theories of political rights and obligations. Thomas Hobbes attacked such ideas strongly. To his way of thinking, people were naturally selfish. They entered into societies simply to protect themselves from the viciousness of others.

Mercantilism

As an economic theory, mercantilism tried to create or foster a powerful state. To achieve this goal, mercantilists recommended building a country's stock of gold and silver by exporting as much as possible, while limiting imports. Further, local industries should be protected against foreign competition.

In general, mercantilists favored active state intervention to promote economic growth. In France, for instance, the government actually ran a number of businesses such as the Gobelins tapestry factories. Mercantilists also looked on colonies as important sources of economic strength, for colonies could supply raw materials, often at regulated prices, as well as a guaranteed market for goods produced in the mother country. Although some businesspeople welcomed such policies, others found that extensive state intervention stifled economic growth.

Glossary

Divine right of kings: Claim made in the seventeenth century that the king derived his authority directly from God. In some countries it was argued that the claim meant the king was not answerable to any other earthly power. Supporters of divine right claimed that it went back to time immemorial. John Locke, however, argued that the theory only appeared in the seventeenth century.

Fronde: Series of civil wars in France during the 1650s. Although alliances were often based on pure expedience, the basic issues were the attempts of the French nobility and the Parlement of Paris to exploit the weakness of the king.

Parlement of Paris: The French *parlements* were not representative assemblies like the English parliament. They were powerful legal bodies that had jurisdiction over various areas of France. The Parlement of Paris was especially troublesome because the king's laws were supposed to be registered there. The king could override the parlement when he was powerful, but in times of weakness the Parlement of Paris was a powerful source of opposition to royal authority.

Timeline

Place each of the following events on the timeline. In some cases you may have to specify a roughly defined period of time rather than a precise date.

1. Glorious Revolution in England.
2. Execution of Charles I.
3. Outbreak of fighting in the English Civil War.
4. Publication of Locke's *Of Civil Government.*
5. Accession of James I.
6. Death of Louis XIV.
7. Lifetime of Corneille.
8. Publication of Hobbes's *Leviathan.*
9. Death of Oliver Cromwell.
10. Murder of Henry IV.
11. Return of Charles II to England.

1600   1750
├───┤

Map Exercise

Find the following locations on the map.

1–2. Two areas outside England where Charles I faced rebellion in 1641.
3. Kingdom of Louis XIV.
4–5. Two countries outside France where aristocrats conducted much of their social and political life in French.

6–7. Two areas outside England subdued by Cromwell.
8. Brandenburg.
9. Homeland of William of Orange.
10. Versailles

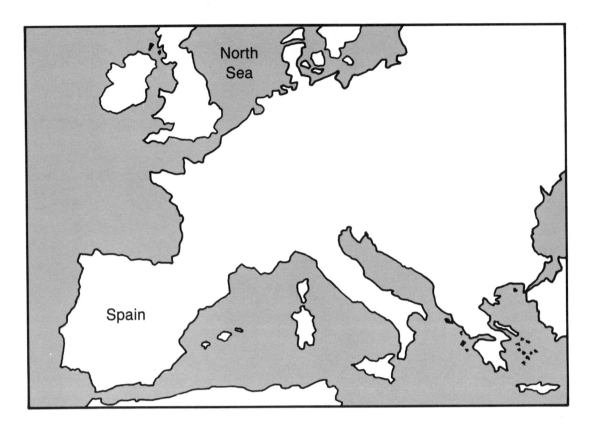

Self-Test

Part I of the self-test asks about important factual material. Part II is interpretive. The answers in Part II are keyed to Professor Weber's interpretations. If you disagree with an answer, be prepared to defend your own understanding of the material. Check your answers at the end of Unit One.

Part I

1. Louis XIV permanently moved his court from _____Paris_____

   to the great palace at ___Versailles___.

2. The political absolutism of the seventeenth century entrusted absolute power to
   a. the feudal lords.
   b. the church.
   c. the cities.
   d. the monarch.

3. For long periods in the seventeenth century, ___France___ was governed by regents because both Louis XIII and ___Louis XIV___ became kings when they were children, long before they could govern in their own right.

4. Which of the following was *not* one of the French statesmen who tried to create public order by concentrating power in the central monarchy?
   a. Richelieu.
   b. Louis XIII.
   c. Pascal.
   d. Louis XIV.

5. The Glorious Revolution in the year _____1688_____ deposed _____James II_____ and replaced him with _____William + Mary_____

Part II

1. In the series of civil wars known as the Fronde, the _____nobles_____ and the _____Parliament of Paris_____ tried to assert their rights against the French crown.

2. Mark the false choice. In an attempt to build a strong monarchy, Louis XIV
   a. created a splendid court for his nobility, while depriving them of real power.
   b. chose most of his ministers from the middle class.
   c. followed a mercantilist economic policy.
   d. extended religious toleration to all his subjects willing to live in peace.

3. Mark the false choice. Mercantilism was an economic system
   a. that advocated exporting as much as possible and importing as little.
   b. under which countries tried to build up their stock of gold and silver.
   c. aimed at making a state more powerful than its rivals.
   d. that advocated the free play of market forces.

4. Mark the false choice. During 1641–1642 parliament refused to grant taxes to Charles I to pay for an army
   a. because they feared that with a strong army he could force parliament to vote however he wanted.
   b. because they feared that with a strong army he could collect other taxes, even if they had not been voted.
   c. because parliament sympathized with the Irish rebels.
   d. because they feared that with a strong army he could govern permanently without parliament.

5. Mark the false choice. In *The Leviathan,* Thomas Hobbes
   a. argued that the natural state of man is a state of war.
   b. argued that the most important function of a ruler is to maintain peace.
   c. argued that the basic principle of life is selfishness.
   d. argued that this selfishness justifies the overthrow of rulers.

Optional Activity

Although the following activity is not required for the course unless assigned by the instructor, students are encouraged to use it as a source of interesting topics for further study.

Literature and Society

Professor Weber argues that Corneille's play *The Cid* reveals many concerns that troubled seventeenth-century France. In particular, he argues that the play tried to teach political and moral lessons to the nobility.

France's other great tragedian during this period was Jean Racine. To test Professor Weber's thesis, examine one of Racine's plays to determine if it is concerned with the same moral and political issues that are found in Corneille.

For this assignment, Racine's *Phedre* (or *Phaedra*) and *Andromaque* (or *Andromache*) are recommended. Many translations are available in English; those by Richard Wilbur, C. H. Sisson, and Wallace Fowlie are recommended. Avoid the translation of *Phaedra* by Robert Lowell.

Write a paper of 3–5 pages in which you analyze one scene from the play you have chosen. How does Racine treat the conflict between public duty and private passion? At what audience do you think Racine was aiming his play? Describe the similarities or differences in the moral visions of Corneille and Racine. Antoine Adam's *Grandeur and Illusion* (1972) (see Further Reading) gives important background.

Films

You may wish to view some of the following films, which deal with matters discussed in this unit.

- *Cromwell,* starring Richard Harris, gives some sense of the political unrest of the 1640s and 1650s.
- *The Devils,* directed by Ken Russell, dramatizes an actual case in the reign of Louis XIII in which a priest was accused of demonic possession. However, the film has only the slightest resemblance to reality.

Review Questions

The following questions are designed to help you think critically and to construct explanations from factual knowledge. Remember that whenever you learn a new piece of information you should always ask yourself "so what?" questions.

Keep in mind that historians continually disagree on emphases, interpretations, and even on simple matters of fact. Many of the following questions emphasize Professor Weber's particular point of view and ask you to compare it to what you find in your textbook. When you find important disagreements, you should remember that historians are always struggling with each other; this struggle is one that you can enter yourself.

1. Who were the most important kings or statesmen who tried to centralize the French state in the seventeenth century? What classes or institutions were their greatest opponents? Why were so many French subjects willing to support such a great concentration of power?
2. The French kings of the seventeenth century were great patrons of art, especially of architecture. What were the principal features of the styles they favored? Both the baroque style, which is discussed in earlier units, and the neoclassical style of Louis XIV were intended to glorify the power of rulers. What were some of the common features of these styles? How did they differ?
3. In part of his discussion of Corneille's *Le Cid,* Professor Weber treats the play as a didactic work directed at an audience "that couldn't be touched by sermons, by moralizing, by sentimentalism." To what audience is Professor Weber referring? What were the principal lessons embodied in this play? Corneille was also a considerable moral thinker. What is the principal conflict in *Le Cid*? In what ways is this conflict more complex than a simple struggle between right and wrong?
4. England experienced two civil wars in the seventeenth century: a bloody, protracted war in the 1640s and a nearly bloodless coup in 1688. What were the causes of the first civil war and why was the fighting so drawn out? What were the causes of the second civil war and why was there almost no fighting at all?
5. Both Hobbes and Locke begin their arguments by imagining the condition of the human race before the creation of governments. Compare and contrast the two thinkers on the following issues. What were the principal features of this early condition? Why did people originally create governments? What are the duties of rulers to their subjects? What rights do subjects have to resist their rulers?

Further Reading

Sources

de Sevigne, Madame. *Letters.* Madame de Sevigne was one of the great letterwriters of all time. She was well connected at the court of Louis XIV and had many friends in intellectual and literary circles.

Locke, John. *Two Treatises of Government.* The Second Treatise is the classical statement of Locke's political theories.

Weber, Eugen. *The Western Tradition,* 2nd ed. (1965). "The Seventeenth Century," pp. 392–446. "The Political Debate," pp. 448–475.

Studies

Adam, Antoine. *Grandeur and Illusion: French Literature and Society, 1600–1750.* (1972). Excellent study on the relationship between social and literary issues.

Church, William F., ed. *The Greatness of Louis XIV: Myth or Reality?* (1972). A good collection of scholarly articles. Opposing viewpoints about the importance of Louis XIV.

Goubert, Pierre. *Louis XIV and Twenty Million Frenchmen.* (1970). Excellent short work on social and economic life.

Lewis, W. H. *The Splendid Century: Life in the France of Louis XIV.* (1953). Good popular history of social life. Good anecdotes.

Saint-Simon, Louis. *Historical Memoirs,* 2 vols. (1967 and 1968). Great gossipy accounts of life at the court of Louis XIV.

Prall, Stuart E. *The Puritan Revolution: A Documentary History.* (1968). A large collection of sources on the English Civil War.

Treasure, G. R. R. *Seventeenth Century France.* (1981). One of the best surveys.

Wolf, John B. *Louis XIV.* (1968). Good political biography.

Answer Key

Timeline
1. 1688.
2. 1649.
3. 1642.
4. 1688.
5. 1603.
6. 1715.
7. 1605–1684.
8. 1651.
9. 1658.
10. 1610.
11. 1660.

Map Exercise
1–2. Ireland and Scotland.
   3. France.
4–5. Russia and Germany are mentioned in the lectures. Your textbook may provide additional examples.
6–7. Scotland and Ireland.
   9. Holland.

Self-Test

Part I

1. Paris; Versailles.
2. (d) the monarch.
3. France; Louis XIV
4. (c) Pascal.
5. 1688; James II; William and Mary.

Part II

1. Nobility; Parlement of Paris
2. (d) extended religious toleration to all his subjects willing to live in peace.
3. (d) advocated the free play of market forces.
4. (c) because parliament sympathized with the Irish rebels.
5. (d) argued that this selfishness justifies the overthrow of rulers.

The French caption reads, "The genius of Voltaire and Rousseau conducts these celebrated writers to the temple of glory and immortality." The scene is meant to be a model of dignity and simplicity, with children playing along the path as the two great men make their way to a classical temple. (SNARK/Art Resource, NY.)

UNIT SEVENTEEN

Program 33: The Enlightened Despots

Program 34: The Enlightenment

LEARNING OBJECTIVES

After completing Unit Seventeen students should understand the following issues:

- The relationship between warfare and economic growth. Consult your textbook for examples of eighteenth-century wars that were motivated largely by economic considerations. Find examples of wars for which a purely economic interpretation seems too limited.
- The rise or decline of major European powers. As you compare your notes with your textbook, look for similar ways in which rulers tried to make their states more powerful. Consider the countries in which these methods were most successful.
- The relationship between the enlightened despots and the French philosophes. The lecture discusses Voltaire and Diderot. Compare Professor Weber's arguments to those in your textbook.
- The relations between the enlightened despots and their subjects. Use your textbook to supplement Professor Weber's discussion. Find examples of the problems faced by reforming rulers in different countries.
- The ways in which the rococo style was a reaction against the more ponderous style of the age of Louis XIV. From the images in the lectures and in your textbook, consider ways in which this style reflects important changes in personal and social life.

━━━━━━━ *TV INSTRUCTION* ━━━━━━━

OVERVIEW
PROGRAM 33: THE ENLIGHTENED DESPOTS

Because maritime powers tend to be the most economically advanced nations, many eighteenth-century countries fought wars to expand overseas or to gain access to the sea. Professor Weber argues further that many Central and Eastern European powers, who had only limited access to the sea, tried to make their realms stronger and more prosperous through enlightened administration. These enlightened despots found support among many of Western Europe's leading intellectuals, the philosophes.

I. Throughout history, access to the sea has often been the key to prosperity.
  A. Until the invention of the railroad, travel by land was slow, dangerous, and expensive.
  B. Rivers were enormously important to traders but river travel had its own problems:
    1. Rapids.
    2. Sand banks.
    3. Shallows.
    4. Varying water level.
    5. Tolls that could make even short journeys expensive.
  C. Therefore, many of the leading trading powers had based their prosperity on sea routes:
    1. The Italian city-states of the Renaissance.
    2. Spain and Portugal in the sixteenth century.
    3. England and Holland in the seventeenth century.
  D. Loss of sea routes meant economic decline.
    1. In 1571 the loss of Cyprus to the Turks sealed the economic decline of Venice.
    2. In 1588 the English defeated the Spanish armada and marked a first step in the long, slow decline of Spain.
    3. By the middle of the seventeenth century English fleets were beginning to defeat the Dutch.

II. Many countries in Central and Eastern Europe possessed only limited access to the sea.
  A. Some of these countries were able to expand whatever access they had.
    1. The Russians drove to acquire ports on
      a. The Baltic.
      b. The Black Sea.
    2. The Austrians tried to revive Antwerp in the Austrian Netherlands.
      a. The Dutch, however, were able to prevent this revival.

       b. The Austrians created the port of Trieste at the head of the Adriatic.

    3. Prussia, which had ports on the Baltic, established overseas trading companies.

  B. None of these enterprises was very successful because the continental powers had to concentrate on land wars.

    1. Nevertheless, Professor Weber argues that a pragmatic business mentality was gaining ground.

    2. This pragmatism imposed a curb on the destructiveness of warfare.

III. Professor Weber argues that warfare became less destructive in the eighteenth century.

  A. One cause was revulsion at the savagery of earlier wars, especially those of the seventeenth century. The French, for instance, destroyed Heidelberg in 1689 and then again in 1694.

  B. Wars were also fought with a more businesslike mentality.

    1. It made little sense to destroy territory a nation wanted to exploit.

      a. Therefore, destruction should be kept to a minimum.

      b. Civilians should be involved as little as possible.

    2. Armies did not aim at total destruction of the enemy.

      a. They maneuvered to outflank one another or to gain position.

      b. They tried to cut off the enemy from its base of supplies.

      c. Generals were not eager for pitched battles.

    3. As far as possible, armies brought their own provisions, instead of living off the land.

IV. Nevertheless, the eighteenth century was a time of widespread warfare, especially in Central and Eastern Europe where boundaries were still fluid.

  A. Russia now became a great power under the rule of

    1. Peter the Great.

    2. Catherine the Great.

  B. Prussia became an increasingly important power under

    1. Frederick-William I.

    2. Frederick the Great.

  C. The Austrian Habsburgs rolled back the Turks in Central and Eastern Europe under

    1. Maria-Theresa.

    2. Joseph II.

  D. These wars also involved many other powers:

    1. England.

    2. France.

    3. Sweden.

    4. Holland.

  E. European politics had become so thickly intertwined that nations would intervene simply to prevent one country from becoming too powerful. This policy is known as the balance of power.

   F. By 1795, as the result of three separate partitions, Poland had been divided among
     1. Prussia.
     2. Russia.
     3. Austria.

   G. European wars were also fought over world dominion and world trade.
     1. Spanish trade and possessions in the Americas were fought over by the
       a. English.
       b. French.
       c. Dutch.
       d. Spanish.
     2. French possessions in North America and India were also crucial issues,
     3. As were the British colonies in North America and the West Indies.

V. Professor Weber argues that, because Central and Eastern European powers were shut out of the action overseas, they tried to strengthen their realms through more efficient administration at home. Some of the maritime powers also tried to strengthen themselves in these ways.
   A. More efficient administration was the goal of enlightened despots in
     1. Naples.
     2. Tuscany.
     3. Spain.
     4. Portugal.
     5. Prussia.
     6. Russia.
     7. Austria.
     8. Scandinavia.
   B. Frederick the Great (ruled 1740–1786) was one of the most powerful of the enlightened despots.
     1. He was a great general.
     2. He was a patron of Voltaire.
     3. He described himself as "the first servant of his people."
   C. Such rulers tried to rationalize government administration through such measures as
     1. Censuses, which were useful for
       a. Taxation.
       b. Conscription.
     2. Surveys of their lands.
     3. Training an efficient bureaucracy.
   D. Although religious laws often remained on the books, the enlightened despots were generally tolerant.

E. This was an age of migrations in which people persecuted in one country would move to another that was more tolerant:
 1. Irish Catholics fled English rule.
 2. Supporters of the exiled Stuarts fled Scotland.
 3. French Protestants fled to
    a. England.
    b. North America.
    c. Prussia.

VI. Many of the enlightened despots put pressure on the church, even to the point of outright attacks.
 A. Some simply wanted the church's money and property.
 B. Some wanted the church to perform certain duties:
    1. To care for the poor.
    2. To represent the central government.
 C. Some limited the church's powers in order to
    1. Limit or abolish ecclesiastical censorship.
    2. Improve education.
 D. The Jesuits played a paradoxical role in this struggle between church and government.
    1. In 1773 Catholic powers persuaded the pope to abolish the order:
       a. France.
       b. Spain.
       c. Portugal.
    2. The Jesuits, however, were welcomed as educators in a number of non-Catholic countries:
       a. Prussia.
       b. Russia.
    3. Finally, the order was restored in 1814.

VII. The enlightened despots were continually looking to other countries, especially England and France, to find people who could help them.
 A. They needed trained personnel:
    1. Teachers.
    2. Writers.
    3. Scientists.
 B. To attract such people, rulers abolished censorship.
 C. Western ideas were thought to be connected with western superiority in
    1. Technology.
    2. Weaponry.
    3. Productivity.

VIII. The enlightened despots believed that a well-ordered state was a strong state.
 A. They wanted their subjects to be
    1. Educated.

    2. Prosperous.
    3. Content.
  B. They wanted wise laws
    1. Consistently administered by royal officials.
    2. Not capriciously enforced by local nobles.
  C. They wanted prosperous cities.
  D. Above all, they wanted regular taxes, collected from everyone, to pay for the
    1. Army.
    2. State machinery.

IX. Professor Weber argues that the enlightened despots failed because what they wanted was a contradiction in terms.
  A. They would have needed a social revolution to achieve their aims.
  B. In fact, they didn't really want to revolutionize society. They only wanted to make it more efficient.
  C. The enlightened despots met opposition from all ranks of society.
    1. The nobles opposed them in
      a. Prussia.
      b. Hungary.
    2. In Belgium the middle class objected.
    3. The church protested in
      a. Russia.
      b. Catholic countries.
    4. Peasants revolted in
      a. Transylvania.
      b. Hungary.

X. An unlikely alliance sprang up between the enlightened despots and some of Europe's leading intellectuals, or philosophes.
  A. These rulers drew support from some of Europe's leading thinkers:
    1. Diderot.
    2. Voltaire.
    3. Hume.
    4. Bentham.
    5. Kant.
  B. The philosophes had acquired a new function in society.
    1. They were no longer retired seekers of wisdom.
    2. They looked for possibilities for social reform.
  C. Although they were a disparate group of thinkers, the philosophes shared a number of characteristics:
    1. They were often hostile to the accepted versions of revealed religion.
    2. They were rationalists, determined to teach the world the power and rights of the human intelligence.
    3. They were heavily influenced by

       a. Newton.
       b. Locke.
    4. They assumed that everything can be understood by the human mind.
  D. Like the enlightened despot, the philosophes wanted
    1. Order.
    2. Prosperity.
    3. Tolerance.
    4. Education.
    5. Fair administration of the law.
  E. In social matters, both despots and philosophes
    1. Wanted to encourage the middle class as a source of prosperity and enlightenment.
    2. Distrusted aristocratic privileges.
  F. Although most of the philosophes were from Western Europe, it was farther east that they found rulers most ready to take their advice.

Key to the Images

Corvée: During the Middle Ages peasants often worked on their lord's estate as part of their feudal obligations. By the eighteenth century, however, most European peasants paid rent for their land. A number of medieval obligations survived, however, such as the obligation to contribute labor (in France, this obligation was known as the corvée).

Several images in Program 33 show peasants at work on such projects as building roads. Although this obligation was not crushing for most peasants, it was bitterly resented because it prevented them from making the most efficient use of their time. The corvée was among the obligations that were abolished on the night of August 4, 1789, in the early days of the French Revolution.

Eighteenth-century tactics: A striking image in Program 33 depicts the victory of Frederick the Great over the Austrians at Leuthen in 1757. Professor Weber argues that warfare in the eighteenth century depended on the clever maneuvering of complex formations of troops.

Frederick the Great of Prussia was one of the most brilliant generals of his time, and in this battle he faced an Austrian army that outnumbered him two to one. By sending his troops into battle in staggered formations, however, Frederick caught the Austrians off guard and won one of his greatest victories.

Salons: Several images in Program 33 show eighteenth-century writers at the center of great social scenes. Voltaire is portrayed reading a new work at the salon of Madame Geoffrin in 1755. It was at social gatherings like this that the philosophes and other writers of the time often spread their ideas by reading and discussion.

The salon remained a feature of French literary life well into the twentieth century. Hostesses tried to patronize famous writers who brought glamour to their social life. It was known, for instance, that Voltaire was a regular fixture at the salon of one hostess, Diderot at another.

Focus Questions

1. How did access to sea routes contribute to economic prosperity and political strength?
2. What were the most important patterns of emigration in the eighteenth century?
3. In what ways did warfare become more pragmatic in the eighteenth century? How did pragmatism affect the destructiveness of warfare?
4. What states emerged as major European powers in the course of the eighteenth century?
5. Who were some of the eighteenth-century rulers described as enlightened despots? What were the most important features of their policies?
6. Why did the policies of the enlightened despots often bring them into conflict with the Catholic church?
7. Why did the ideals of the philosophes seem to be compatible with the political goals of the enlightened despots?

OVERVIEW
PROGRAM 34: THE ENLIGHTENMENT

The alliance between philosophes and enlightened despots was based on mutual misunderstanding. Despite their shortcomings, however, the despots were often better rulers than potentates who made no pretensions to enlightenment. By the eighteenth century, a new, wittier, more frivolous style—the rococo—had touched European art. This new style also reflected changes in sentiment and feeling.

    I. Because many Western European countries seemed firmly established, it often happened that the rulers of more malleable countries to the east were most ready to listen to the advice of the philosophes.
      A. Voltaire carried on a long correspondence with Frederick the Great.
      B. Diderot carried on an equally long correspondence with Catherine the Great.
      C. Despite quantities of good advice, however, the enlightened despots rarely lived up to their intentions.

1. The privileges of the nobility, for instance, were not abolished.
    a. In Prussia, for instance, the nobility maintained close to a monopoly on the officer corps.
    b. The rulers needed the nobles to fill positions of command.
2. In some countries serfdom was abolished,
    a. But only on the royal estates.
    b. Nobles kept their serfs.
3. The philosophes talked about freedom but the rulers needed discipline.

II. Many reforms of the enlightened despots were only for show.
    A. Catherine the Great, for instance, had her ministers draw up a new constitution.
        1. It was widely circulated in Europe, where it won great admiration.
        2. It had almost no relation to the truth about Russia.
    B. Catherine, in particular, let herself be deluded about the strength and prosperity of her nation.

III. Relations between the philosophes and the enlightened despots were based on mutual misunderstanding.
    A. The philosophes were concerned with the progress and dignity of humanity.
    B. The despots were trying to increase the power of the state.
    C. Both groups promoted individualism.
        1. The philosophes thought they were advancing the dignity of humanity.
        2. The despots were interested in administrative convenience.
            a. It was easier to govern isolated individuals,
            b. Instead of people who belonged to collective groups with strong collective powers.

IV. The philosophes were so concerned with injustices in their own countries that they were tempted to believe that their distant patrons were trying to establish real utopias.
    A. Disillusion often set in when philosophes visited these distant lands.
        1. Voltaire in Prussia.
        2. Diderot in Russia.
    B. Even so, the philosophes often missed the great injustices in the countries they visited.

V. Nevertheless, the enlightened despots were often better rulers than many of their unenlightened contemporaries.
    A. Germany, in particular, was a patchwork of states, whose rulers varied widely in competence and decency.
        1. There were between two and three hundred states.
        2. There were nearly ten times that number of sovereign entities.
    B. As the century wore on, many of the smaller states fell under

French influence, because they maintained their position by playing off

1. France.

2. The emperor.

C. Many of these rulers still maintained their medieval rights over
commoners.

   1. In many places only the ruler and nobility could hunt.

   2. Peasants could not even protect their crops with their

      a. Dogs.

      b. Firearms.

D. Some of these minor rulers gave free rein to their eccentricity,
insanity, or simple stupidity.

VI. In this same period a new style, the rococo, appeared in art and
architecture.

   A. It was daintier and lighter than earlier styles.

      1. Partly it was a reaction to the solemnity of the styles of Louis
XIV.

      2. It also gave freer rein to frivolity and imagination.

      3. Furniture grew less massive.

      4. Clothing became lighter and brighter.

   B. Professor Weber describes the painters of the eighteenth century
as reveling in color, freedom, and enchantment.

      1. The exuberance of Boucher.

      2. The dramatic paintings of Tiepolo.

      3. The enchanted mirages of the Guardi brothers.

      4. The erotic flippancy of Fragonard.

   C. Jean-Antoine Watteau was perhaps the most representative
painter of the eighteenth century.

      1. His colors shimmer.

      2. Much of his work appears bright and misty.

      3. His people seem as shimmering and evanescent as an autumn
day.

      4. He loved scenes of pleasure:

         a. Games.

         b. Dances.

         c. Picnics.

         d. Music.

      5. At the same time, this pleasure is delicate, as though it were
about to vanish.

   D. Rococo gardens abandoned the rigidity so loved in the age of
Louis XIV.

      1. They were full of irregularities, whimsy, unexpected twists and
turns.

      2. Some even tried to create an artificial wilderness or artificial
ruins.

   E. A taste developed for exotic fashions from

      1. Turkey.

      2. China.

F. Professor Weber suggests that music may have been the greatest rococo art.
   1. It was the great evanescent art.
   2. Although the notes survive on paper, every performance vanishes as soon as it ends.
   3. Rococo architecture even looks musical. Some of its greatest buildings were
      a. Theaters.
      b. Opera houses.
      c. Even rococo churches look like opera houses.
      d. In such churches, it almost seems that joy has driven hellfire out of the building.

VII. Professor Weber argues that such changes in art and style reflect important developments in other areas of social life.
  A. It was in this period that people began to speak out against
   1. Torture.
   2. Public execution.
   3. Repressive legislation.
  B. Some of these people may have wanted reform simply because their tastes had changed.
   1. They found cruelty repulsive.
   2. Their manners had become gentler.
   3. Their feelings were more humane.
  C. Changes in taste can be as profound as changes in beliefs or ideas.

Key to the Images

Enlightened despots: Many of the enlightened despots of Central and Eastern Europe tried to encourage economic growth in their realms. Monarchs had always been portrayed as great warriors and wise judges. Now they were also appearing as clever businesspeople or improving landlords.

An image in Program 34 shows Frederick the Great on a visit to a spinning factory. Although Frederick was one of the greatest soldiers of his time, he also wanted to show his interest in practical affairs. Similarly, Joseph II appears on a visit to a farm. Agriculture was no longer the concern solely of peasants. Even a gentleman could show an interest in farming, in this case the greatest gentleman of his realm.

Boucher (1703–1770): Francois Boucher was an especially popular painter of the eighteenth century. In paintings such as "Angelica and Medoro" and "The Toilet of Venus" he showed his love for the human body. Professor Weber emphasizes the delicate, fleeting scenes that rococo painters loved to portray. Boucher is an especially good example. In real life the plump rosy flesh he loved to paint can only keep its tone and color for a short time. Beauty this delicate is always fleeting.

Fragonard (1732–1806):   Jean Honore Fragonard was another popular eighteenth-century painter. In "Portrait of a Lady with a Dog" and "The Swing," he painted social scenes, often with a heavy dose of flirtation delicately painted.

Watteau (1684–1721):   Professor Weber considers Antoine Watteau to be one of the most characteristic painters of the eighteenth century. Like other artists of his time, he painted scenes of pleasure or entertainment, as in "Assembly in a Park" and "Embarcation for Cythera." Often the subdued lighting and outlines of Watteau's work create a sense of melancholy in the midst of pleasure, a sense that all these pleasures will soon be gone.

Focus Questions

1. Why did some of the French philosophes act as advisers to the despots of Central and Eastern Europe?
2. Why were the achievements of the enlightened despots so much more limited than their initial goals?
3. In what ways were the enlightened despots an improvement over many other European rulers?
4. Why was equality before the law an important issue for the enlightened despots and for the philosophes?
5. How did the smaller states of Europe preserve their independence?
6. What were the most important features of the rococo style?
7. How was the rococo style reflected in social and political life?

—————— ASSIGNMENTS AND ACTIVITIES ——————

IN CONTEXT

Themes and issues that set Unit Seventeen in context with other units include the following:

• Professor Weber argues that warfare became less harsh in the eighteenth century. Care was taken to spare civilians at least a few of the horrors of war, and armies tried to outmaneuver their enemies rather than to annihilate them. Contrast the wars of the eighteenth century to the Thirty Years' War and the campaigns of Louis XIV. This civilized style of warfare did not survive the eighteenth century. Napoleon's troops often moved so quickly and in such great numbers that they were forced to live off the land. His tactics also depended on committing great numbers of soldiers in pitched battles so as to destroy the enemy's army.

- In their attempts to make their countries strong through administrative reform, the enlightened despots of Central and Eastern Europe adopted many of the policies of Louis XIV. Unlike Louis, however, they usually did not try to impose religious uniformity on their subjects. In their attempts to create administrative efficiency and to impose the ideal of equality before the law, the enlightened despots anticipated some of the demands of the French Revolution.

- In Unit Seventeen Professor Weber emphasizes some of the factors that promoted or hindered the growth of trade in various European countries. In later units look for ways in which England, the great trading country of the eighteenth century, would become the first great industrialized nation. Do trade and industry always go hand in hand?

- The eighteenth century was a great age of emigration. In some cases emigration simply continued trends that had begun in the seventeenth century. The emigration of French Huguenots to North America and to Protestant parts of Europe is an especially prominent example.

- Europe had long had important scholars and thinkers, but during this period the philosophes adopted a stance that we still associate with intellectuals today. They thought of themselves as social reformers. They expected that their ideas would change society for the better. Look back to earlier units for examples of other writers and thinkers who expected their ideas to change the world. In Units Five – Eight of Semester I on the ancient Greeks, Plato, with his ideal of the philosopher king, and Aristotle, the teacher of Alexander the Great, are notable figures. In the units that follow examine Karl Marx and Lenin as examples of intellectuals in politics.

Textbook Assignment

Read the following pages in your assigned text book:

Text: *Western Civilizations* (Eleventh Edition, 1988)
Read: From Chapter 18, "The Age of Absolutism," pp. 595 – 628; and from Chapter 19, "The Scientific Revolution and Enlightenment," pp. 649 – 665.

Text: *The Western Experience* (Fifth Edition, 1991)
Read: Chapter 18, "Absolutism and Empire 1715 – 1770s," pp. 705 – 737; and Chapter 19, "The Age of Enlightenment," pp. 738 – 768.

Text: *The Western Heritage* (Fourth Edition, 1991)
Read: Chapter 17, "Empire, War, and Colonial Rebellion," pp. 591 – 621; and Chapter 18, "The Age of Enlightenment: Eighteenth-Century Thought," pp. 625 – 655.

Issues for Clarification

Partitions of Poland

The partitions of Poland are the most notorious examples of eighteenth-century diplomacy. During this period, Austria, Russia, and Prussia were fierce rivals, as they all tried to expand in Central Europe. The partitions allowed these nations to enjoy the spoils of victory without having to win them in war.

On three separate occasions — 1772, 1793, and 1795 — Austria, Russia, and Prussia each annexed large sections of Poland, until finally, in 1795, the country ceased to exist as an independent state.

For more than a hundred years, Polish revolutionaries tried to regain their country's independence, although Poland did not become a sovereign state until after World War I.

Tolls

Transportation was expensive throughout the eighteenth century. The problem was aggravated because in many countries the roads, rivers, bridges, and canals were subject to tolls levied by local lords or other authorities. In countries like Germany, where political authority was fragmented, the problem was especially severe. A merchant might have to pay several heavy tolls over the course of only a few miles. Pictures and travelogues of the Rhine Valley often show great numbers of castles along the river. Many of these places were the seats of local magnates who supported themselves by levying tolls.

The tolls were lucrative and could be one of the principal sources of revenue for a small state, but there was a heavy price to be paid in terms of economic progress.

Jesuits

Professor Weber mentions that after the dissolution of the Jesuit Order many of the members emigrated to non-Catholic countries where they were welcomed as educators and scholars. This was the case in Prussia and Russia, two of the countries mentioned in Program 33, but we should not assume that the Jesuits were universally welcomed. In England, for instance, Protestants often considered Jesuits to be secret agents for Catholicism.

Mercenaries

Throughout the eighteenth century, rulers of the German states, many of them quite small, would raise troops and hire them out as mercenaries. The Hessians, who played a prominent role in trying to suppress the American Revolution, were mercenaries hired by the British.

Glossary

Philosophe: Some of the differing connotations of the word *philosophe* appear in this definition taken from the dictionary of the French Academy of Sciences: "(1) a student of the sciences; (2) a wise man who lives a quiet life; (3) a man who by free thought puts himself above the ordinary duties and obligations of civil life." The definition comes from the end of the seventeenth century. By the middle of the 1700s, the word had come to mean a man who studied society to bring about social reforms.

Rococo: A style of art and architecture that developed in eighteenth-century France. In architecture the style uses elaborate ornamentation, such as imitations of rocks, leaves, and seashells. Modeling is usually delicate and involved.

Timeline

Place each of the following events on the timeline. In some cases you may have to specify a roughly defined period of time rather than a precise date.

1. Cyprus conquered by the Turks.
2. Destruction of Heidelberg by the French.
3. Final partition of Poland.
4. Reign of Frederick the Great.
5. Period of abolition of the Jesuits.
6. Death of Louis XIV.

1550   1850

Map Exercise

Find the following locations on the map.

1–2. Two areas where Russia tried to gain access to the sea.
3. Adriatic Sea.
4. Port in the Low Countries that the Austrians tried to revive unsuccessfully.
5–6. Two areas in Europe where Hugeunot refugees settled.
7. Rhineland.
8. Port established by the Austrians to gain access to the Mediterranean.
9. Prussia.
10. Saint Petersburg.

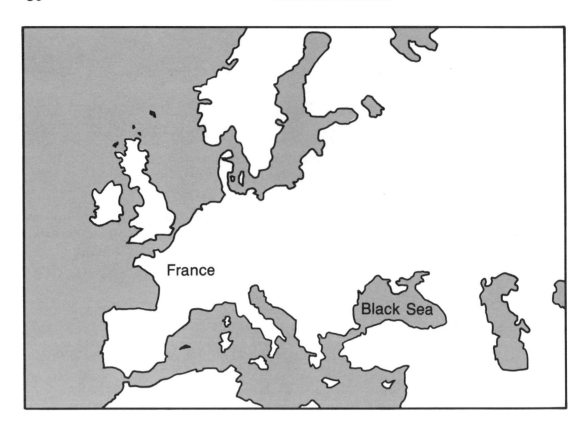

Self-Test

Part I of the self-test asks about important factual material. Part II is interpretive. The answers in Part II are keyed to Professor Weber's interpretations. If you disagree with an answer, be prepared to defend your own understanding of the material. Check your answers at the end of Unit One.

Part I

1. To gain access to the sea, the Austrians tried to revive the old port of _____Antwerp_____ in the Low Countries. Although the Dutch blocked this project, the Austrians were able to create a port at _____Trieste_____ at the head of the Adriatic Sea.

2. Among the rulers who enjoyed reputations as enlightened despots were Catherine the Great of _____Russia_____, Frederick the Great of _____Prussia_____, and Joseph II of _____Austria_____.

3. In the eighteenth century Poland lost lands to _____Russia_____, _____Russia_____, and _____Austria_____, until finally in the year _____1795_____ the Polish state ceased to exist.

4. Under the so-called enlightened despotism of Frederick the Great
   a. serfdom was abolished.
   b. men from all classes could become army officers.
   c. nobles lost their special privileges.
   d. a considerable degree of religious toleration was granted.

5. Which of the following was *not* an important painter of the eighteenth century?
   a. Watteau.
   b. Tiepolo.
   c. Poussin.
   d. Boucher.

Part II

1. In the Holy Roman Empire of the eighteenth century
   a. the rulers of Prussia and Austria were the foremost sovereigns.
   b. the smaller states survived by remaining completely loyal to the emperor.
   c. the smaller princes tried to protect their states from the cultural influence of any country outside of Germany.
   d. Germany finally achieved political and religious uniformity.

2. Name two of the great maritime powers of seventeenth- and eighteenth-century Europe: ___England, Dutch___ and ___France___ .

3. Mark the false choice. In the style of warfare of the eighteenth century,
   a. armies took some pains to spare civilian targets.
   b. armies developed complex maneuvers with which to outflank each other.
   c. armies tried to bring along their own supplies to avoid having to live off the land.
   d. aristocrats were driven from the officer corps well before the French Revolution.

4. In one or two sentences, describe the diplomatic principle of maintaining the balance of power:
   No one power would dominate, if it tried others would prevent

5. According to Professor Weber, the rococo style
   a. was a reaction against the stately, ponderous, restrained style popular in the age of Louis XIV.
   b. received little support from figures at the French court.
   c. was too frivolous to have much influence on the building of churches.
   d. was not influenced by styles from outside Europe.

Optional Activity

Although the following activity is not required for the course unless assigned by the instructor, students are encouraged to use it as a source of interesting topics for further study.

The Dark Side of the Enlightenment

At first sight much eighteenth-century art seems light-hearted and frivolous. The characteristic thinkers of the Enlightenment, such as Voltaire and Diderot, are often accused of naive optimism, as though they believed that all problems of the world could be solved with a little common sense and courtesy. A closer reading of their works, however, reveals a darker vision.

For this assignment, read one of the following works: *Candide* by Voltaire or *Rameau's Nephew* by Denis Diderot. Numerous translations of both works are available, but those listed in Further Reading are recommended. If you have studied French, try reading the works in their original language.

Write a paper of 3 – 5 pages in which you deal with one of the following topics. For your chosen topic, you should discuss only a short section of the work.

- What literary devices does Voltaire or Diderot use to describe eighteenth-century Europe? In your opinion do the devices create an effective indictment of European customs and institutions? If not, why not?
- What does the author consider to be the greatest causes of social misery? Does the author have a comprehensive theory about the causes of Europe's problems or does he simply list one problem after another without attempting to tie the points together?
- Is the author optimistic about the possibility of changing things for the better? What episodes from the work are especially revealing on this point?

Review Questions

The following questions are designed to help you think critically and to construct explanations from your factual knowledge. Remember that whenever you learn a new piece of information you should always ask yourself "so what?" In one sense or another these are all "so what?" questions.

Keep in mind that historians disagree continually on emphases, interpretations, and even on simple matters of fact. Many of the following questions will emphasize Professor Weber's particular point of view and ask you to compare it to what you find in your textbooks. When you find important disagreements, you should remember that historians are always struggling with each other; the contest is one that you can enter yourself.

1. Why was access to water so important to military and commercial strength? What were the advantages and disadvantages of river routes and sea routes? In what areas did the countries of Central and Eastern Europe try to gain access to the sea or to expand the access they already had?

2. Professor Weber argues that the relationship between the philosophes and the enlightened despots was based on mutual misunderstanding. The two groups sometimes favored the same reforms but for different reasons. What were the different reasons for which each group favored administrative and judicial reforms? Why were both groups often hostile to the Roman Catholic church? Why were the two groups interested in the concept of equality before the law?

3. What were the principal features of the rococo style in art and architecture? In what ways did it differ from the classical style of the seventeenth century? Professor Weber describes many eighteenth century painters as "enchanted" or "enchanting." What are some of the features of the style to which these words might apply? State your reasons for agreeing or disagreeing with Professor Weber's description.

4. Professor Weber argues that the grace and delicacy of eighteenth-century style may be related to changes in social and political attitudes. If people wanted an art of pleasure or delight, as Professor Weber claims, what does this taste reveal about their attitudes toward human nature? Professor Weber argues that some people wanted, or at least accepted, reforms simply because their tastes had changed. State your reasons for agreeing or disagreeing.

5. Professor Weber argues that styles of warfare changed in the course of the eighteenth century. State your reasons for agreeing or disagreeing. Examine this argument in light of the following considerations: To an eighteenth-century statesman, what was the relationship between military power and economic prosperity? If rulers now commanded highly trained professional troops, would generals be more or less inclined to risk their troops in bloody pitched battles?

Further Reading

Sources

Gendzier, Stephen J., ed. *Denis Diderot: The Encylopedia: Selections.* (1967). The *Encyclopedia* was one of the greatest projects of the philosophes and the most important source for understanding what they meant by useful knowledge.

Voltaire. *The Portable Voltaire.* (1949); (1977). A good selection, including all of *Candide*.

Studies

Behrens, C. B. *The Ancien Regime.* (1967). A synthetic text. Good illustrations.

Dorn, Walter. *Competition for Empire: 1740–1763.* (1940). Especially good on the relationship between European wars and overseas economic interests.

Gagliardo, J. *Enlightened Despotism.* (1967). Especially important for its comparison of various European countries.

Krieger, Leonard. *Kings and Philosophers, 1689–1789.* (1970). Discusses important political thinkers in relation to their immediate political backgrounds.

Parry, J. H. *Trade and Dominion: The European Overseas Empires in the Eighteenth Century.* (1971).

Wilson, Arthur. *Diderot.* (1972). Biography of a central figure of the Enlightenment. Diderot was at the center of literary and intellectual life, and his correspondence with Catherine the Great of Russia is a classic example of the relationship between a philosophe and an enlightened despot.

Woloch, Isser. *Eighteenth-Century Europe: Tradition and Progress, 1715–1789.* (1982). A thorough introduction to the period.

Answer Key

Timeline
1. 1571.
2. 1689, 1693.
3. 1795.
4. 1740–1786.
5. 1773–1814.
6. 1715.

Map Exercise
1–2. The Baltic coast and the coast of the Black Sea.
   4. Antwerp.
5–6. England and Germany (especially Prussia).
   8. Trieste.

Self-Test

Part I
1. Antwerp; Trieste
2. Russia; Prussia; Austria (Joseph II was also Holy Roman Emperor).
3. Russia; Prussia; Austria; 1795
4. (d) a considerable degree of religious toleration was granted.
5. (c) Poussin.

Part II

1. (a) the rulers of Prussia and Austria were the foremost sovereigns.
2. England; France; Holland.
3. (d) aristocrats were driven from the officer corps well before the French Revolution.
4. Following this principle, several nations, especially England, tried to make sure that no one power dominated the continent of Europe. Because France was the strongest power on the continent at the time, the English generally involved themselves in alliances against the French.
5. (a) was a reaction against the stately, ponderous, restrained style popular in the age of Louis XIV.

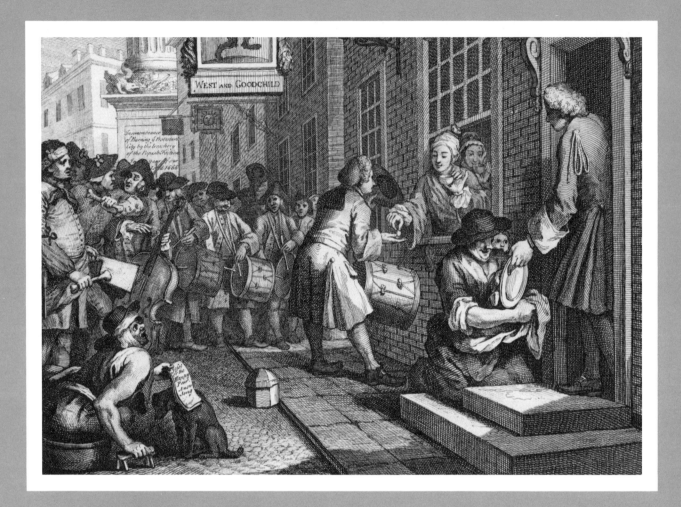

The Industrious Apprentice (1747) Part of a series in which William Hogarth contrasted an industrious apprentice to one of his idle fellows. The idle apprentice goes to ruin, while in this scene the industrious apprentice is seen the morning after marrying his master's daughter. The band has come to play for a tip, while a crippled beggar is trying to sell a ballad. (Courtesy of the Print Collection, Lewis Walpole Library, Yale University.)

UNIT EIGHTEEN

Program 35: The Enlightenment and Society

Program 36: The Modern Philosophers

LEARNING OBJECTIVES

After completing Unit Eighteen students should understand the following issues:

- The relationship between economic growth, on the one hand, and political and social ideas, on the other.
- The causes of economic growth in the eighteenth century. Use your textbook to trace the principal patterns of growth. Which countries became most prosperous in the eighteenth century? Which countries lagged behind?
- The influence of science on religious ideas. Use your textbook to supplement Professor Weber's discussion of Newton and deism.
- The development of utilitarianism and the growth of laissez-faire economics. Your textbook provides additional information about such figures as Jeremy Bentham and Adam Smith.
- The growth of intellectual relativism. How does your textbook supplement or rebut Professor Weber's argument?

TV INSTRUCTION

OVERVIEW
PROGRAM 35: THE ENLIGHTENMENT AND SOCIETY

As the European economy expanded throughout the eighteenth century, the middle classes became increasingly influential, to such an extent that the leading ideas of the times had bourgeois origins. Further, middle-class politicians spoke of the rights of all people, not simply the rights of a certain class or nation.

I. The European economy expanded in the eighteenth century, partly as a result of improvements in transportation.
   A. Water transport was improving.
      1. Ships were larger and stronger.
      2. A network of canals was spreading across Europe.
   B. Decent roads were appearing in some parts of Europe.
      1. France, probably the leader, had a network of good roads radiating from Paris. Apart from their commercial advantages, roads were important for
         a. Moving troops.
         b. Sending out tax collectors and other officials.
      2. Louis XIV had begun building roads and was soon imitated in
         a. Spain.
         b. Northern Italy.
         c. Germany.
         d. Russia.
      3. By the end of the eighteenth century, Macadam, a Scotsman, had developed a good road surface.
      4. The cost of land transport began to fall.
      5. In many spots bridges replaced fords and ferries.

II. Travel conditions had so improved that something like modern tourism was beginning to appear.
   A. Certain places became favorite tourist spots:
      1. Paris.
      2. Various spas where fashionable people could
         a. Take the waters.
         b. Gamble.
         c. Carry on flirtations.
      3. Italy, especially Venice.
   B. The Venetians even invented a special kind of painting, the *veduta* or view, for rich visitors.
      1. Views of Venice were turned out in workshops operated by some of the greatest Venetian painters:
         a. Canaletto.
         b. Bellotto.
         c. The Guardi brothers.

       2. These painters would be imitated in other European cities, to give rise to a whole school of "urban landscape".

III. Two of the most popular works of the eighteenth century masqueraded as travel books.
- A. *The Persian Letters*, published by Montesquieu in 1721.
  - 1. It pretends to be the impressions of two Persian ambassadors in Paris.
  - 2. It is actually a commentary on French society that displays how the commonplaces of one society can look absurd to members of another.
- B. Voltaire's *Candide* tells of the imaginary travels of a young man through Europe and South America.
  - 1. It too compares different customs.
  - 2. It makes fun of optimistic philosophies.
- C. Both books have a strong dose of moral relativism.
  - 1. They argue that attitudes vary with environment.
  - 2. Professor Weber argues that this sort of relativism develops as travel brings different people in contact with one another.

IV. The general standard of living rose in the eighteenth century.
- A. Agriculture was in a better state.
  - 1. Farm technology was improving.
  - 2. Agriculture was more productive.
  - 3. Fewer crops were destroyed by armies.
  - 4. Crops were stored better.
  - 5. Consequently, the population grew.
- B. Because most people still lived on the land, healthy agriculture meant a healthy economy.
  - 1. There was a greater rate of exchange.
  - 2. Buying power increased.
  - 3. Manufacturing grew.
- C. Economic development spurred the growth of towns and ports.
  - 1. Merchants and shipowners became more powerful.
  - 2. Lawyers were coming into increasing prominence.

V. Economic growth took off most quickly in England.
- A. England had suffered less in the wars that drained other countries.
- B. England possessed important resources:
  - 1. Wool.
  - 2. Waterpower.
  - 3. Access to cotton.
  - 4. Iron.
  - 5. Coal.
- C. Scotland also produced important contributors to the Industrial Revolution:
  - 1. John Macadam developed an important process for surfacing roads.

    2. James Watt greatly improved the steam engine.
      a. Steam engines were first used in the 1730s.
      b. By the 1770s they were coming into wide use.

VI. When Voltaire visited England, he came to believe that trade was the foundation of a healthy state.
  A. He argued that "trade has made them rich."
  B. Trade "has helped make them free."
  C. "Freedom in turn has spread trade further."
  D. Voltaire believed that countries everywhere should follow this pattern:
    1. The middle classes had already gained political power.
    2. Soon they would demand political power to go with it.

VII. The middle classes, or bourgeoisie, were coming into economic and intellectual prominence.
  A. The middle classes followed a wide range of pursuits:
    1. Businesspeople.
    2. Craftspeople.
    3. Public servants.
    4. State employees.
    5. Lawyers.
    6. Financiers.
    7. Manufacturers.
    8. Writers.
  B. Nevertheless, Professor Weber argues that they held certain ideas in common, a bourgeois philosophy.
    1. They also believed that this philosophy applied to all people, not just to the middle classes.
    2. They believed in universal human rights, as seen in a number of eighteenth-century documents:
      a. The American Bill of Rights.
      b. The French Declaration of the Rights of Man.
    3. Professor Weber argues that the bourgeois thinkers of eighteenth century thought in broader terms than many nineteenth-century radicals.
      a. Marxists, for instance, would argue from a narrower, proletarian perspective.
      b. Although bourgeois claims were often hypocritical, they did believe in general improvement for all people.

VIII. In the eighteenth century ideas spread more quickly and widely than ever before.
  A. Mass communications were developing through
    1. Broadsheets.
    2. Gazettes.
    3. Newspapers.
    4. Clubs.
  B. Social life was often organized around the exchange of ideas in
    1. Drawing rooms.

     2. Cafes.

     3. Debating societies.

     4. Secret societies.

  C. The freemasons were one of the most important secret societies involved in spreading the ideas of the Enlightenment.

     1. Freemasonry began in England and was spread throughout the continent by the French.

     2. Many prominent men were freemasons:

       a. Voltaire.

       b. Diderot.

       c. The Duke of Orleans.

       d. Frederick the Great.

       e. Mozart.

       f. Washington.

       g. Franklin.

     3. The masons celebrated a cult of humanity.

     4. Masons believed in God but they did not restrict themselves to the god of any one church or revelation.

     5. They believed in natural religion that can be wholly understood by reason.

IX. Many social ideas were influenced by the discoveries of seventeenth-century science.

  A. It was assumed that through reason and science people could understand nature and come to live in harmony with its laws.

  B. By living in harmony with these laws, people could progress toward happiness and perfection.

X. The seventeenth century had been a great age of scientific discovery.

  A. Galileo had invented, perfected, or improved a number of crucial scientific instruments:

     1. The telescope.

     2. The thermometer.

     3. The mechanical clock.

  B. His pupil, Torricelli, invented the barometer.

  C. These instruments permitted more exact and extensive measurements, which were crucial to the scientific method.

  D. The seventeenth century saw a great number of discoveries:

     1. William Harvey discovered the circulation of the blood through the heart and lungs.

     2. Anton Leeuwenhoek developed lenses powerful enough to see bacteria and spermatozoa.

     3. Robert Boyle became the father of modern chemistry through his work on the behavior of gases at different temperatures and pressures.

     4. Great advances in mathematics were made by

       a. Isaac Newton.

       b. John Napier.

       c. Rene Descartes.

     5. The foundations of higher mathematics were laid with
       a. Logarithms.
       b. Differential calculus.
       c. Integral calculus.
   E. In the eighteenth century magnetism and electricity were investigated by
     1. William Gilbert.
     2. Benjamin Franklin.
     3. Alessandra Volta.
     4. Luigi Galvani.

XI. Professor Weber argues that the Scientific Revolution fundamentally affected the ways educated people thought.
   A. In 1600, for instance, many educated people still believed in witches.
     1. By 1700 such beliefs were dying out among the educated,
     2. Because no scientist believed in the supernatural forces on which witches were supposed to base their power.
     3. The proportion of educated people was still low in 1700 but their number was growing.
   B. Scientific discoveries also altered religious belief.
     1. Many of the greatest scientists had been religious:
       a. Newton.
       b. Descartes.
     2. Their discoveries, however, took on an independent life.
       a. Many believers thought of God as a kind of great clockmaker.
       b. God was a kind of constitutional monarch who reigned over a universe that operated quite independently according to the laws He had ordained.
   C. Advances were also being made in the fight against certain diseases:
     1. Scurvy.
     2. Smallpox.
   D. Even air travel was possible.
     1. In 1783 the Montgolfier brothers demonstrated the first hot-air balloon.
     2. In 1785 an American and a Frenchman crossed the English Channel by balloon.
   E. Many great men of letters dabbled in science.
     1. Voltaire studied mathematics and explained Newton's work in popular articles.
     2. D'Alembert wrote popular works on science and philosophy.
     3. Diderot performed experiments in anatomy and chemistry.

XII. Professor Weber argues that the eighteenth century was possessed of a profound belief in happiness.
   A. Happiness was not an important theme in earlier thinkers such as
     1. Aquinas.
     2. Luther.

    B. As religious restraints relaxed in both Protestant and Catholic countries, thinkers increasingly wrote about the possibilities of human happiness.

    C. Scientific progress seemed to be making these possibilities real.

Key to the Images

Public works: Many of contemporary images in Program 35 portray highways and great bridges. The transportation revolution would not begin in Europe until the nineteenth century, with the building of the railroads. Even so, the eighteenth century made considerable improvements of its own.

France in particular developed a network of good roads radiating from Paris, and the government was now building bridges at many places where there had once been only ferries or fords.

Canaletto (1697–1768): Giovanni Antonio Canaletto was one of the great Venetian painters of the eighteenth century. Among his most famous works are great panoramas of Venice, which became popular among travelers who wanted to take home views of the cities they had seen.

Canaletto, as well as painting such masterpieces as "The Grand Canal" and "The Dock at Saint Mark's" in Venice, also painted other cities as in "The View of London and the Thames."

Canaletto had been trained originally as a stage designer, a craft that required mastery of perspective and architectural detail. He is also notable for the skill with which he related his cityscapes to great expanses of water.

Focus Questions

1. What were the signs of economic growth in eighteenth-century Europe?
2. What were some of the improvements in transportation that fostered economic growth?
3. How did increased travel throughout Europe affect intellectual and artistic life?
4. How were the ideas of the philosophes related to Europe's growing prosperity?
5. How were the social and political ideas of the philosophes influenced by discoveries in mathematics and the natural sciences?
6. What social classes found these ideas especially appealing? Especially repugnant?
7. What were the social and intellectual channels through which the new ideas spread?

OVERVIEW
PROGRAM 36: THE MODERN PHILOSOPHERS

Eighteenth-century philosophers were continually exploring the relationship between the happiness of the individual and the general welfare of
society. Rousseau argued, for instance, that society corrupted the individual. British economists and social thinkers argued that society prospered
best when individuals pursued their own enlightened self-interest.

I. The works of Jean-Jacques Rousseau (1712–1778) show how
changes in personal taste affected social ideas.
   A. Rousseau argued that society corrupted the natural goodness of
   human beings.
   B. He encouraged a taste for natural beauty in
      1. Wilderness.
      2. Forests.
      3. Mountains.
      4. Fields.
   C. In earlier times wild places had been considered a nuisance or a
   danger.
      1. Rousseau, however, conceived of them as magnificent
      landscapes.
      2. People derived deep spiritual benefits from contemplating
      such things.
   D. Further, nature was innocent.
      1. It never led people astray,
      2. Unlike the corruptions of society.

II. Rousseau's philosophy was at odds with the work of many other
eighteenth-century philosophers.
   A. He attacked other philosophers for their crude
      1. Rationalism.
      2. Materialism.
   B. Other philosophers attacked his notion of happiness as too
   dreamy and private.
      1. They thought of happiness as something that had to be earned.
      2. The best way of earning happiness was by making others
      happy.
      3. In this way private good coincided with public good.

III. Eighteenth-century moral thinkers greatly expanded their notion of
virtue.
   A. In the ancient world virtue had meant courage or manly strength.
   B. In the eighteenth century, however, virtue was more social.
      1. The virtuous man was useful to his fellow creatures.
      2. Virtue was not just private, as it might be in the case of a good
      Christian.

C. Further, virtue was secularized.
　　1. It did not depend on faith in God.
　　2. It was reasonable, other-directed behavior.

IV. Much eighteenth-century thought depended on the notion of utility, or usefulness, as explained by such thinkers as Jeremy Bentham (1748–1832).
　A. Bentham defined utility as the property or tendency of a thing to procure good or to avoid pain.
　　1. For the individual utility was anything that increased his or her well-being or happiness.
　　2. In society utility was judged by the ability of a measure to bring the greatest happiness to the greatest number.
　B. Bentham and others like him stressed the importance of enlightened self-interest.
　　1. They argued that the general good is best promoted by individuals who pursue their own self-interests.
　　2. This line of thought was followed by such thinkers as
　　　a. Benjamin Franklin.
　　　b. Adam Smith.
　　　c. Voltaire.
　　　d. Beccaria.

V. Many of these thinkers had a specific program for social reform.
　A. Many of them concentrated on reforming the law.
　　1. Arbitrary arrest should be ended.
　　2. Torture should be abolished.
　　3. The death penalty should be abolished.
　　4. Punishments should be moderated to fit the crime.
　　5. The law should apply to all classes without exception.
　B. There should be open discussion of all these matters.
　　1. Voltaire in particular clashed with the church because
　　　a. It stifled free thought.
　　　b. It punished free expression.
　　2. Voltaire defended numerous victims of religious persecution:
　　　a. The Calas family.
　　　b. The Chevalier de la Barre.

VI. *The Great Encyclopedia,* published in the 1750s and 1760s by Voltaire, Diderot, and their friends, is a great tribute to technical and economic progress.
　A. By treating subjects in alphabetical order, the *Encyclopedia* abandoned the traditional notion that some forms of knowledge were intrinsically superior to others.
　B. The mechanical arts were treated in loving detail, often with illustrations.
　C. When Diderot wrote the article on political man, he concentrated on

1. Agriculture.
2. Demography.
3. Wealth.
D. The idea was that material wealth led to
   1. Intellectual progress.
   2. Individual well-being.

VII. The best and worst aspects of Diderot's "material humanism" can be seen in the painters he admired.
  A. Chardin was one of the greatest painters of the century. His treatments of everyday life were
    1. Clean.
    2. Direct.
    3. Intimate.
    4. He was the Vermeer of his times.
  B. Greuze, on the other hand, showed the weakness of Diderot's taste. The paintings are
    1. Melodramatic.
    2. Moralistic.
    3. Sentimental.

VIII. England was the true home of economic progress and utilitarian thinking.
  A. The British differed greatly from the enlightened despots of the continent.
    1. The English did not want a strong bureaucratic state.
    2. Nor did they want the government to control economic life.
  B. In part the British were enjoying the luxury of their position.
    1. Protected by the sea, they did not need a huge army or bureaucracy to support it.
    2. They could channel resources to promote economic growth.
  C. British economists and social thinkers argued that individuals could operate most efficiently when they were left alone and not regulated by the government.
    1. In 1723 Bernard Mandeville's *The Fable of the Bees* described a prosperous beehive that was ruined by strict supervision.
    2. Mandeville believed that private selfishness could contribute to the good of society.
  D. The greatest work of British economic theory was Adam Smith's *Inquiry into the Nature and Causes of the Wealth of Nations,* published in 1776.
    1. Smith believed that individual self-interest is socially harmonious.
    2. He wrote in favor of
      a. Free trade.
      b. Competition.
      c. Production.
      d. Profit.
    3. Above all, he was against government regulation.
    4. The state should simply maintain order and enforce the law.

IX. The career of Benjamin Franklin (1706–1790) illustrates many of the trends discussed in Unit Eighteen.
   A. Franklin began work as a printer.
      1. He printed currency for Pennsylvania and some of the other colonies.
      2. He published *Poor Richard's Almanac*.
         a. Almanacs were popular, especially because they were easy to read.
         b. Franklin published jokes, anecdotes, and a great deal of practical information.
   B. Eventually, Franklin became a public figure and promoted
      1. A lending library.
      2. A fire department.
      3. The school that eventually became the University of Pennsylvania.
   C. He was also a scientist, concentrating on projects that were immediately useful:
      1. The Franklin stove.
      2. Bifocals.
      3. The lightning rod.
   D. In national politics Franklin was
      1. A delegate to the Second Continental Congress.
      2. One of the drafters of the Declaration of Independence.
      3. A diplomat in England and France.
   E. Even at this stage of his life, Franklin remained involved in many practical projects:
      1. Draining swamps.
      2. Improving watering troughs.
      3. Curing smoky chimneys.
      4. Cleaning the streets.
   F. Despite his many reforms and improvements, Franklin's view of human nature was not especially sanguine.
      1. The world was a place where the strong oppressed the weak.
      2. The privileged were in control.
      3. He did think, however, that life could be improved by small gradual acts.
   G. Despite his belief in small, gradual improvements, Franklin and others like him soon became revolutionaries.

Key to the Images

Joseph Wright: One of the most arresting images in Program 36 is Joseph Wright's painting of an experiment with an air pump. The scientist has placed a bird inside a glass bell, from which the pump removes air until the bird dies. Although this is supposed to be a purely scientific experiment, the scene's lighting spectators' faces make it seem that a magical rite is in progress.

William Hogarth (1697–1764): Following the advice of the Roman poet Horace to use humor to reform morals, Hogarth became one of Europe's greatest satirical artists. Many of his best pieces were series of works such as "The Harlot's Progress," "The Rake's Progress," and "Marriage a la Mode." Many of his works were widely distributed as engravings.

Although much of Hogarth's work has a clear moral purpose, it is often crowded by too much life to suffer from the single-mindedness that mars so many other didactic artists. "Gin Lane," for instance, shows nearly every conceivable evil of drink, even a baby falling away from the breast of its drunken mother, but the scenes are so crowded with the details of Hogarth's imagination that they become a kind of realistic surrealism.

Focus Questions

1. How did Rousseau's ideas about human happiness differ from those of Diderot or Voltaire?
2. What did the philosophers of the eighteenth century mean by "virtue"? How was virtue related to happiness and to social responsibility?
3. How did *The Great Encyclopedia* of Voltaire and Diderot differ from earlier assemblages of knowledge?
4. For the utilitarians, what was the relationship between personal self-interest and the public good?
5. For Adam Smith, what was the principal economic function of the state? How did his ideas differ from those of the mercantilists? From those of the enlightened despots?

ASSIGNMENTS AND ACTIVITIES

IN CONTEXT

Themes and issues that set Unit Eighteen in context with other units include the following.

• In the period covered by Unit Eighteen a number of European countries, especially France and the states of northern Italy, created systems of improved roads and bridges. Look back to earlier units for discussions of the difficulty of overland travel in the ancient and medieval worlds. In many respects overland travel in 1700 was not much better than it had been during the Roman Empire. In Unit Twenty-One on the Industrial Revolution we learn how economic progress was accompanied by great advances in transportation, the railroad being the most important example. Keep in mind that for more than a hundred years before the first railroad, Europeans had been looking for ways to improve transportation.

• One could write a history of European social thought simply by tracing the evolution of the word *virtue*. In Unit Eighteen Professor Weber defines *virtue* as a set of qualities that make a person a useful member of society. In Roman times *virtus* was a combination of courage and strength. Julius Caesar, for instance, was always praising the *virtus* of his soldiers. Machiavelli also discussed *virtu* at great length. For him, the word still had many of its Roman connotations. He thought that the securest foundation for a state was the *virtu* of its citizens. Citizens possessed *virtu* if they were ready to defend their country, even at the risk of their own life. In later units, especially in Program 20 on the French Revolution, we learn how virtue broadens into a general sense of public morality.

• During the Enlightenment, European agriculture became significantly more productive. Look back to earlier units in which Professor Weber argues that the flowering of medieval culture was based on the improvements in agriculture carried out in the Dark Ages. In many countries improvements in eighteenth-century agriculture were accompanied by a rapid growth in population. England, for example, grew from a population of 5.5 million around the end of the seventeenth century to nine million by the time of its first census in 1801. This growth may not seem impressive by modern standards, but it was astounding for the eighteenth century. In the units that follow watch for the economic and political consequences of rapid growth in population.

• Professor Weber speaks of the eighteenth century as the first great age of mass advocacy. Look back to Unit Fourteen on the Protestant Reformation. The Reformation would have been impossible without the printing press, which produced vast numbers of Bibles and religious tracts. In later units watch for the rise of a truly popular press. The last units discuss the political effects of mass media, such as radio and television. In general, whenever we study the ideas of a period, we must ask how widespread the ideas actually were at the time, and how people came to know of them.

Textbook Assignment

Read the following pages in your assigned textbook:

Text: *Western Civilizations* (Eleventh Edition, 1988)
Read: From Chapter 19, "The Scientific Revolution and Enlightenment," pp. 629–649.

Text: *The Western Experience* (Fifth Edition, 1991)
Read: Chapter 20, "Revolutions of the Eighteenth Century," pp. 769–820.

Text: *The Western Heritage* (Fourth Edition, 1991)
Read: Chapter 18, "The Age of Enlightenment: Eighteenth-Century Thought," pp. 625–655.

Issues for Clarification

Bourgeois

In the Middle Ages and after, a bourgeois was a town-dweller; not simply one who lived in a town, however, but one who was substantial enough to be a freeman of the town and to take part in public life.

By the time of the Enlightenment, the word *bourgeois* had broadened to include public officials, writers, teachers, merchants, and substantial businesspeople. The word is often used to mean middle-class, but in most places the bourgeoisie probably accounted for only 10 percent of the population.

Universal Rights

The Enlightenment witnessed a number of the great statements of universal rights, such as the American Bill of Rights and the French Declaration of the Rights of Man. We are so used to the notion of universal rights that it is easy to overlook the importance of such claims in the eighteenth century.

For most people, rights were assumed to be highly individualized. A king had certain rights that he and his family received directly from God. A nobleman had rights that he or his ancestors received from a king, a pope, or an emperor. A bishop had rights to which all holders of his office were entitled.

Most rights belonged the individuals or restricted groups. The church, however, did have at least a limited concept of universal rights, for all Christians in good standing were entitled to the sacraments of the church. Secular rulers also made some progress toward a notion of universal rights. In England, for instance, everyone was entitled to the protection of the king's peace.

One of the most important accomplishments of the eighteenth century was the notion that many other rights extended to all people. During this same period, feminists such as Mary Wollstonecraft began to argue that the rights of man should extend to all people, including women.

Glossary

Deism: A belief, common among the philosophes and other thinkers of the eighteenth century, that God did not intervene directly in the affairs of the world even though He created the universe and the laws that govern it.

Macadamizing: A process for improving road surfaces with crushed stone, invented by John L. Macadam (1756–1836).

Veduta: The Italian word for a view. During the eighteenth century many painters specialized in views of Italian cities, especially of Venice.

Timeline

Place each of the following events on the timeline. In some cases you may have to specify a roughly defined period of time rather than a precise date.

1. First flight over the English Channel by air.
2. Spread of Macadamized roads.
3. Steam engines first used.
4. Declaration of Independence.
5. Publication of *The Great Encyclopedia*.
6. Publication of *The Fable of the Bees*.
7. Publication of *The Wealth of Nations*.
8. Birth of Benjamin Franklin.

1700   1800
├──┤

Map Exercise

Find the following locations on the map.

1. The country with best roads in mid-eighteenth century.
2. Homeland of Rousseau.
3. Homeland of Volta and Galvani.
4. Homeland of Macadam.
5. First country to exploit steam power on a large scale.
6. Hub of French road system.
7. Homeland of Adam Smith.
8. English Channel.
9. Homeland of James Watt.

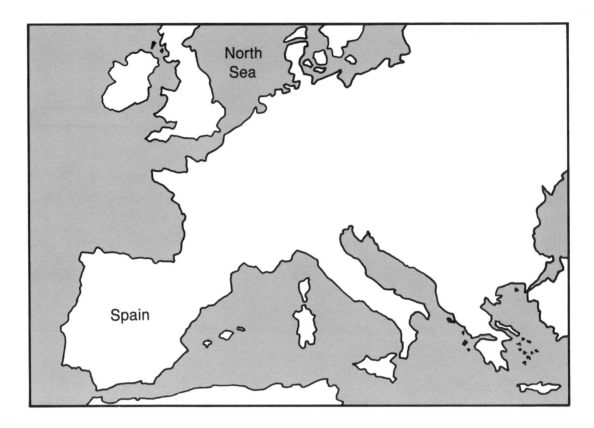

Self-Test

Part I of the self-test asks about important factual material. Part II is interpretive. The answers in Part II are keyed to Professor Weber's interpretations. If you disagree with an answer, be prepared to defend your own understanding of the material. Check your answers at the end of Unit One.

Part I

1. Name one of the great eighteenth-century painters who specialized in *vedute* of Venice. Guardi Bros.

2. Which of the following was *not* a member of the Masonic Lodges?
   a. Frederick the Great.
   b. Louis XVI.
   c. George Washington.
   d. Mozart.

3. Among the great scientists of the seventeenth century were
   _____Harvey_____, who discovered the circulation of the blood
   through the heart and lungs; ___Leuwenhoek___, who developed lenses powerful enough to detect bacteria; and

_____Boyle_____ , who discovered laws governing the behavior of gases at varying temperatures and pressures.

4. Galileo invented or made important improvements in all but one of the following.
  a. The barometer.
  b. The telescope.
  c. The thermometer.
  d. The mechanical clock.

5. _____Montesquieu_____ , author of the *Persian Letters,* and _____Voltaire_____ , author of *Candide,* wrote fictionalized travel books that were actually commentaries on contemporary Europe.

Part II

1. All but one of the following were among the reasons for England's strong economic growth in the eighteenth century.
  a. Plentiful sources of wool.
  b. Abundant access to sea and river routes.
  c. The largest army of the eighteenth century.
  d. Abundant coal resources.

2. Mark the false choice. Deists believed that
  a. the cosmos operated in accordance with universal laws.
  b. God intervened directly in human affairs.
  c. God created the universe.
  d. science could discover the mysteries of creation.

3. Mark the false choice. Among the signs or causes of increasing prosperity in the eighteenth century were
  a. fewer crops destroyed by war.
  b. improved agriculture.
  c. declining population.
  d. increasing trade.

4. Mark the false choice. Voltaire opposed the Roman Catholic church because he
  a. objected to its persecution of other religions.
  b. was an atheist.
  c. thought it blocked free expression.
  d. objected to the political power of the clergy.

5. The editors and writers of *The Great Encyclopedia*
  a. neglected mechanical and technical knowledge.
  b. rejected the possibility of social progress.
  c. tended to subordinate politics to the economy.
  d. arranged their work to demonstrate the kinds of knowledge they considered most important.

Optional Activity

Although the following activity is not required for the course unless assigned by the instructor, students are encouraged to use it as a source of interesting topics for further study.

Tom Jones

Tom Jones by Henry Fielding is one of the great novels of the eighteenth century. As Tom wanders about England he encounters people from every section of society. In addition, Fielding inserts essays throughout the novel in which he discusses almost every idea current in the eighteenth century.

Write a paper of 3 – 5 pages in which you discuss one of the following topics:

• What is Fielding's notion of virtue? How did this idea conflict with the conventional morality of the eighteenth century?
• Tom Jones is an orphan. How does his lack of a clear social status influence his views on society? Why is Tom an especially good witness?

Because *Tom Jones* is a long novel, confine your discussion to one brief episode but be sure to include one of Fielding's essays in your discussion. Does the action of the novel fit in well with the ideas Fielding develops?

Films

You may wish to view some of the following films, which deal with matters discussed in this unit.

• *Tom Jones,* directed by Tony Richardson, is worth seeing, although only the most obvious sources of humor come through.
• *Barry Lyndon,* directed by Stanley Kubrick, is highly recommended. Barry Lyndon, although much less intelligent than Tom Jones, is another young man who wanders about England and Europe, trying to make his way in the world.

Review Questions

The following questions are designed to help you think critically and to construct explanations from your factual knowledge. Remember that whenever you learn a new piece of information you should always ask yourself "so what?" In one sense or another these are all "so what?" questions.

Keep in mind that historians disagree continually on emphases, interpretations, and even on simple matters of fact. Many of the following questions will emphasize Professor Weber's particular point of view and ask you to compare it to what you find in your textbooks. When you find important disagreements, you should remember that historians are always struggling with each other; the contest is one that you can enter yourself.

1. What were the principal improvements in land travel during this period? How did easier travel affect tastes in art? How did people begin to think differently about their own society?
2. How would you define the bourgeoisie? What were some of the ideas shared by this class throughout Europe? How did these ideas reflect their social and economic position?
   Professor Weber argues that when the bourgeoisie talked about human needs and rights, they really meant the needs and rights of the bourgeoisie. Why did they claim to be speaking for all people? Was this simply bad faith on their part?
3. Who were some of the most influential writers or groups of writers in the eighteenth century? What were some of the great publishing projects? What organizations were important in spreading ideas?
4. Apart from their scientific importance, how did the discoveries of Isaac Newton affect the thinking of ordinary educated people? How did they influence people's general conception of the universe? How did ideas about God change in the eighteenth century?
5. Professor Weber argues that before the eighteenth century few moralists or social thinkers wrote about happiness. What does the new emphasis on happiness reveal about attitudes toward human nature?
6. How do Rousseau's views of happiness differ from those of Diderot and Voltaire? How do these differing views derive from differing notions about human development? From differing notions about the individual's responsibilities to other people?
7. Define *utilitarianism*. Who were some of the thinkers influenced by it in the eighteenth century? According to a utilitarian, why should an individual act in such a way as to benefit other people? What assumptions does utilitarianism make about human nature?

Further Reading

Sources

Fielding, Henry. *Tom Jones.*

Gay, Peter. *The Enlightenment: A Comprehensive Anthology.* (1973).

Weber, Eugen. *The Western Tradition,* 2nd ed. (1965).
   "The Eighteenth Century," pp. 482–510.

Studies

Baumer, Franklin L. *Modern European Thought: Continuity and Change in Ideas, 1600–1950.* (1977). A fine intellectual history. Especially good for tieing together strands of thought that run throughout the units.

Hampson, Norman. *A Cultural History of the Enlightenment.* (1969).   A good introduction. Useful for connecting different ideas of the unit.

Hazard, Paul. *The European Mind: The Critical Years (1680–1715).* (1953). Traces the climate of opinion that preceded the Enlightenment.

Manuel, Frank. *The Eighteenth Century Confronts the Gods.* (1959).   One of the best discussions of the philosophes' ideas about religion.

Shklar, Judith. *Men and Citizens, a Study of Rousseau's Social Theory.* (1969).

Answer Key

Timeline

1. 1785.
2. Late eighteenth century.
3. 1730s.
4. 1776.
5. 1750s–1760s.
6. 1723.
7. 1776.
8. 1706.

Map Exercise

1. France.
2. Switzerland.
3. Italy.
4. Scotland.
5. England.
6. Paris.
7. Scotland.
9. Scotland.

Self-Test

Part I

1. Canaletto, Bellotto, or the Guardi brothers.
2. (b) Louis XVI.
3. William Harvey; Anton van Leeuvenhoek; Robert Boyle
4. (a) The barometer.
5. Montesquieu; Voltaire

Part II

1. (c) The largest army of the eighteenth century.
2. (b) God intervened directly in human affairs.
3. (c) declining population.
4. (b) was an atheist.
5. (c) tended to subordinate politics to the economy.

Benjamin West began this painting to commemorate the Peace Treaty Conference at the end of the American Revolution (1783) The American commissioners appear from left to right: John Jay, John Adams, Benjamin Franklin, Henry Laurens, and William Temple Franklin. The British commissioners, however, would not sit for their portraits, and the picture was never finished. (Courtesy of the Henry Francis du Pont Winterthur Museum.)

UNIT NINETEEN

Program 37: The American Revolution

Program 38: The American Republic

LEARNING OBJECTIVES

After completing Unit Nineteen students should understand the following issues:

- European myths about America. What do these myths reveal about European society? Use your textbook to supplement Professor Weber's discussion.
- The patterns of European settlement throughout North and South America.
- The ways in which the American colonies became important factors in international politics of the eighteenth century. Look at the sections in your textbook on the War of the Austrian Succession and the Seven Years' War.
- The ways in which England's role as an imperial power created tensions with its North American colonies. Look at the sections in your textbook on England's relations with France.
- The social and political divisions in the new republic.
- The tensions between political ideals and political practice.
- The social and economic conditions that lay behind the political ideals of the United States.

TV INSTRUCTION

OVERVIEW
PROGRAM 37: THE AMERICAN REVOLUTION

From the moment of its discovery, America became a symbol of European dreams and ideals. The Spanish created a rich and complex culture in Central and South America, at a time when French and English colonies amounted to no more than a few fishermen and trappers. By the eighteenth century, however, the British colonies in North America were growing restive under the restrictions imposed by England. Finally, with help from France and other enemies of England, the thirteen colonies became free.

  I. Myths grew about America from the moment it was discovered.
    A. There was the myth of the noble savage who
      1. Shared his possessions.
      2. Had few needs.
      3. Lived a harmonious life.
      4. Was naturally good.
    B. The noble savage never existed, of course, and most of America's original inhabitants were
      1. Exploited.
      2. Infected with European diseases.
      3. Conquered in war.
      4. Driven from their lands.
    C. America was seen as a land of limitless riches:
      1. Gold.
      2. Silver.
      3. Land.
      4. Tobacco.
    D. Political idealists saw America as a land where it would be possible to establish
      1. Liberty.
      2. Democracy.

  II. The Spanish were the first to establish extensive colonies in the New World, in South America, and the Caribbean Basin.
    A. The Spanish colonies were closely modeled on the mother country. They were
      1. Bureaucratic.
      2. Prosperous.
      3. Stable.
      4. No more oppressive than Spain.
      5. Less heavily taxed than Spain.
    B. At a time when the North American colonies of England and France were still primitive, the Spanish had established
      1. Great churches.

    2. Universities at
      a. Santo Domingo.
      b. Mexico City.
      c. Lima.
    3. Great cities with
      a. Paved streets.
      b. Lighting.
      c. Water supplies.

III. Only gradually did the colonies in North America catch up.
    A. In the 1530s the French sailed up the Saint Lawrence River.
    B. In the 1580s the English
      1. Settled Newfoundland.
      2. Tried to settle Virginia.
    C. European settlement began slowly in North America.
      1. There was no treasure to loot.
      2. Trapping and fishing did not require a great deal of manpower.
      3. Further, the North American Indians were more warlike than those of the South.
    D. Real colonization began in North America in the seventeenth century.
      1. The French settled
        a. Quebec.
        b. Montreal.
      2. The English settled
        a. Virginia.
        b. Massachusetts.
        c. Other colonies along the Atlantic Coast.
      3. The Dutch settled New Amsterdam, in what is now New York.
      4. The Swedes founded New Sweden, in what is now Delaware.

IV. Many European social theories would be worked out in North America.
    A. John Locke wrote a constitution for the colony of Carolina.
    B. The Pilgrims signed a compact among themselves that was a kind of social contract.
    C. Far from cutting itself off from Europe, America would develop many trends from
      1. Renaissance humanism.
      2. The Enlightenment.

V. Thomas Jefferson was an example of the way that some Americans were tied to European intellectual life.
    A. He was a gifted architect in the Palladian style, as seen in
      1. His home at Monticello.
      2. Buildings at the University of Virginia.
    B. As well as being a politician, Jefferson was a
      1. Linguist.

     2. Scientist.
     3. Farmer.
     4. Town planner.

VI. By the eighteenth century the North American colonies of England and France were considered to be worth fighting about.
  A. In general, France and England most highly valued their colonies in the West Indies, which produced
    1. Sugar.
    2. Coffee.
    3. Tobacco.
  B. In the eighteenth century the great wars between England and France were really fought to see who would rule the sea and command the colonies.

VII. The English were the natural allies of their North American colonies.
  A. The colonists aided the home country against
    1. The French.
    2. The Indian allies of the French.
  B. Soldiers like George Washington learned their trade in the French and Indian War.
  C. The colonists had greatly gained as a result of these wars.
    1. The French could no longer oppose westward expansion.
    2. The French could no longer arm the Indians to withstand colonial advance.

VIII. After the end of the French and Indian War in 1763, the British colonies began to resent the home country.
  A. The British wanted to tax the colonies for services rendered by the home country.
  B. The colonists preferred to provide these services themselves.
  C. The British wanted to harness the colonies to serve the economic interests of England.
    1. The British followed a mercantilist policy.
    2. The Americans wanted free trade.
  D. Professor Weber argues that part of the problem was that, for more than a century, the colonies had enjoyed a considerable degree of self-government.
    1. The English government had more pressing concerns at home and in Europe.
    2. Colonial affairs had followed a policy of benign neglect.
    3. The great resentment came when British governments tried to reassert control.
  E. Professor Weber argues that to some extent the American Revolution was conservative, as Americans fought to preserve the independence they had long enjoyed.

IX. At first the arguments between colonies and home country were fought as legal battles.
  A. Parliament would impose a tax on the colonies.

    1. The colonists would object that such a tax was illegal because they were not represented in parliament.

    2. Sometimes parliament would repeal the tax, only to impose another.

  B. The real issue was that the colonists did not want to pay taxes to an empire they no longer needed.

  C. The terms of the debate changed as the struggle wore on.

    1. At first colonists demanded their rights as Englishmen.

    2. Eventually, they began to argue in terms of the natural rights of all men.

      a. Natural law arguments were intellectually fashionable.

      b. Natural law was usefully ambiguous.

      c. Natural law condemned governments that did not rest on the support of the governed.

  D. The colonists appealed to different parts of the British government.

    1. Sometimes they petitioned parliament that they were being oppressed by the king.

    2. They also petitioned the king against parliamentary oppression.

X. The American Revolution was an exercise in international politics.

  A. The enemies of England were glad to encourage rebellion in the colonies.

  B. The French in particular provided

    1. Military aid.

    2. Naval support.

XI. The American Revolution was also a victory for economic liberalism.

  A. Mercantilist policies were discredited.

  B. Free trade policies began to replace the old colonial system.

  C. Because the English themselves were divided on these issues, the colonists found allies even in England.

  D. The Revolution was seen throughout Europe as a victory for rational reform.

Key to the Image

Palladian architecture: Professer Weber points out the importance of Palladian architecture in eighteenth-century America, especially in the hands of Thomas Jefferson. The style, with its emphasis on clarity and proportion, had a number of qualities that made it especially suitable for the New World.

First, it could be adapted to an enormous range of uses. There were Palladian palaces and great churches, but the style is also suited to private homes and the estates of country gentlemen like Jefferson himself. Much baroque architecture is magnificent, but it requires a grand scale. In the wrong hands a private house in the baroque style can look like a doghouse in the shape of a cathedral.

The Palladian style also embodies principles that can be acquired by amateurs. Jefferson was a gifted builder but he did not devote his entire life to architecture. Nevertheless, he was responsible for a number of beautiful buildings. The baroque, on the other hand, is a style for geniuses.

The idea of amateur builders is a part of Jefferson's greater vision of a good society. He believed that culture should not be left to the experts. Jefferson hoped that every decently educated person would be able to draw and play a musical instrument. He believed that people should know enough about agronomy to manage their farms scientifically. Jefferson also maintained that people should know enough about architecture to create their own buildings.

Focus Questions

1. In what ways did European myths about the New World reflect Europe's own troubles?
2. Compare and contrast the European settlements in Latin America to those in North America. Concentrate on the seventeenth century.
3. In what ways did thinkers in the North American colonies reflect European humanism and political thought?
4. How did the European colonies in the New World participate in to the great wars of the eighteenth century between England and France?
5. After the French and Indian War, why did tensions grow between the English government and the American colonies?
6. What were some of the legal and philosophical principles with which the English colonists justified their resistance to the home government?

OVERVIEW
PROGRAM 38: THE AMERICAN REPUBLIC

After the American Revolution, a political struggle broke out between those who favored maximum independence for the individual states and those who wanted a strong central government. The struggle did not, however, lead to civil war but to the compromises of the American Constitution. Professor Weber argues that although Europeans looked to the American Revolution as a model, the American experience was different from anything in Europe. Americans could build a new country without having to destroy the old.

I. After the Revolution a struggle began among the victors over the government of the new country.
  A. One group consisted of early revolutionary leaders, who were among the first to call for a war of independence:
    1. Thomas Jefferson.
    2. Richard Henry Lee.
  B. These men favored the Articles of Confederation because they
    1. Were fairly loose and unrestrictive.
    2. Allowed the individual states a great deal of independence.
  C. The second group consisted of men who joined the revolution more reluctantly:
    1. Alexander Hamilton.
    2. Robert Livingston.
  D. They believed that the country should have a central government with power to coerce
    1. State governments.
    2. Individuals.
  E. The second group was conservative in politics and social attitudes.
    1. At times the preservation of property seemed to be their main social principle.
    2. The country should be governed by "the rich, the well born, and the able."
  F. Professor Weber argues that the two groups are represented in two classic American documents.
    1. Jefferson's ideals appear in the Declaration of Independence.
    2. Hamilton's resulted in the Constitution, which Professor Weber sees as the result of compromise and fear of further revolution.

II. The two groups differed even in their assessment of human nature.
  A. Jefferson and his followers feared the corruptions of power.
    1. People would do well for themselves,
    2. As long as they were freed from tyranny.
  B. Hamilton and his followers feared the corruptions of human nature.
    1. People needed to be saved from themselves.
    2. Governments needed power to do so.
    3. Therefore, they argued that the loose government of the Articles of Confederation had been a failure.
  C. Professor Weber argues that, while the Jeffersonians made the Revolution, the Hamiltonians made the Constitution.
  D. Although all men were created equal, a great number of people were not treated as equals:
    1. Blacks.
    2. Indians, who were driven from their lands.
    3. Women.
    4. Illiterates and paupers, who were excluded from the vote.

III. The old monarchical ruling class was replaced by a new republican one.
    A. Americans, however, were reluctant to admit that their society, like every other, was based on hereditary and social distinctions.
    B. This split between theory and truth was one that would last throughout American history.

IV. Europeans often saw America as a reflection of their own ideals, not as it actually was.
    A. Europe was now divided between
        1. Old ideas of inherited status and privilege.
        2. New ideas of personal merit.
    B. On the one hand, there was a demand for equality and social mobility.
    C. On the other, there was growing elitism among
        1. The aristocratic reaction.
        2. The bureaucracies.
    D. Finally, Europeans who had been excluded from political life now wished to take part in affairs.
    E. America seemed to be the place where these dreams had come true.
        1. Americans were not supposed to care about inherited privileges.
        2. They recognized personal merit, without regard to birth or rank.

V. Some believed that America had created a new order of human society.
    A. Washington became a republican hero because he did not make himself a king or emperor as other successful generals might have done.
    B. The Revolution, based as it seemed to be on universal principles, was seen as a model for aspirations throughout the world.

VI. Professor Weber argues that the American Revolution was fundamentally different from those in Europe.
    A. It was set in a new country, unlike the revolutions in
        1. Seventeenth-century England.
        2. Eighteenth-century France.
    B. The hopes of the revolutionaries could be tested in a great, unexploited continent.
        1. The founding fathers had a chance to build.
        2. They were not forced to turn on one another.

VII. Jefferson was an unusual revolutionary.
    A. On his tombstone, he wanted to be remembered for
        1. The Declaration of Independence.
        2. The Virginia Statute for Religious Freedom.
        3. The University of Virginia.
    B. Unlike many other revolutionaries, Jefferson
        1. Defended freedom of thought for others.

    2. Did not emphasize his great offices, especially the presidency.

    3. Was a founder of a university.

  C. On the other hand, he thought that "a little revolution was good now and then."

VIII. Men like Jefferson could build on their revolutionary ideals because America enjoyed numerous advantages.

  A. The oceans gave the country protection from attack.

  B. The country could go its own way, without fear of interference.

  C. By 1801 Jefferson was president and presided over the construction of Washington, D.C.

    1. The city was laid out by L'Enfant on rational, enlightened lines.

    2. It was supposed to reflect republican virtues:

      a. Dignity.

      b. Virility.

      c. Solemnity.

Key to the Image

Images of the Republic: The American Revolution presented new challenges for social and political thinkers, but the challenge extended to artists as well. How does one glorify a republic? Images that worked well for kings and princes of the church would not work for citizens of a republic.

In some cases the problem was not difficult. John Trumbull's "The Death of General Mercer at the Battle of Princeton" is indebted to many other scenes of heroic death painted in the eighteenth century. It does not matter that General Mercer was a republican rather than a royal general. Many republican works of art portray acts of state, as in Trumbull's painting of the signing of the Declaration of Independence. The Constitutional Convention was another favorite theme of American painters.

Portraits of George Washington presented more of a problem. One painting of the Constitutional Conventional portrays George Washington with the sun at his back. The sun may have been intended to represent the dawn of the New Republic, but it looks suspiciously like the nimbus that often surrounds a king or saint. John Trumbull solved this problem in a revealing manner. To complement his painting of the Declaration of Independence, Trumbull also portrayed Washington's resignation at the end of the American Revolution.

Washington's greatness as a republican hero is that, instead of using his military power to make himself king or dictator, he returned to private life once the fighting ended.

Focus Questions

1. Describe the differences of opinion over the form that the new American government should take.
2. What classes came to power after the Revolution? What classes were excluded from power?
3. What were some of the conflicts that divided European societies of the time? How did these conflicts shape the vision that Europeans formed of the new American Republic?
4. What were some of the myths that Europeans created about America?
5. Why were the American revolutionaries able to put so many of their ideals into practice?
6. What were some of the most important achievements of Thomas Jefferson? What was the central vision that lay behind these achievements?

—————— *ASSIGNMENTS AND ACTIVITIES*——————

IN CONTEXT

Themes and issues that set Unit Nineteen in context with other units include the following:

- During the period covered by Unit Nineteen, all of Europe turned its attention to North America. Look back to the discussion of John Locke to find some of the ways North Americans seemed to carry his principles into action. In later units watch for resemblances and differences between the American and French revolutions. Pay special attention to the new constitutions and to statements of revolutionary principles.
- Professor Weber contrasts the Spanish colonies of Latin America, which were controlled by a highly centralized administration, to the English colonies in North America, which had their own legislatures and a high degree of self-government. In Unit Nineteen look for ways in which this training in self-government affected the American government and the formation of a new constitution.

Textbook Assignment

Read the following pages in your assigned textbook:

Text: *Western Civilizations* (Eleventh Edition, 1988)
Read: Chapter 18, "The Age of Absolutism," pp. 587–628; and Chapter 19, "The Scientific Revolution and Enlightenment," pp. 629–665.

Text: *The Western Experience* (Fifth Edition, 1991)
Read: From Chapter 18, "Absolutism and Empire," pp. 718–737; and from Chapter 20, "Revolutions of the Eighteenth Century," pp. 794–800.

Text: *The Western Heritage* (Fourth Edition, 1991)
Read: Chapter 17, "Empire, War, and Colonial Rebellion," pp. 591–621.

Issue for Clarification

"Taxation Without Representation Is Tyranny"

Because the phrase "taxation without representation is tyranny" was one of the most important slogans of the American Revolution, it deserves comment. First, remember that this principle was just as important in England as in the American colonies. When the colonists created the slogan, they were demanding their rights as Englishmen.

Much of the quarrel centered on a disagreement about the nature of representation. The American colonies had assemblies in which they passed laws and levied taxes. When the colonists objected to taxes passed by the English parliament, they argued that the taxes were illegal in that the colonies could not vote for members of parliament. The English argued, however, that even though the colonists could not vote for members of parliament, they were nevertheless represented indirectly. For the most part, the American colonists were not convinced by these arguments, but they were very much a part of eighteenth-century political thinking.

Many members of parliament were sympathetic to the colonists and believed that the Stamp Act and other such measures were badly conceived. But even the best friends of the colonies objected to the American claim that parliament simply did not have the right to pass certain sorts of laws.

The principle of "no taxation without representation" has remained fundamental in British and American political thought. The suffragist Susan B. Anthony once refused to pay taxes on these grounds. She argued that, because women did not have the right to vote, they could not rightly be asked to pay taxes.

Glossary

Articles of Confederation: The agreement passed by Congress in 1777 that bound the former colonies into a confederation known as the United States of America. Dissatisfaction with these articles led to the calling of the constitutional convention in 1787.

Declaratory Act: After the repeal of the Stamp Act, parliament declared in 1766 that the king and parliament had the right to pass laws binding the colonies in all respects.

Stamp Act: A measure passed by parliament in 1765 requiring the North American colonists to buy revenue stamps for newspapers, pamphlets, almanacs, and certain kinds of legal and commercial documents. Even dice and playing cards required a stamp. In protest the colonists called the Stamp Act "Congress."

Timeline

Place each of the following events on the timeline. In some cases you may have to specify a roughly defined period of time rather than a precise date.

1. Period when the French first explored the St. Lawrence River.
2. Period when the English settled Newfoundland and first tried to settle Virginia.
3. Treaty of Paris ended the French and Indian War.
4. Year of the Constitutional Convention.
5. Death of Thomas Jefferson.
6. Treaty that ended the American Revolution.
7. Jefferson founding of the University of Virginia.
8. When French Estates General assembled.
9. When George Washington became president.
10. When Thomas Jefferson became president.
11. Declaration of Independence.

1500   1850
├───┤

Map Exercise

Find the following locations on the map.

1. Area of North America explored by France in the 1530s.
2. Home state of Thomas Jefferson.
3. One area settled by the English in the 1580s.
4. New Amsterdam.
5. Quebec.
6. Area of North America lost by France in the French and Indian War.
7. Area of North America settled by Swedes in the seventeenth century.
8. Montreal.
9. Saint Lawrence River.

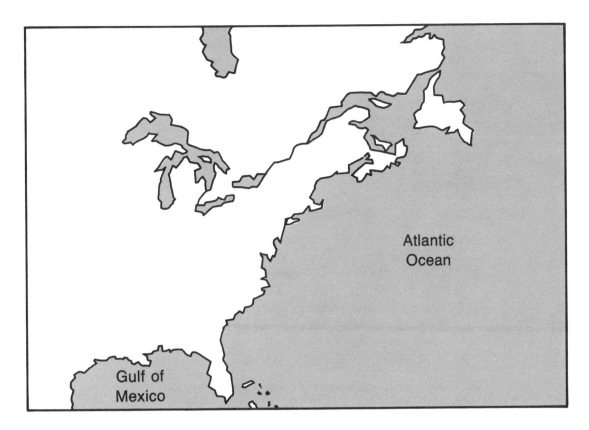

Self-Test

Part I

1. Which of the following cities was *not* founded in the seventeenth century?
   a. New Amsterdam.
   b. Boston.
   c. Quebec.
   d. Lima.

2. During the French and Indian War
   a. the French were unable to make alliances with the Indians.
   b. the English colonists tried to gain French help in order to break free of England.
   c. the French lost all but a small part of their empire in North America.
   d. both sides restricted their operations to North America.

3. Which of the following did *not* participate in the constitutional convention?
   a. Thomas Paine.
   b. Thomas Jefferson.
   c. James Madison.
   d. Alexander Hamilton.

4. Mark the false choice. During the American Revolution, the French
   a. were the only European nation to aid the rebels.
   b. supplied the rebels with weapons and gunpowder.
   c. gave the colonists important naval support.
   d. gave the colonists extensive loans.

5. Mark the false choice. The following groups were not allowed to vote under the new Constitution of 1787:
   a. Women.
   b. Slaves.
   c. Catholics.
   d. Indians.

Part II

1. Mark the false choice. Thomas Jefferson
   a. was one of the drafters of the Declaration of Independence.
   b. was a talented architect.
   c. favored a strong central government with extensive powers to coerce state governments.
   d. was one of the founders of the University of Virginia.

2. The English colonies in North America
   a. only allowed Englishpeople to immigrate.
   b. were far more lucrative to investors than the islands of the West Indies.
   c. were usually allowed extensive powers of self-government.
   d. all broke free from England in the American Revolution.

3. For the most part, in the years before the American Revolution
   a. the English colonies were cut off from the main currents of the Enlightenment.
   b. the English colonists had no defenders in the English parliament.
   c. the English armies did much to make the colonies safe from attack.
   d. English colonial administration was becoming increasingly negligent.

4. Mark the false choice. One of the important grievances that lay behind the American Revolution was
   a. the English attempt to levy taxes that the American colonists had not approved.
   b. the English decision to abolish religious toleration in the colonies.
   c. the English attempt to harness the American economy in the interests of the home country.
   d. the belief that England intended to increase its control over the governments of the colonies.

5. The constitutional convention was divided between men like
   __Thomas Jefferson, Rich Lee__, who wanted the individual states
   to have as much independence as possible, and others such as

Alex Hamilton Rob Livingston, who wanted the central government to coerce the states. (Name one person in each group.)

Optional Activity

Although the following activity is not required for the course unless assigned by the instructor, students are encouraged to use it as a source of interesting topics for further study.

Historical Novels

A good historical novel does more than tell a story in which the characters wear old fashioned clothes. It has a vision of the period it treats, a vision that is in fact a kind of historical interpretation.

Three especially good novels that treat the American Revolution from different points of view are:

- _Rabble in Arms_ by Kenneth Roberts treats the war from the point of view of the rebels. It includes an especially good description of Benedict Arnold.
- _Oliver Wiswell_, also by Kenneth Roberts, tells the story of a young American whose family remains loyal to the British crown. The work is especially valuable in that Americans who opposed the Revolution are not often portrayed elsewhere.
- _Sergeant Lamb's America_ by Robert Graves is told from the point of view of a British soldier.

After reading one of these novels, write a paper of 3 – 5 pages in which you discuss some unexpected aspect of the Revolution. Concentrate on a short episode and compare the novel's interpretation of events to what you have learned from other sources.

Films

You may wish to view some of the following films, which deal with matters discussed in this unit.

- _The Devil's Disciple_ (1959), starring Kirk Douglas, Burt Lancaster, and Laurence Olivier, is a screen version of George Bernard Shaw's play.
- _Lafayette_ (1962) tells the story of the French soldiers who came to aid the revolutionaries.
- _The Adams Chronicles_ is a series produced by public television about the family of John and Abigail Adams. John Adams, who became our second president, was a leading figure in the Revolution and in the early days of the New Republic.
- _George Washington_ (1984) is an eight-hour miniseries, starring Barry Bostwick, about the life of our first president.

Review Questions

1. What was the myth of the noble savage? How else did Europeans idealize the New World?

2. Professor Weber argues that for some Americans the Revolution was a conservative affair to protect old rights. In their eyes it was the British who tried to introduce innovation. In what ways did the relationship between England and the colonies seem to take a new direction? Why did the colonists object so strongly? Why did the English begin these new policies?

3. What were some of the philosophical ideas with which the American colonists justified their rebellion against England? Many of the causes of the Revolution were involved with the details of the special relationship between England and her colonies. Why then did the American experience become a model for the rest of the world?

4. During the Constitutional Convention there was a continuing debate between those who wanted the individual states to be as independent as possible and those who wanted a strong federal government. Who were some of the politicians on each side of the debate? On what other issues did these factions disagree? How did each side contribute to the final form of the Constitution?

5. Professor Weber argues that in every country there is a gap between political ideals and political practice. According to Professor Weber, what are some of the contradictions in American political life? State your reasons for agreeing or disagreeing with his analysis.

6. Professor Weber argues that during the late eighteenth century many European countries were experiencing a growing elitism, along with a growing desire for social equality. State your reasons for agreeing or disagreeing. While formulating your answer, pay special attention to France.

7. In what ways did a myth of the American Revolution begin to develop even before the war was over? What were some of the features of this myth and how did they conflict with the truth? The myth was especially strong in Europe. What did Europeans consider to be the most important lessons of the American Revolution?

Further Reading

Sources

Weber, Eugen. *The Western Tradition*, 2nd ed. (1965).
    "The Declaration of Independence," pp. 534–537.
    "The Federalist," pp. 537–543.

Studies

Bailyn, Bernard. *The Ideological Origins of the American Revolution*. (1967). An important study that traces links between English radical traditions and the ideas of the American revolutionaries.

Becker, Carl. *The Declaration of Independence: A Study in the History of Political Ideas*. (1922).

Dorn, Walter. *Competition for Empire*. (1940). One of the best surveys of the great wars of the mid-eighteenth century.

Godechot, Jacques. *France and the Atlantic Revolutions of the Eighteenth Century*. (1965). Important comparative history.

Palmer, R. R. *The Age of the Democratic Revolution: A Political History of Europe and America*. (1959–1962). Good on the similarities and differences of various revolutionary movements.

Wills, Gary. *Inventing America: Jefferson's Declaration of Independence*. (1978). Covers much the same ground as Becker (see above), but offers different interpretations.

Wood, G. S. *The Creation of the American Republic, 1776–1787*. (1969). Concentrates on political thought.

Answer Key

Timeline
1. 1530s.
2. 1580s.
3. 1763.
4. 1787.
5. 1826.
6. 1783.
7. 1816.
8. 1789.
9. 1789.
10. 1801.
11. 1776.

Map Exercise
1. The valley of the Saint Lawrence River.
2. Virginia.
3. Newfoundland or Virginia.
4. Now the city of New York.
6. Roughly the area of modern Canada in the provinces of Montreal and Quebec.
7. The state of Delaware.

Self-Test

Part I

1. (d) Lima.
2. (c) the French lost all but a small part of their empire in North America.
3. (a) Thomas Paine.
4. (a) were the only European nation to aid the rebels.
5. (c) Catholics.

Part II

1. (c) favored a strong central government with extensive powers to coerce state governments.
2. (c) were usually allowed extensive powers of self-government.
3. (c) the English armies did much to make the colonies safe from attack.
4. (b) the English decision to abolish religious toleration in the colonies.
5. For the first group, the lecture mentions Thomas Jefferson and Richard Henry Lee; for the second, Alexander Hamilton and Robert Livingston. Your textbook may supply other names as well.

Revolutionary Enthusiasm *(left)* French citizens of all classes shout the slogan "Liberty or Death." *(right)* A volunteer is about to depart for the army. For many Frenchmen, the great story of the Revolution was the stand their country took against all of Europe. (GIRAUDON/Art Resource, NY.)

UNIT TWENTY

Program 39: The Death of the Old Regime

Program 40: The French Revolution

LEARNING OBJECTIVES

After completing Unit Twenty students should understand the following issues:

- The stabilizing factors in the United States in the years after the Revolution.
- The fiscal weakness of the French crown. Your textbook will supplement Professor Weber's description.
- The factors working for and against reform in France. Look in your textbook for the fiscal status of the nobility and the clergy.
- The reforms of 1789.
- The transition from reform to Revolution. Use your textbook to distinguish the various phases of the revolution.
- New styles of warfare. How does your textbook support or rebut Professor Weber's arguments about the changing nature of warfare?
- The creation of the French Empire.
- The enduring legacy of the Revolution.

—————————————— *TV INSTRUCTION* ——————————————

OVERVIEW
PROGRAM 39: THE DEATH OF THE OLD REGIME

After the separation from England, the American Revolution did not continue indefinitely. The American Constitution resulted from a working compromise between conservatives and radicals. The French Revolution, however, developed a powerful momentum of its own. It quickly became more radical and more dangerous than its leaders had ever intended.

I. The American Constitution resulted from compromises between conservatives and radical leaders.
   A. Conservatives such as Alexander Hamilton wanted a strong central government.
      1. Conservatives distrusted democracy.
      2. They wanted to keep power in the hands of "the best people in the land."
   B. The Constitution adopted in 1787 had to quiet these fears, while remaining democratic enough to win the support of more radical leaders.
      1. The propertied classes retained their control of American society.
      2. The Revolution was no longer a revolution.
   C. Even the most radical leaders had a conservative side.
      1. Slavery continued to be protected.
      2. The Constitution avoided direct representation.

II. Radicals and conservatives were able to compromise for several reasons.
   A. The most conservative groups, those who remained loyal to the king, had been driven from the country.
   B. Because America had never known harsh repression, radical resentment was moderate enough to permit compromises.

III. In Europe the American Revolution was seen as a model:
   A. The Revolution showed how certain abstract principles could be "reduced to practice":
      1. The Rights of Man.
      2. The Sovereignty of the People.
   B. People began to think more concretely about political issues.
      1. England was no longer the model of an enlightened nation.
      2. People more readily criticized their own governments in light of the American Revolution.
   C. New political practices became real possibilities:
      1. Written constitutions.
      2. Declarations of rights.
      3. Constitutional conventions.

IV. By the last quarter of the eighteenth century, the idea of revolution had become popular, even widespread, throughout Europe.
  A. Even village priests sometimes read
    1. *The Great Encyclopedia.*
    2. The works of the philosophes.
  B. The philosophes themselves did not advocate revolution but their works promoted ideals of social reform.
  C. The American Revolution had made celebrities of men like
    1. Lafayette.
    2. Franklin.
  D. Arguments for radical change could be heard everywhere, in
    1. Salons.
    2. Cafes.
    3. Agricultural societies.
    4. Philanthropical societies.
    5. Provincial academies.
    6. Correspondence societies.
  E. The Masonic Lodges were especially receptive to radical ideas, for they were already committed to such ideals as
    1. Civil equality.
    2. Religious toleration.
    3. The liberation of the personality.
  F. Even the theater and opera spread radical ideas.
    1. The playwright Pierre de Beaumarchais
      a. Wrote the *Marriage of Figaro.*
      b. Supplied arms to the American rebels.
    2. Wolfgang Amadeus Mozart
      a. Composed an opera based on the *Marriage of Figaro.*
      b. Wrote *The Magic Flute*, which was based on Masonic symbols and ideas.
  G. Painters such as Jacques-Louis David portrayed scenes that glorified republican virtues:
    1. "The Oath of the Horatii" (1784).
    2. The scene of Brutus receiving the corpses of his traitorous sons (1789).
    3. These paintings were seen as indictments of the aristocracy and glorifications of republican virtues, such as
      a. Stoicism.
      b. Courage.
      c. Civic virtue.
  H. Eventually, even men's and women's fashions would come to imitate those of ancient Rome.

V. Even the court and nobility played a part in promoting revolutionary ideas.
  A. Louis XVI had aided the American Revolution.
  B. The Marquis de Lafayette had fought alongside the Americans and returned to France a popular hero.

   C. Part of the reason was that the French had a long tradition of aiding the enemies of their enemies:
1. They had allied with the Turks against the Habsburgs.
2. They had allied with foreign Protestants against Catholic Spain.
3. They were happy to aid any enemy of England.

VI. By the end of the 1780s France was in an enormous crisis.
   A. Aid to the American rebels had cost the equivalent of four years' revenue.
   B. Because most of the money had come from borrowing, more than half of each year's income went to pay interest.
   C. The general economy was weak.
1. The weather had been bad.
   a. Therefore, crops had been bad.
   b. The price of bread was rising.
2. Wages were stagnant.
3. Taxes and prices were rising.

VII. Many of the crown's problems were caused by an inequitable system of taxation.
   A. Many people were exempt from taxation.
1. The nobility.
2. The clergy.
3. Officers of the crown.
   B. Because these were among the most prosperous people, the burden of taxation fell on those who were least able to pay.
   C. Even so, the system of taxation may not have been beyond salvation.
1. Privileged classes would have had to pay their fair share.
2. Pensions to royal favorites would have had to be cut.

VIII. Revolution or unrest was breaking out in many parts of Europe.
   A. In 1786 Prussian troops put down a revolution in Holland.
   B. In 1788 there was a revolution in Belgium.
   C. There was unrest in many parts of the Habsburg Empire.

IX. The French government tried to rationalize the management of the country.
   A. Minister of Finance Charles de Calonne tried to reform the financial system.
   B. When its first attempt failed, the government convened the Estates General in the spring of 1789.
1. This institution was so anachronistic that it had not met in 175 years.
2. The government wanted to play the Third Estate, or commoners, against the privileged orders: the clergy and aristocracy.
3. The Third Estate seized control and declared itself the National Assembly.

4. Eventually, representatives of clergy and nobility joined. This was the Constitutional Revolution of June 1789.
C. Violence broke out all over the country.
  1. The storming of the Bastille on July 14, 1789, was only one incident of violence in the cities.
  2. There were violence and unrest in the countryside in "the Great Fear."
D. On August 4, 1789, the Assembly abolished the most important special privileges:
  1. No more economic privileges.
  2. No more forced labor.
  3. No more personal serfdom.
  4. No more tax exemptions.
  5. No more hunting rights.
  6. Guilds and corporations were dissolved.
  7. Clergy gave up their tithes.
  8. Magistrates gave up the offices they had bought.
E. Three weeks later the Assembly proclaimed the "Declaration of the Rights of Man," which
  1. Echoed the ideals of the American Revolution.
  2. Derived much from philosophers such as
    a. Locke.
    b. Rousseau.

X. The Revolution was becoming increasingly violent.
  A. The Third Estate had tried to exploit the violence of the Paris mob but soon found that the violence could not be controlled.
  B. In October 1789, a Paris mob marched on Versailles and forced the king and royal family back to Paris.

Key to the Images

Jacques-Louis David (1748–1825): Even before the French Revolution, David had painted scenes of republican virtue, many of them taken from the history of ancient Rome: "The Oath of the Horatii" and "The Lictors Bringing Brutus the Bodies of His Sons" both appear in Program 39. David painted to illustrate an idea that had become widespread in Europe since the American Revolution. As the French writer Chamfort once said, "Only free peoples have history. Slaves have nothing but anecdotes."

When the Revolution came, David portrayed one of its greatest events, "The Oath of the Tennis Court," the occasion on which members of the Estates General swore not to disband until they had drawn up a constitution.

Great days: The French Revolution, especially in Paris, was marked by a number of "great days" on which the Revolution seemed to take dramatic steps forward. In addition to "The Oath of the Tennis Court," many other paintings celebrated such days. In Program 39 we see "The Triumph of Marat" and "The Plundering of the Invalides."

Political cartoons: Political cartoons had appeared long before the French Revolution, but many events and currents of feeling seemed more suited to cartoons or cartoonlike works than to more formal paintings. An image in Program 39 portrays a group of peasants with flails, beating a pile of mitres, officers' hats, pieces of armor, and coats of arms—symbols of the old ruling classes that were supposedly being displaced.

Focus Questions

1. What were the major political divisions in the United States in the years after the Revolution? Why did these differences not plunge the country into civil war?
2. How widespread was the desire for reform in France in the years before the Revolution? How did the example of America influence these desires?
3. What other European countries had revolutionary movements in the 1780s?
4. How did the painting of Jacques-Louis David reflect the social and political attitudes of the 1780s and 1790s?
5. What groups benefited from the fiscal policies of the French crown?
6. What common threads unite the various reforms of 1789?
7. What were the stages of increasing violence in the Revolution?

OVERVIEW
PROGRAM 40: THE FRENCH REVOLUTION

The first years of the French Revolution brought important political and administrative reforms. By 1793, however, France was at war with most of Europe and the period of revolutionary terror had begun. Eventually, Napoleon seized control of the state and spread French power and influence across the continent.

    I. The first years of the French Revolution brought important political and administrative changes.
      A. France now had a written constitution, with
        1. Representative government.
        2. Universal male suffrage.
      B. The old provinces were replaced with more convenient administrative units known as departments.

    C. The government replaced the old chaotic systems of measurements.
        1. The metric system was introduced.
        2. New months with new names were introduced.
        3. The week was replaced with a ten-day period.
    D. The government tried to make French a truly national language that would replace dialects such as
        1. Flemish.
        2. Breton.
        3. Basque.
    E. All children were to be taught in public schools.
    F. It was decreed that careers would now depend only on talent, not on birth or status.

  II. Some of these reforms would only gradually be implemented in the course of the next one hundred years.
    A. Universal suffrage.
    B. Public education.
    C. The spread of the French language.
    D. The adoption of the metric system.

 III. The religious policy of the French Revolution was complex and potentially troublesome.
    A. The Revolution stood for religious toleration and emancipated
        1. Protestants.
        2. Jews.
    B. Such toleration was not pleasing to good Catholics.
    C. Even worse, however, the church was subjected to even greater control than under the Old Regime.
        1. The state confiscated church property.
        2. The priests became salaried employees of the state.
        3. The clergy had to swear to an oath of loyalty.

 IV. Religious policy created a political crisis.
    A. The pope forbade the clergy to take the oath of loyalty.
        1. All those who took it were excommunicated.
        2. The French clergy were split in two:
            a. The minority who took the oath.
            b. The majority who refused and were imprisoned, exiled, or driven into hiding.
    B. Further, the king would not enforce this religious policy.
        1. Louis XVI now became estranged from the revolutionaries.
        2. Ultimately, both he and the queen would be executed.

  V. The French Revolution was becoming more radical and violent.
    A. The monarchy was abolished.
    B. The liberation constitution was jettisoned.
    C. Dictatorship and terror were taking control.

 VI. By 1792 the French Revolution had taken a new course.
    A. Thousands of people were executed.

B. Hundreds of thousands died in the civil wars.

C. The government also embarked on a number of disastrous internal policies.
  1. Fixed prices were set for many commodities.
    a. These goods disappeared from the market.
    b. Great food shortages resulted.
  2. Paper currency was introduced, which soon lost its value.
  3. A police state was imposed to
    a. Enforce decrees.
    b. Stifle dissent.

VII. Many of these measures were caused or aggravated by the fact that France was going to war with nearly all of Europe.
  A. In 1792 France mobilized volunteers to fight
    1. Prussia.
    2. Austria.
  B. In 1793 the revolutionary government declared war on
    1. England.
    2. Holland.
    3. Spain.

VIII. Professor Weber argues that war and revolution were turning the country into a nation.
  A. The former subjects of the king were now citizens, or in Professor Weber's phrase, "equal shareholders in the nation."
  B. The sovereignty of the people was more powerful than the sovereignty of the king had been.
    1. The revolutionary governments could raise heavier taxes than the kings had ever done.
    2. The state could mobilize soldiers in ever greater numbers.

IX. European warfare was about to be transformed.
  A. Military conscription as such was not new in Europe.
    1. The Swedes had had a sort of military draft during the Thirty Years' War.
    2. Louis XIV's war minister, Louvois, had tried to introduce a military draft, although the idea was dropped in the face of opposition.
    3. Prussia had begun universal military service for all healthy males.
      a. By 1789 Prussia had nearly 200 thousand troops.
      b. The French kings could support only 180 thousand even though France was much larger.
      c. Further, the French army cost three times as much to support.
  B. By 1792 France was beginning mass conscription.
    1. By 1794 the French army had nearly one million soldiers.
    2. This enormous manpower changed styles of warfare.
  C. Under the Old Regime armies had consisted of highly trained men marching in files.

1. Training took so long that generals were reluctant to waste their troops,
2. Because replacements could not quickly take the place of the dead or wounded.

D. The generals of the French Revolution sent soldiers into battle in columns.
1. These formations were well suited to hastily trained soldiers.
2. Because replacements could quickly make up losses, the revolutionary generals were more ready to risk their men in bloody, decisive battles.

E. The French Revolution had revived the idea of total war.

X. As the French won battles throughout Europe, they claimed that they were spreading the ideals of the Revolution to the rest of the world.
A. They declared that they would aid any country that was trying to overthrow oppression.
1. In some countries the French armies were welcomed as liberators.
2. In others, however, people did not want to be liberated or to adopt French institutions.

B. Revolutionary rhetoric sometimes became a disguise for French imperialism.
1. French occupiers had to "teach people to be free."
2. The French also conquered countries that already had republican institutions:
a. Switzerland.
b. Venice.

XI. French military power reached its height under Napoleon Bonaparte.
A. In 1795 and 1796 Napoleon crushed the armies of
1. Austria.
2. Sardinia.

B. Before long he had conquered
1. Italy.
2. Switzerland.

C. Napoleon's military power eventually made him head of the state.
1. In 1799 he issued a new constitution that amounted to a one-man rule.
2. In 1804 he had himself crowned emperor.

D. Under Napoleon's rule the French conquered or dominated Europe from the Baltic to the Adriatic seas.
1. For a few years there were French kings or princes in
a. Madrid.
b. Naples.
c. Dubrovnik.
d. Stockholm.

e. Munster.

f. Florence.

2. Napoleon's fall only began in 1812, when he overextended himself by trying to conquer Russia.

E. Napoleon was a lawmaker as well as a general.

1. His Civil Code, later known as the Napoleonic Code, gave permanent form to many of the gains of the Revolution:

a. Individual liberty.

b. Freedom to work.

c. Freedom of conscience.

d. Equality before the law.

2. His code, however, showed little interest in the rights of women.

XII. Napoleon's armies transformed Europe.

A. They destroyed the remnants of medieval privileges and restrictions.

1. Serfdom was abolished.

2. Jews were emancipated.

3. Free enterprise was established.

B. By introducing people to new ideas and institutions, Napoleon also created new desires for

1. National sovereignty.

2. National self-determination.

Key to the Images

More great days: When a painter portrays an act of state, he is trying to preserve its memory and significance for ages to come. During the French Revolution, however, events proceeded at such a pace that sometimes the paint was barely dry on canvas before history had taken a quite different turn.

Le Clerc portrayed the "Signing of the National Pact of the Constitution of 1791 by Louis XVI." In theory at least, France was now a constitutional monarchy. In two years, however, the monarchy was destroyed, as seen in Demachy's portrayal of "Destruction of the Royal Emblem," on August 10, 1793.

The French National Guard: Once the French Revolution was underway, political and economic life were in disarray. The National Guard, as well as providing security, was now assigned to watching over daily life. An image in Program 40 portrays officers of the guard exhorting citizens to return to work.

The French army: By early 1793 France was at war with most of Europe. Many images in Program 40 show the growth of the new French army, such as Edouard Detaille's "The Departure of the Volunteers" and the painting of the Paris National Guard leaving to join the army.

Battles: The victories of the French army, especially those of Napoleon, provided abundant subjects for painters. In Program 40 we see images of the battles of Eylau, Marengo, and Friedland.

Focus Questions

1. What were the revolutionary reforms in such practical areas as political administration, education, and the standardization of weights and measures?
2. How did policies affecting the Catholic clergy create political tensions?
3. What caused the terror of the French Revolution?
4. With what countries did the revolutionary governments go to war in the 1790s?
5. How did the new French armies differ from those of other European powers?
6. What were the French policies toward the countries they conquered in the years after the Revolution?
7. What were Napoleon's principal achievements?

—————— *ASSIGNMENTS AND ACTIVITIES* ——————

IN CONTEXT

Themes and issues that set Unit Twenty in context with other units include the following:

• Professor Weber discusses the Terror of 1793–1794. Keep in mind that France was at war with nearly the whole of Europe during these years and that large sections of the army's high command had deserted to the enemy. In later units we learn that many of those who fled from France during this period returned to their homes long before the restoration of the monarchy. Napoleon, in particular, welcomed many of the emigres back to France. In units to come, especially those that discuss the Russian Revolution, pay special attention to patterns of violence.

• In Unit Twenty Professor Weber explains many of the administrative reforms carried out under the Revolution and during the Napoleonic period. Look back to the administrative reforms of the seventeenth century. Many writers, especially Tocqueville, argued that the Revolution continued a trend of centralization and reform that began more than a century before.

- In previous units Professor Weber argues that in the eighteenth century warfare became less savage than it had been in earlier periods. During the revolutionary period warfare became bloodier than ever. After the French introduced mass conscription, they were able to use great numbers of soldiers to smash enemy armies. In later units look for resemblances between the revolutionary wars of this period and the total wars of the twentieth century.

- In Unit Nineteen Professor Weber emphasizes the disagreements among American politicians over the form of the New Republic. These divisions, however, did not lead to open fighting in the early days of the United States. Compare the American and French situations. Why were social divisions in France so much more bitter? Look ahead to the revolutions of the twentieth century, especially the Russian Revolution.

Textbook Assignment

Read the following pages in your assigned textbook:

Text: *Western Civilizations* (Eleventh Edition, 1988)
Read: Chapter 20, "The French Revolution," pp. 673–714.

Text: *The Western Experience* (Fifth Edition, 1991)
Read: From Chapter 20, "Revolutions of the Eighteenth Century," pp. 801–820; and Chapter 21, "The Terror and Napoleon," pp. 821–864.

Text: *The Western Heritage* (Fourth Edition, 1991)
Read: Chapter 19, "The French Revolution," pp. 657–691; and Chapter 20, "The Age of Napoleon and the Triumph of Romanticism," pp. 693–727.

Issues for Clarification

Confiscation of Lands

During the French Revolution enormous parcels of land were confiscated from the clergy and the nobility. Because France was at war throughout the period, most of this land was soon sold to raise money. The land sales created support for the Revolution. Even though they might disapprove of government policies, the new landholders had a strong incentive to remain loyal in that they feared a restored monarchy would return the lands to their original owners.

The French Language

Several languages were spoken in France apart from French itself. Breton, a Celtic language related to Welsh and Gaelic, was spoken in Brittany.

Flemish, which is related to Dutch, was spoken along the Belgian border. Basque, which is unrelated to any other European language, was spoken in the Pyrenees. German was spoken in Alsace and Lorraine.

Even within French-speaking areas, Parisian French was only one dialect among many. The *langue d'oc* spoken in the south is more closely related to the Catalan of Northwest Spain than to the northern dialects of French.

Even before the Revolution, however, Parisian French was spreading throughout the kingdom. Many educated people in the provinces were familiar with it, even though they may have spoken a local dialect as well. Under the Revolution, it was decreed that Parisian French would be the language of education. Even today, however, many of the local dialects survive.

Price Controls

To lower the price of food for the armies and the cities, some of the revolutionary governments decreed that grain could not be sold above a certain price. As a result, grain producers kept their products off the market rather than sell them at an artificially low price. For a time, the government sent agents into the countryside to confiscate food. Before this policy was dropped, it created enormous resentment, especially among the peasantry.

The *Taille*

The *taille*, a tax on land, was one of the most important sources of revenue for the French crown. Unfortunately, because the clergy and the nobility were exempt, much of the kingdom's wealth could not be tapped.

Further, many government offices automatically conferred noble status so that the number of people exempted tended to grow. To make matters worse, if a nobleman or clergyman sold land, it sometimes remained exempt from the *taille*, even if the new owner was a member of the Third Estate.

Glossary

Departments: The administrative units that replaced the old French provinces.

Estates General: The great French assembly convoked in 1789 to reform French finances. The Estates General had last been called in the early seventeenth century.

Guillotine: A device for beheading people, widely used during the French Revolution and afterwards. The victim is strapped down horizontally and a heavy, slanted blade slides down guiderails to sever the neck. The guillotine was named for Dr. J. L. Guillotin, who advocated its use as a humane measure.

Loyalists: North American colonists who remained loyal to England during the American Revolution. After the Revolution many loyalists emigrated to Canada. The pejorative term for loyalist was *Tory*.

Timeline

Place each of the following events on the timeline. In some cases you may have to specify a roughly defined period of time rather than a precise date.

1. French assembly abolishes most feudal privileges (give full date).
2. Napoleon invades Russia.
3. Oath of the Horatii first exhibited in Paris.
4. Napoleon becomes emperor.
5. Foreign troops suppress revolution in Holland.
6. French introduce mass conscription.
7. Storming of the Bastille (give full date).
8. Italy and Switzerland fall under French control.
9. Revolution breaks out in Belgium.
10. Napoleon's new constitution essentially creates one-man rule.

1750   1850
├──┤

Map Exercise

Find the following locations on the map.
1. Country that suppressed the Dutch rebellion.
2. Country where revolution broke out in 1788.
3. Country invaded by Napoleon in 1812.
4. Area of Breton speakers.
5. Area of Flemish speakers in France.
6–7. Two countries with which France was at war in 1793.
8. Area of French conquests in 1795.
9. France's great naval enemy.
10. Area of Basque speakers in France.

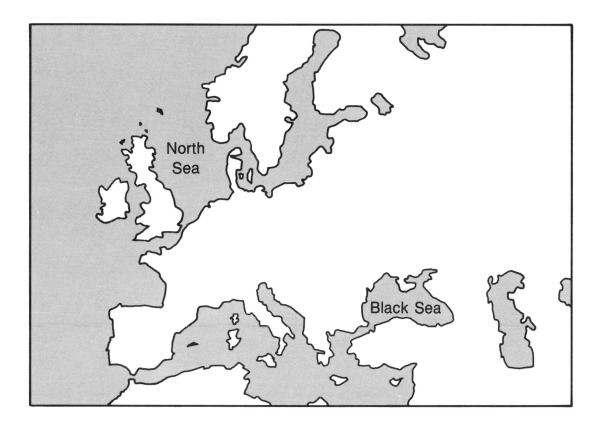

Self-Test

Part I

1. Which of the following men did *not* help supply the American rebels with money or arms?
   a. Diderot.
   b. Beaumarchais.
   c. Louis XVI.
   d. Lafayette.

2. Mark the false choice. In 1789
   a. the Estates General met for the first time since the early seventeenth century.
   b. the Assembly abolished most feudal privileges.
   c. the Paris mob forced the king and royal family to move back to Paris.
   d. the revolutionary government declared war on Austria, Prussia, and England.

3. Which of the following was *not* one of the achievements of the French Revolution?
   a. The emancipation of the Jews.
   b. A stable economy in France.

    c. The abolition of feudal privileges.

    d. The principle that all citizens were liable to taxation.

4. By 1800 all but one of the following had experimented with universal male conscription:

    a. England.

    b. France.

    c. Prussia.

    d. Sweden.

5. Which of the following was *not* one of Napoleon's conquests?

    a. England.

    b. Spain.

    c. Switzerland.

    d. Italy.

Part II

1. Mark the false choice. By 1789 the French government was in severe economic trouble because

    a. many of the wealthiest people in the kingdom paid little or nothing in taxes.

    b. interest payments on the national debt consumed at least half of each year's revenues.

    c. the French economy was one of the most underdeveloped in Europe.

    d. nearly a quarter of the budget went to maintain the court and pay pensions to the nobility.

2. Mark the false choice. The religious policy of the revolutionary governments

    a. demanded that all clergy take an oath to the state.

    b. confiscated church property and made the clergy employees of the state.

    c. was condemned by the pope.

    d. was supported by the king.

3. Mark the false choice. The French tactic of fighting in columns

    a. required less training than other eighteenth-century tactics.

    b. required an abundant supply of troops.

    c. was designed to spare manpower.

    d. was able to concentrate great numbers of troops at key spots in a battle.

4. Mark the false choice. In their policy of conquest the revolutionary and Napoleonic governments

    a. declared that they would aid any people who were trying to free themselves from dynastic rulers.

    b. set up French rulers or dynasties in many parts of Europe.

    c. did not invade countries that already had a republican form of government.

   d. introduced French practices to their allies and subjects.

5. Mark the false choice. The Napoleonic Code protected
   a. freedom of conscience.
   b. freedom to work.
   c. women's suffrage.
   d. equality before the law.

Optional Activity

Although the following activity is not required for the course unless assigned by the instructor, students are encouraged to use it as a source of interesting topics for further study.

Charles Dickens

Charles Dickens was a novelist of generally liberal opinions whose books show great sympathy for victims of oppression. Dickens's sympathy comes across clearly in *A Tale of Two Cities*, a novel about the French Revolution. Nevertheless, like many other writers in the English-speaking world, Dickens portrayed the Revolution as an endless sequence of violence and horror.

   After reading *A Tale of Two Cities*, write a paper of 3–5 pages in which you address one of the following issues:

- According to Dickens, what were the causes of the French Revolution? To what degree were the French aristocrats responsible for what happened?

- Why did the French Revolution become so violent and unjust? How does Dickens portray the revolutionaries who appear in the novel?

- How does Dickens contrast England and France? In *A Tale of Two Cities* what makes London so different from Paris? How were English aristocrats different from the French?

- You may also wish to consider Dicken's work from the perspective of Unit Twenty–One. Dickens wrote more than two generations after the Revolution. Why might an Englishman of the mid-nineteenth century have looked at the Revolution from this point of view?

   You may also wish to look at one or more of the films that have been made from the book. Ronald Coleman's version (1935) is recommended and is available on videocassette. The 1958 version with Dirk Bogarde is also good.

Review Questions

1. With the exception of Alexander Hamilton who was killed in a duel, most of America's founding fathers died in their beds. How was the American Republic able to achieve stability so soon after the war of independence? In what ways was the situation in America different

from that in France or in the other European countries that went
through revolutions during this period?

2. How did the American Revolution affect political thinking in Europe?
What features of the American experience were especially admired or
condemned? How widespread was the desire for social and political
reform in France?

3. What were some of the principal reasons behind the fiscal crisis of the
French state? What were the crown's greatest expenses? Many French-
people realized that fiscal reform was necessary. Why then did the
crown find it so difficult to increase its revenues or cut its expenses?

4. What were some of the principal reforms enacted in the year 1789?
Which of these reforms would endure beyond the revolutionary period?
Although the period of revolutionary terror came a few years later,
what were some of the signs of increasing violence that had already
appeared in 1789?

5. What were the policies of the revolutionary governments toward Cath-
olic clergy? What were the effects of these policies on the clergy itself?
On relations between France and the papacy? On relations between
Louis XVI and the revolutionary governments?

6. By 1793 France was at war with most of Europe. Why were the French
not crushed by the combined force of the great powers? In what ways
did the French depart from the tactics and strategies of most eighteenth-century armies? In what ways did the French foreshadow the
total wars of more recent times?

7. To what extent did Napoleon continue or preserve the work of the
French Revolution? In what ways did he spread revolutionary ideas and
practices throughout Europe? What were some of his other achievements, apart from his military conquests?

Further Reading

Original Sources

Burke, Edmund. *Reflections on the Revolution in France.* (1969).   Written
    in England during the early years of the revolution. In denouncing the
    revolutionaries, Burke constructed a social philosophy that would
    become influential among conservative thinkers.

de Caulaincourt, Armand. *With Napoleon in Russia.* (1935).   One of the
    classic memoires of Napoleon's campaigns.

Higgins E. L., ed. *The French Revolution as Told by Contemporaries.* (1939).

Stewart, J. H. *A Documentary Survey of the French Revolution.* (1951).

Weber, Eugen. *The Western Tradition*, 2nd ed. (1965).
    from "A Dawn of Revolution," pp. 559–572.
    "The Reaction," pp. 573–590.

Wollstonecraft, Mary. *A Vindication of the Rights of Women.* (1976).

Studies

Chandler, David. *The Campaigns of Napoleon.* (1966).

Cobban, Alfred. *Aspects of the French Revolution.* (1968). Essays on a wide range of topics.

de Tocqueville, Alexis. *The Old Regime and the French Revolution.* (1955). By one of the great political thinkers of the nineteenth century. His interpretations are still fruitful.

Geyl, Pieter, ed. *Napoleon: For and Against.* (1964). Essays on controversial issues. Compiled by one of Europe's greatest historians.

Godechot, Jacques. *The Counter-Revolution: Doctrine and Action.* (1971). On opposition to the revolution.

Lefebvre, Georges. *The Coming of the French Revolution.* (1947). By one of the greatest historians of the subject. The following two works by Lefebvrc form a continuous history of the period.

———. *The French Revolution*, 2 vols. (1962–1964).

———. *Napoleon*, 2 vols. (1969).

Answer Key

Timeline
1. August 4, 1789.
2. 1812.
3. 1785.
4. 1804.
5. 1786.
6. 1793.
7. July 14, 1789.
8. 1795.
9. 1788.
10. 1799.

Map Exercise
1. Prussia.
2. Belgium.
3. Russia.
4. Brittainy.
5. Northern France, along the Belgian border.
6–7. England, Holland, Spain, Prussia, Austria, and the states of Italy are all good answers.
8. Switzerland and Italy.
9. England.
10. Southern France, along the Pyrenees.

Self-Test

Part I

1. (a) Diderot.
2. (d) the revolutionary government declared war on Austria, Prussia, and England.
3. (b) A stable economy in France.
4. (a) England.
5. (a) England.

Part II

1. (c) the French economy was one of the most underdeveloped in Europe.
2. (d) was supported by the king.
3. (c) was designed to spare manpower.
4. (c) did not invade countries that already had a republican form of government.
5. (c) women's suffrage.

Rotary Presses   These great machines transformed journalism. Previously, newspapers had circulated in editions of only a few thousand. By the end of the
nineteenth century, newspapers in the great cities had circulations in the
hundreds of thousands. The press had become a political force in its own right.
(Culver Pictures.)

UNIT TWENTY-ONE

Program 41: The Industrial Revolution

Program 42: The Industrial World

LEARNING OBJECTIVES

After completing Unit Twenty-One students should understand the following issues:

- The relationship between the revolutions in industry, commerce, communications, and agriculture. Compare Professor Weber's interpretation to that in your textbook.
- The network of markets and sources of raw materials created by the Industrial Revolution.
- The political and military effects of economic interdependence. Use your textbook to trace specific patterns of dependence between industrialized nations and their sources of raw materials.
- The most important improvements in the European standard of living. Use your textbook to trace the interdependence of these various improvements.
- The effect of the popular press on social and political life.
- The ways in which the economic developments of the nineteenth century created a new kind of city.

TV INSTRUCTION

The eighteenth-century revolution in agriculture made possible the Industrial Revolution of the nineteenth century. Textiles were the first industry to be transformed, soon to be followed by transportation and communications. By the beginning of the twentieth century the European population had more than doubled since 1800, and the standard of living was much higher.

I. The Industrial Revolution began with the mass production of textiles.
  A. The textile mills were powered by
    1. Water.
    2. Steam engines.
  B. Within a generation after 1800, the mills were producing clothing that even working people could afford:
    1. Calicos.
    2. Ginghams.
    3. Other cheap clothing.
  C. Cheap clothing transformed the lives of the poor. In earlier times poor people had worn
    1. Secondhand clothes or hand-me-downs.
    2. At best, one or two sets of durable clothing that had to last a lifetime.
  D. Isaac Singer patented the sewing machine in 1851.
    1. Ready-made clothing became increasingly affordable.
    2. By 1900 women could afford to own their own sewing machines.

II. The revolution in transportation was equally striking.
  A. The railroads did the most to transform travel.
    1. In 1848 there were only around 16,000 miles of track in Europe.
    2. By 1914 there were 220,000 miles of track.
  B. Apart from the mileage of tracks, the railroads required a huge infrastructure of
    1. Bridges.
    2. Tunnels.
    3. Stations.
    4. Workshops.
  C. The railroads were part of an even larger structure of public works:
    1. Canals.
    2. Subways.

    3. Aqueducts.
    4. Drains.
    5. Sewers.
    6. Roads.
  D. Professor Weber estimates that these projects consumed more stone and metal than all the monuments of antiquity.
  E. It has been estimated that the nineteenth century produced
    1. More buildings in the Gothic style than had the Middle Ages.
    2. More classical buildings than had the Classical Age.
  F. Within a century the scale and speed of travel had been transformed.
    1. In 1815 the armies of Napoleon had not been able to travel much faster than those of Julius Caesar.
    2. By 1900 it was possible to cross Europe by railroad in three to four days.

III. Communications were speeding up at an even greater rate.
  A. Before 1800 improvements in communications had proceeded slowly.
    1. In ancient times people occasionally sent messages by pigeons, which were likely to be diverted or eaten along the way.
    2. By the seventeenth century a fast courier might be able to cover sixty miles a day.
    3. By the French Revolution the Semaphore telegraph could send simple messages when the weather was clear.
  B. This situation changed completely in the nineteenth century.
    1. By the 1870s a telegram could be sent around the world in a few hours.
    2. By 1900 radio messages could cross the oceans.
    3. The telephone, which had seemed no more than a toy in the 1870s, had 2.5 million European subscribers by 1900.

IV. News reporting and publishing were industrialized.
  A. Daily newspapers had been published in the eighteenth century.
    1. Because they were expensive to produce, only the well-off could afford them.
    2. In 1815, for instance, the *London Times* sold five thousand copies a day at seven pence.
  B. By mid-century the rotary press permitted large-scale circulation at lower prices.
    1. By 1850 the *London Times* was selling fifty thousand copies a day at five pence.
    2. Eventually, some newspapers sold for a penny.
    3. By the 1890s some of the great papers had circulations of more than one million.
  C. News could be reported at much greater speeds.
    1. In 1815 news of Waterloo took four days to reach London.

    2. By mid-century such news could be transmitted in a few hours, especially after the laying of
      a. The underwater cable between Dover and Calais in 1851.
      b. The cable between England and the United States in 1866.

V. This information revolution created powerful new political forces.
  A. The newspapers could inflame public opinion to create political crises, even wars and revolutions:
    1. The Revolution of 1830.
    2. The Revolution of 1848.
    3. The Franco-Prussian War of 1870–1871.
    4. The Dreyfus affair of the 1890s.
    5. The Spanish-American War of 1898.
  B. Professor Weber argues that the mass media tended to create a lurid, sensational picture of the world.
    1. Exotic, bizarre, or violent subjects made more exciting stories.
    2. The mass media could report stories from all over the world, which would have been forgotten or neglected in earlier times.
    3. Consequently, the world may have begun to seem more dangerous or threatening.

VI. It became possible to reproduce images on a mass scale.
  A. The lithographic process was invented in 1798. Even people of modest means could afford
    1. Prints.
    2. Etchings.
    3. Caricatures.
    4. Portraits.
    5. Reproductions of art.
    6. Religious pictures.
  B. After 1839 photography developed rapidly.
    1. Even people of modest means could have portraits of themselves and their relatives.
    2. Pictures of public figures could be circulated on a huge scale.

VII. Professor Weber argues that the new means of communications emphasized novelty and change.
  A. Earlier periods had also gone through phases of rapid transition.
  B. In the nineteenth century, however, all these changes were documented and reported.
  C. Nobody could overlook or ignore them.

VIII. The scale of travel and communications grew enormously.
  A. In 1900 people were sending one hundred times as many pieces of mail as in 1800.
  B. By 1900 five billion passengers used the railroads every year.
  C. Travel across the oceans multiplied.

    1. In 1830 fewer than twenty thousand people crossed the Atlantic each year.

    2. By the 1850s clipper ships could travel between Boston and Liverpool in only twelve days.

    3. Steamships soon appeared that were even faster and more reliable.

    4. By 1900 one million people crossed the Atlantic each year.

IX. The Industrial Revolution would have been impossible without the revolution in agriculture.

    A. The occupational structure of the population changed.

        1. In 1800 75 percent of the population was engaged in growing food.

        2. By 1900 only 50 percent of the population was growing food.

    B. Until the nineteenth century the population lived constantly on the verge of famine.

    C. Even in the nineteenth century there were times when starvation was widespread:

        1. In the years after Waterloo in 1815.

        2. In the 1840s the potato famine devastated Ireland. Within a few years 20 percent of the population had died or emigrated.

    D. Europe needed increasing supplies of food.

        1. In 1800 only 10 percent of the population lived in cities.

        2. By 1900 about 40 percent of the population was urban.

    E. Some of the needed food was imported from outside of Europe:

        1. North America.

        2. South America.

        3. Australia.

    F. Most of the extra food, however, was produced in Europe itself.

        1. More land was cultivated.

        2. Production was rationalized.

        3. Crop rotation was improved.

        4. More fertilizer was used.

        5. New tools were introduced:

            a. The scythe.

            b. Harvesters.

            c. Threshers.

    G. More food could be produced by fewer workers.

        1. In Britain 25 percent of the population was engaged in farming in 1850.

        2. By 1900 only 8 percent still worked the land.

X. Life in the countryside was transformed.

    A. In some places the natural environment was damaged.

        1. Forests were cut down.

        2. Water tables were affected.

    B. The standard of living had vastly improved in the countryside.

   1. Homes had improved.
   2. Roads were better.

XI. The biggest changes came in the cities.
   A. The distribution of population drastically changed.
      1. In 1800 there were seventeen cities with populations greater
         than one hundred thousand.
      2. By 1900 one hundred cities were this large.
   B. Cities now dominated society and culture.

Key to the Images

Communications: The dramas of daily life had long been a popular
subject for European painters. In the nineteenth century, however,
communications had so shrunk the world that the dramas of daily life
could involve events miles, even thousands of miles, away.

W. F. Witherington's "The Village Post Office" is one of the calmest
such pictures. The viewer, however, is invited to speculate about the
news that is coming into the sleepy countryside. Thomas Webster's
"A Letter from Abroad" and W. P. Frith's "Bad News in the Break-
fast Room" are more openly dramatic. These paintings look like
episodes from a play. One half expects the characters to begin reading
aloud so that the next act can begin. Thomas Roberts's "The Opinion
of the Press" portrays a painter reading an unfavorable review of his
work.

Labor: As the Industrial Revolution proceeded, workers and laborers
were made the subject of paintings, as in the work of such artists as
Ford Madox Brown. In Program 41 Sir Hubert von Herkamer's "On
Strike" depicts suffering during the great London Dock Strike.

Focus Questions

1. How did the patterns of European agriculture change between 1800
   and 1900? How were these changes related to industrialization and
   urbanization?
2. How did new techniques transform older industries and create new
   ones?
3. How did developments in transportation and communications transform the European economy?
4. How did mass-produced goods affect the standard of living in Europe?
5. What social and technological factors created the popular press?
6. In what ways did the communications revolution bring different parts
   of the world into closer contact with one another?
7. How did changes in industry and agriculture affect Europe's relationships with the rest of the world?

OVERVIEW:
PROGRAM 42: THE INDUSTRIAL WORLD

The Industrial Revolution was accompanied by a revolution in consumption. The European standard of living rose dramatically, both in personal terms and in public goods and services. Among the greatest monuments of the nineteenth century were the railroad stations, bridges, and ships.

I. The nineteenth century also created a revolution in the ways that goods were bought and sold.
   A. Until the nineteenth century, most shops followed a centuries' old pattern:
      1. Goods in front.
      2. Workshops behind.
      3. Living quarters upstairs or at the very back.
   B. Originally, salespeople (or tallymen) were illiterate.
   C. Because people made many of their own goods at home, the volume of retail trade remained low.
   D. Around 1800 shops as we know them began to appear, especially in England.
      1. Plate glass was now becoming inexpensive enough to use for show windows and in some homes.
      2. Later in the nineteenth century, gaslight would greatly improve interior lighting.

II. The cities themselves were changing shape.
   A. Streetlights appeared in some of the greatest cities.
   B. Even in such cities as London and Paris streets were still badly paved, although they were greatly improved in the course of the century.
   C. In the second half of the nineteenth century sidewalks began to be common.
   D. In the bigger cities shopkeepers built enclosed galleries and arcades, which
      1. Gave protection from the weather.
      2. Gathered many stalls under one roof.
   E. Around 1850 the first department stores appeared.

III. A consumers' revolution was under way.
   A. Great numbers of people could now afford to buy goods, as a result of such techniques as
      1. Mass production.
      2. Bulk buying.
      3. Economies of scale.
   B. England led the way in these developments.
      1. English cities improved streets for goods and customers.
      2. London's Regent Street (developed in the 1830s and 1840s) was praised for its space and grandeur.

C. After mid-century, Paris built great new thoroughfares throughout the city, which
1. Made shopping and traffic easier.
2. Allowed more air and breathing space.
3. Were lined with
    a. Trees.
    b. Benches.
    c. Lamps.
D. Great public parks were built all over Europe, such as
1. Hyde Park in London.
2. The gardens of the Tuileries in Paris.
E. Pleasures that once could be enjoyed by only a few were now
open to many.

IV. Cities were becoming safer and more comfortable.
A. Regular police forces appeared in the 1830s.
B. Public facilities were constructed in greater numbers:
1. Public baths.
2. Drinking fountains.
3. Standpipes for water.
4. Public washhouses.
5. Museums and exhibitions.
C. Lithography transformed the streets with posters and advertisements.
1. Some of these posters acquainted people with new trends in
art.
2. The public was exposed to a new pictorial shorthand.

V. The nineteenth century was a great age for public transportation.
A. As streets were widened, tramways appeared. The trams themselves were
1. First pulled by horses.
2. Electrified later in the century.
B. Omnibuses also appeared, which were
1. First pulled by horses.
2. Eventually powered by internal combustion engines.
C. Trains made it easier for city people to visit the country or the
seaside.
D. There was a great democratization of goods and services, even in
such areas as
1. Leisure.
2. The enjoyment of nature and fresh air.

VI. The nineteenth century was the age of coal.
A. Most cities were enveloped in clouds of soot and smoke.
1. Coal was the greatest source of heat and power. About 95
percent of all commercial power was generated by coal.
2. The cities also suffered pollution from
    a. Gin works.

      b. Dye works.

      c. Gas works.

      d. Chemical works.

B. England was fortunate to have extensive coal-fields within easy reach of water:

    1. Near the Tyne River.

    2. Near the Clyde River.

    3. In Wales.

C. Industries clustered around the coal-fields in

    1. Northwest England.

    2. Belgium.

    3. Lorraine.

    4. The Ruhr Valley.

    5. South Wales.

D. These areas drew streams of immigrants looking for work.

E. Throughout the nineteenth century coal output doubled every twenty years.

    1. By 1913 thirty times as much coal was produced as in 1820.

    2. Most of the coal was used to produce

      a. Iron.

      b. Steel.

      c. Steam power.

VII. The nineteenth century admired the symbols of its grandeur.

A. Artists were excited by steam and power:

    1. Turner.

    2. The Impressionists, especially Monet.

B. The railroad stations were symbols of triumphant technology.

C. A number of projects came to represent the age:

    1. The Crystal Palace, built in 1851.

    2. St. Lazare Station in Paris.

    3. The Eiffel Tower, built in 1889 to mark the first century of the French Revolution.

    4. The Brooklyn Bridge, designed in 1867.

D. The ocean liners were among the greatest technical achievements of the time.

    1. By the 1870s ships of between five and eight thousand tons had been built.

    2. The Atlantic could be crossed in seven days.

E. Naval vessels kept up with these developments.

    1. Iron- and then steel-plated warships.

    2. Submarines, although those used in the American Civil War were not especially successful.

    3. Coal- and then oil-burning ships.

F. These fleets made possible the age of gunboat diplomacy.

    1. Fleets could be dispatched to intimidate enemies around the world.

    2. Fleets could protect the shipping lanes that linked the economic core to peripheral countries.

Key to the Images

Iron, steel, and glass: By the middle of the nineteenth century, iron, steel, and glass could be used as construction materials. The Crystal Palace, built for the Exposition of 1851, was one of the first great structures to depend largely on metal and glass, a form of construction that has become commonplace in the twentieth century.

Many of the great structures of the nineteenth century depended on the new possibilities of iron and steel. I. K. Brunel's single-span suspension bridge at Clifton, finished in 1864 after Brunel's death, was one of the greatest triumphs of a great engineer. Other images in Program 42 show the construction of the Forth Bridge in Scotland and the Brooklyn Bridge in the United States.

In Paris the Gare Saint Lazare, one of the great train stations, was a favorite subject for painters, especially for Monet. Other new structures were not so well received. The Eiffel Tower, for instance, was so unpopular at first that for some years there was talk of tearing it down.

Ironclads and dreadnoughts: During the American Civil War a new form of naval architecture came into use. At first, wooden ships were armored with iron plates, which gave them enormous protection against enemy fire. Before long, however, ships were built entirely of metal. Almost overnight, wooden warships became obsolete.

The navies of the world embarked on an enormous arms race, for against the new warships the older ships were useless. In the years before World War I, the growth of the German navy, one of the most advanced in the world, created great tensions between England and Germany. It was the superiority of the American navy that allowed the United States to acquire its overseas empire in the Spanish-American War.

By the early twentieth century, the English were building dreadnoughts, great battleships that could hit targets many miles away.

Focus Questions

1. How did the distribution of fuel and raw materials influence industrial development?
2. In what ways did material life become more comfortable in the nineteenth century?
3. What were the most important civic improvements that were carried out in the great cities of Europe?
4. What arts were created or transformed by the Industrial Revolution? How did art reflect new styles of life?
5. In what ways were different parts of the world becoming more interdependent?

6. How did the Industrial Revolution affect ship-building, especially the building of warships?
7. How did economic interdependence affect diplomacy and warfare?

——————— *ASSIGNMENTS AND ACTIVITIES* ———————

IN CONTEXT

Themes and issues that set Unit Twenty-One in context with other units include the following:

- The period of industrialization in the nineteenth century saw an enormous growth in the power of the popular press. Look back to Unit Twenty on the years before the French Revolution and note some of the channels through which ideas and information traveled. In later units look at the influence of the press on twentieth-century politics. How did Fascists and Communists create propaganda on a large scale?

- In Unit Twenty-One Professor Weber traces some of the relationships between industrial nations and their sources of raw materials. Look back to earlier units and examine the relationship between European powers and their colonies in the Western Hemisphere. Remember that the American colonists greatly resented the mercantilist policies that defined their economic relationship to Great Britain. Look forward to Units Twenty-Five and Twenty-Six, in which Professor Weber discusses the economic problems of the Third World.

- Professor Weber emphasizes improvements in the standard of living during this period. Look back to Unit Twenty and note the industries that formed the basis of the first stages of the Industrial Revolution. In England the manufacture of cloth was of special importance. Many of the early industries concentrated on mass-produced goods. This influx of cheap goods — clothing is an especially good example — greatly improved the material life of the average person. Look back also to earlier discussions of nutrition and disease. During this period, improvements in public health and transportation saved lives and raised the general standard of living. Look ahead to later units to see how nations in the Third World now cope with similar problems.

- The world economy became increasingly interdependent during this period. In later units watch for ways in which this interdependence strengthened some nations at the expense of others. In Unit Twenty-Six Professor Weber shows how this issue is responsible for many of the problems of the Third World.

- During this period warfare became industrialized. The American Civil War made extensive use of railroads, mass-produced weapons, telegraphs, and iron-clad vessels. In later units we see industrialized warfare on a massive scale in World Wars I and II.

Textbook Assignment

Read the following pages in your assigned textbook:

Text: *Western Civilizations* (Eleventh Edition, 1988)
Read: Chapter 21, "The Industrial Revolution," pp. 715–734; and Chapter 22, "Consequences of Industrialization: Urbanization and Class Consciousness," pp. 735–768.

Text: *The Western Experience* (Fifth Edition, 1991)
Read: Chapter 23, "Industrialization and Social Change 1800–1860," pp. 908–955; and Chapter 25, "The Age of Progress," pp. 1004–1052.

Text: *The Western Heritage* (Fourth Edition, 1991)
Read: Chapter 22, "Economic Advance and Social Unrest (1830–1850)," pp. 765–803; and from Chapter 24, "The Building of European Supremacy (1860–1914): Society and Politics," pp. 843–883.

Issues for Clarification

Omnibus

Omnibus, literally meaning "for all," is the original form of our word *bus.* The origin of the word is especially revealing in that buses were the first form of transportation available to everyone. Only the well-to-do could afford carriages and coaches. Stage-line travel existed before the Industrial Revolution but was expensive and generally used only for long trips.

Semaphore Telegraph

Toward the end of the eighteenth century the French constructed a network of watchtowers for relaying messages rapidly across the country. Each tower was equipped with a set of long arms, rather like the vanes of a windmill. The arms were moved to various positions to spell out messages in a semaphore code.

The system did work, although it was liable to enormous difficulties. The system, for instance, required a great many links in the network because towers had to be easily visible to their neighbors. Nor could the system work when weather interfered with visibility. Further, messages passed through so many hands that they easily became garbled.

The system was too cumbersome and expensive to be used for anything but important military or administrative matters. And because the watchtowers operated in the open air, a spy who knew the semaphore code could easily decipher messages.

Thoroughfares

The nineteenth century was a great time of urban renewal. One of the most common forms of rebuilding was to build wide, straight avenues or boulevards through tangled clusters of streets that made up much of the older European cities. These new thoroughfares could handle much more traffic than the old narrow streets, but the city-planners had other considerations in mind beyond convenience and efficiency.

The planners were also guarding against uprisings because street-fighting had been enormously important in the French revolutions between 1789 and 1848. Where the streets were narrow, rebels could easily construct a barricade from one side to another and within a few hours transform a city block into a fortress. Such defenses could put up a strong resistance, even against great numbers of troops.

The new thoroughfares, especially in Paris, were designed to help troops restore order. The streets were too wide for barricades and their long, straight lines gave artillery a clear field of fire.

Glossary

Arcades: Enclosed passageways with shops along either side.

Dreadnought: A class of heavily armored British battleships, first built in 1906. In addition to heavy armor, such ships also possessed batteries of twelve-inch guns that could be fired simultaneously in the same direction.

Fourth Estate: A nickname for the press. The term refers to the three estates of the French Estates General. The implication was that the press had become so powerful that it was practically a branch of government.

Lithography: A printing method that uses flat stones or metal plates to reproduce images.

Plate glass: For centuries glass was very expensive and could not be formed into large, thin panes. Not until the eighteenth century could the middle classes afford large numbers of glass windows.

Timeline

Place each of the following events on the timeline. In some cases you may have to specify a roughly defined period of time rather than a precise date.

1. Publication of *Communist Manifesto*.
2. Battle of Waterloo.
3. Outbreak of Franco-Prussian War.
4. Sewing machine patented.
5. Irish potato famine.
6. Appearance of regular police forces in large European cities.
7. Laying of Trans-Atlantic cable.
8. First passenger train.

9. Construction of the Crystal Palace.
10. Brooklyn Bridge designed.

1800   1900
|———|

Map Exercise

Find the following locations on the map.

1. Country struck by potato famine in the 1840s.
2-3. Two coal-producing areas in Europe.
4. Country that pioneered the industrial production of textiles.

5-6. Major European powers at war in 1870-1871.
7. Path of the first international underwater cable.
8-9. Locations of Hyde Park and the Tuileries.
10. Homeland of Karl Marx.

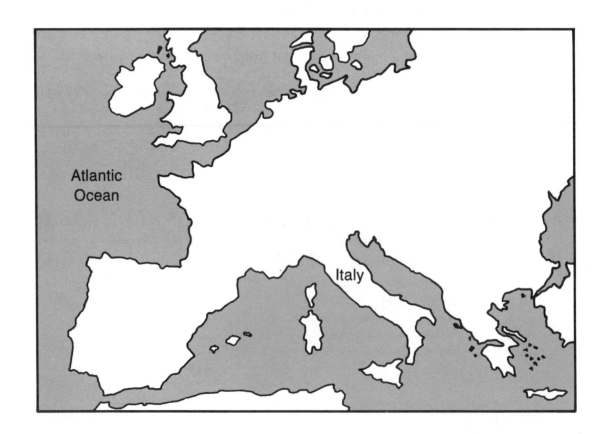

Self-Test

Part I

1. Although daily newspapers appeared in the eighteenth century, they were expensive. Only the invention of _the rotary press_ made newspapers cheap enough for most people to afford.

2. By the late nineteenth century much of Europe's food was being imported from outside the continent. Name two of Europe's major sources: _North America, South America_.

3. Name two inventions that led to the production of cheaper clothing: _knitting frames_ _Sew machine_.

4. The steam engine powered the Industrial Revolution. The steam engine's most important source of fuel was _coal_. The steam engine was quickly put to use in _textiles, transportation_ (name one important industry).

5. In 1800 approximately _75_ (percent) of the European population was engaged in growing food. By 1900 this proportion had shrunk to _50_ (percent). In _England_, the most industrialized of the European countries, this proportion had reached 8 percent by 1900.

Part II

1. Mass-circulated newspapers played an important role in provoking all but one of the following.
   a. Napoleon's invasion of Italy in the 1790s.
   b. The Revolution of 1830.
   c. The Franco-Prussian War.
   d. The Dreyfus affair.

2. Name one of the nineteenth-century inventions that made it possible to reproduce images cheaply: _Photography_.

3. Mark the false choice. During the nineteenth century European agriculture
   a. came under increasing pressure to supply the cities with food.
   b. had to compete with imports from countries that were thousands of miles away.
   c. suffered no widespread famines.
   d. came to use agricultural machinery, much of it imported from America.

4. Mark the false choice. By the end of the nineteenth century Paris and London had
   a. established metropolitan police forces.
   b. set up public water supplies.
   c. replaced coal with less polluting fuels.
   d. set up public transportation systems.

5. Mark the false choice. By the end of the nineteenth century European naval forces were
   a. able to practice gunboat diplomacy.
   b. using radar.
   c. converting from coal to oil.
   d. able to hit targets that were miles away.

Optional Activity

Although the following activity is not required for the course unless assigned by the instructor, students are encouraged to use it as a source of interesting topics for further study.

Industrialists in the Novel

Until the nineteenth century, wealth and power in Europe were usually based on land. With the Industrial Revolution, however, a new and important class appeared: the Industrialists.

Charles Dickens and Elizabeth Gaskell are English novelists who have left vivid portrayals of this new class. In Dickens's novel *Hard Times*, the character of Josiah Bounderby is a fierce caricature. In the story he celebrates his own virtues, especially his self-reliance. He claims that not a single soul ever helped him in the world, and he has no intention of helping anybody.

Elizabeth Gaskell's *North and South* is a more balanced portrait in that its heroine must decide whether to leave the traditional life of southern England to marry a man who has made his fortune in the industries of the north. The novel is also an excellent source for the study of women's issues.

For this assignment, read either *Hard Times* or *North and South*. Write a paper of 3–5 pages on one of the following topics. Instead of treating the entire novel, your paper should deal with its topic by analyzing one or two short episodes.

- How do the Industrialists in the books differ from the other important characters? In what ways are their values different? Are their relations to members of other classes hostile or cordial?
- In both novels marriage is an important issue. Why does the author concentrate on marriage as a way of exploring the relationship between the Industrialists and the other property owning classes? What are the roles of the women in the novel? How do women act as the mediators between classes? (See P. Branca, 1975, listed in Further Reading.)

- What is the relationship between the Industrialists and the workers in the novel? What issues in this relationship does the author emphasize? How does the author try to resolve the conflicts between factoryowners and employees?
- State Dickens's view of the philosophy of utilitarianism. Using examples from the book, show how this philosophy affects human relationships.
- In *Hard Times* compare the world of the factory to the world of the circus.

Review Questions

1. What industries first made use of steam power? How did the growth of these industries lead to the creation of new inventions and to further industrial development? What resources were especially important for industrial development? Which countries had access to these resources?
2. What were the major advances in travel and communications during the nineteenth century? How did advances in communications promote advances in travel? How did developments in both areas make European countries more economically interdependent? What parts of the world outside Europe now became important to the European economy?
3. What were some of the technical and economic causes that lay behind the development of the popular press? How did the popular press alter European politics?
4. Professor Weber argues that the Industrial Revolution would have been impossible without the agricultural revolution. Explain. State your reasons for agreeing or disagreeing. How did the Industrial and the agricultural revolutions strengthen the economic ties between Europe and the rest of the world?
5. What were the most important developments in the growth of the great European cities? How were the cities rebuilding themselves? What were the new public services?
6. How did the Industrial Revolution affect warfare, especially naval warfare, in the nineteenth century? What sorts of weapons could now be built with industrial techniques? What sorts of weapons could be mass produced? How did Europe's military strength affect its relations with the rest of the world?

Further Reading

Original Sources

Dickens, Charles. *Hard Times.*

Engels, Friedrich. *The Condition of Working Class in England.* (1958). Based on Engels's observations of England in the 1840s.

Gaskell, Elizabeth. *North and South*.

Mayhew, Henry. *London Labor and the London Poor*. (1968). Reprint of the 1851 edition. Fascinating descriptions of the ways in which people struggled to make a living. Good account of crime.

Ward, J. T. *The Factory System, 1830–1855*. (1970). Nineteenth-century documents debating the merits of the factory system.

Weber, Eugen. *The Western Tradition*, 2nd ed. (1965). "Economic Revolution," pp. 610–642.

Studies

Ashton, T. S. *The Industrial Revolution*. (1948). A good, generally optimistic survey.

Branca, P. *Silent Sisterhood: Middle Class Women in the Victorian Home*. (1975). Thorough. Useful for Optional Activity.

Briggs, Asa. *Victorian Cities*. (1963). Good comparisons and contrasts.

Heilbroner, Robert. *The Worldly Philosophers*. (1972). Clear presentation of nineteenth-century economic doctrines.

Hobsbawn, Eric. *The Age of Capital, 1848–1875*. (1975). Good on the relationship between economics and politics.

———. *Industry and Empire: 1750 to the Present Day*. (1958).

Houghton, Walter. *The Victorian Frame of Mind, 1830–1870*. (1957). Excellent—not so much an intellectual history as a description of Victorian habits of thought.

Landes, David S. *The Unbound Prometheus*. (1969). The great work on the relationship between technology and economics in the Industrial Revolution.

Mayer, A. J. *The Persistence of the Old Regime in Europe to the Great War*. (1981). Controversial; claims that the Industrial Revolution changed Europe more slowly than most historians believe.

Robertson, P. *An Experience of Women: Pattern and Change in Nineteenth-Century Europe*. (1982).

Taylor, A. J. *The Standard of Living in Britain in the Industrial Revolution*. (1975). A collection of articles debating the effects of industrialism.

Taylor, George Rogers. *The Transportation Revolution, 1815–1860*. (1968).

Thompson, E. P. *The Making of the English Working Class*. (1963). One of the pioneering histories on the lives of ordinary people.

Weber, Eugen. *Peasants into Frenchmen: The Modernization of Rural France*. (1976). Excellent study of modernization in France.

Woodham-Smith, Cecil. *The Great Hunger: Ireland, 1845–1849.* (1962). Shows that the economic doctrines of the nineteenth century may have aggravated the severity of the famine.

Answer Key

Timeline

1. 1848.
2. 1815.
3. 1870.
4. 1851.
5. Mid- to late 1840s.
6. Late 1820s to 1830s.
7. 1866.
8. 1825.
9. 1851.
10. 1867.

Map Exercise

1. Ireland.
2–3. Northwest England, Belgium, Lorraine, the Ruhr Valley, and South Wales are all good answers.
4. England.
5–6. France and Prussia.
7. From Dover, England to Calais, France.
8–9. Hyde Park is in London; the Tuileries in Paris.
10. Germany.

Self-Test

Part I

1. the rotary press
2. North America, South America, and Australia are all good answers. Southern Russia is also acceptable if you consider that area to be outside the mainstream of the European economy.
3. Power looms, knitting frames, and the sewing machine are the most important inventions mentioned in the lectures. Your text may supply additional answers.
4. coal is the answer for the first part, textiles or transportation for the second.
5. 75 percent; 50 percent, England

Part II

1. (a) Napoleon's invasion of Italy in the 1790s.
2. Photography and lithography are mentioned in the lectures. Various forms of engraving were also improved during this period.
3. (c) suffered no widespread famines.
4. (c) replaced coal with less polluting fuels.
5. (b) using radar.

"The Abolition of Slavery" by François Biard (1849)   The painting celebrates the abolition of slavery by the French Assembly on April 27, 1848. Former slaves rejoice at the news, which has just been announced by an emissary from France. By this time, slavery had been abolished in both the French and British empires. American slavery was becoming an anomaly. (© Musées Nationaux, Conservation du Musée de Versailles.)

UNIT TWENTY-TWO

Program 43: Revolution and the Romantics

Program 44: The Age of the Nation-States

LEARNING OBJECTIVES

After completing Unit Twenty-Two students should understand the following issues:

- The revolutionary aspirations that arose in many countries after the American and French revolutions. Use your textbook to supplement the examples discussed by Professor Weber.
- The outlines of romanticism in art, literature, and social thought. As you view the images in your textbook and the programs, watch carefully for examples of painting or sculpture that express nationalist or revolutionary ideals.
- The relationship between romanticism and social reform.
- The similarities and differences among the different European movements for reform. Use your textbook to examine the problems of national liberation faced by various nations.
- The development of a system of great powers during the nineteenth century. Your textbook supplies examples of the strengths or weaknesses of the various powers.
- The patterns of European colonialism.
- The areas of greatest instability in international politics. Does your textbook supplement or rebut Professor Weber on this issue?

TV INSTRUCTION

OVERVIEW
PROGRAM 43: REVOLUTION AND THE ROMANTICS

After the end of the Napoleonic wars, the great powers of Europe tried, unsuccessfully, to prevent further revolutions. Nevertheless, the French Revolution had created hopes for national sovereignty and independence all across the continent. Romantic writers and artists were often sympathetic to revolutionary movements. Romanticism itself was transforming European art and literature.

  I. The American and French revolutions were seen as models for the rest of Europe.
     A. Americans and French alike had rebelled against their rulers.
        1. The Americans had used violence to break away from their British king.
        2. The French had actually executed their king and abolished the monarchy.
     B. Revolutions and struggles for national independence took place all over the world in the years after Waterloo.
        1. Latin America freed itself from
           a. The Portuguese.
           b. The Spanish.
        2. The Greeks freed themselves from Turkey.
        3. The Belgians set up their own independent kingdom.
        4. Insurrections took place in
           a. Italy.
           b. Poland.
           c. Canada.
           d. Switzerland.
           e. Denmark.
           f. Germany.
           g. Spain.
           h. Portugal.
        5. The French changed governments several times themselves.

 II. Political philosophies were now widely accepted that justified the rebellion of subjects against their rulers.
     A. Increasing numbers of respectable people were beginning to believe that the very institution of kingship was evil.
     B. Revolutionary ideologies shared three basic assumptions:
        1. The perfectibility of man.
        2. The sovereignty of the people.
        3. The equality of man.

III. These ideas were unclear or ambiguous, but the very lack of clarity had important consequences.

A. The notion of the perfectibility of man tended to be anti-Christian, or at least anticlerical.
  1. Christianity taught that perfection was impossible in the temporal world.
  2. This new idea, however, claimed that people could be perfect if they were freed from
    a. Kings.
    b. Priests.
B. The idea of sovereignty of the people was equally unclear, but it was generally used to attack the hereditary rule of kings.
C. The notion of equality of man attacked the pretensions of those who claimed to rule others by reason of their
  1. Privileges.
  2. Traditions.
  3. Property.
  4. Right of ancient conquest.
  5. Blood.
  6. Birth.
D. Eventually, the notion of rights of man would be granted even to the disinherited.
  1. Slaves would be freed.
  2. The emancipation of women took considerably longer.

IV. Napoleon was remembered from at least two different points of view.
  A. On the one hand, he seemed to be the last of the enlightened despots, identified with
    1. Law and order.
    2. Repression.
    3. The police.
  B. Others, however, idealized him as a romantic hero who represented
    1. The young against the old.
    2. The "outs" against the "ins."
  C. This second image made Napoleon one of the great heroes of romanticism.

V. The other great shaper of romanticism was Jean-Jacques Rousseau.
  A. Rousseau's *Confessions,* published in the 1780s after his death, is the first modern autobiography in which the writer confesses such weaknesses as
    1. Mean and petty actions.
    2. Sour love affairs.
    3. Sexual hangups.
  B. Professor Weber argues that Rousseau was willing to tell so much because he believed that man is basically good.
    1. Society corrupts man.
    2. Society makes man miserable.
    3. Rousseau argued that to fight oppression people must discover their true nature.

C. Rousseau reacted against the ideas of the early Enlightenment. He did not believe in a world where everything can be calculated or worked out in advance.

VI. The Romantics wanted to get at the invisible and incalculable.
   A. They were obsessed with the forces that move us or reveal us to ourselves:
      1. Dreams.
      2. Fantasies.
      3. Madness.
   B. Romantic painters loved to paint
      1. People under stress.
      2. Madmen.
      3. Nightmares.
      4. Terrible events in which nature overwhelmed human beings.
   C. The Romantics also wanted to discover the hidden currents of society and history. Two of their greatest successors were
      1. Karl Marx.
      2. Sigmund Freud.

VII. Romantic thinkers and writers took a stand against national, political, and social oppression.
   A. In political and legal affairs the Romantics
      1. Opposed slavery.
      2. Opposed the death penalty.
      3. Wanted to mitigate punishments.
   B. In literature, painting, and music the Romantics exalted revolutionaries, bandits, and rebels.
      1. Wordsworth supported the French Revolution until it turned violent and oppressed free peoples abroad.
      2. Goethe admired Napoleon for a time.
      3. Beethoven dedicated the *Third Symphony* to Napoleon, until he learned that Napoleon had crowned himself emperor.
      4. Byron supported revolutionaries in
         a. Italy.
         b. Greece.
      5. Shelley supported
         a. Radicals in England.
         b. Freedom fighters in Greece.
      6. Even Mary Shelley's *Frankenstein* is about a kind of noble savage; naturally good but driven to murder by ill treatment.

VIII. Romanticism also created a historical consciousness in which the great deeds of the past were recalled to inspire the present.
   A. Tales were written about the deeds of
      1. William Tell.
      2. Robin Hood.
      3. The people of Paris.
   B. Sir Walter Scott invented the historical novel.
      1. His books recall the English and Scottish past.

        2. They also inspired other peoples to take pride in their own history.

    C. Although Scott was personally conservative, he continually wrote against injustice and intolerance.

  IX. Other Romantics wrote about injustice and oppression in modern times.

    A. Victor Hugo's *Les Miserables* describes the virtues of people who have been crushed by society.

    B. Shelley wrote against the Massacre of Peterloo in 1819.

    C. Professor Weber cites examples of radicals and revolutionaries who were inspired more by the Romantic novelists than by Marx.

Key to the Images

Romantic suffering: Romantic painters often portrayed scenes of great suffering, perhaps in the belief that suffering revealed aspects of the human soul that would have otherwise remained hidden. One of the greatest romantic paintings of the nineteenth century is Theodore Géricault's (1791–1824) "The Raft of the Medusa," which is based on an account of an actual shipwreck. Another scene of romantic suffering based on fact is Antoine Jean Gros's (1771–1835) portrayal of Napoleon's visit to a plague hospital at Jaffa.

Liberal hopes: After the American and French revolutions, hopes of revolution, reform, or national liberation sprang up all over the world. Some of these hopes would have to wait for new revolutions. Francois Biard's painting of 1849 shows blacks in the West Indies celebrating the abolition of slavery by the French Assembly on April 27, 1848, during the revolution of 1848.

People perceived to be enemies of progress were widely satirized. In Program 43 we view an image of Pope Pius IX, smiling slyly behind a mask representing the face of Christ. To many Europeans, Pope Pius IX seemed to be a turncoat or hypocrite. When he became pope, he showed considerable sympathy for liberal aims. The revolution of 1848, however, frightened him into more conservative views.

Focus Questions

1. How did romanticism differ from the social and artistic thoughts of the eighteenth century?
2. Who were the major romantic writers and artists? Be prepared to discuss their views on the social and political problems of their day.
3. Why were the Romantics so deeply interested in history?
4. What was the relationship between romanticism and nationalism?

5. What countries fought revolutions or wars of national liberation in the century after 1815?

6. What were some of the assumptions about society and human nature used to justify revolution?

OVERVIEW
PROGRAM 44: THE AGE OF THE NATION-STATES

By the middle of the nineteenth century some of the worst horrors were being mitigated through reform, pressure from workers, or the rise in the general standard of living. Although there was no general European war between 1815 and 1914, the great powers keenly competed with one another, often in colonial areas or on the periphery of Europe.

I. The Industrial Revolution came about at great cost in human suffering.
   A. Child labor.
   B. Female labor.
   C. Wretched living conditions.

II. Gradually, much of the suffering was mitigated by
   A. Reform.
   B. Workers organizing to help themselves.
   C. Revolution, or at least the fear of revolution.
   D. The general increase in productivity.

III. By the second half of the century much of the suffering had been mitigated.
   A. Social legislation regulated
      1. Working hours.
      2. Working conditions.
   B. Social services were being provided:
      1. Medical services.
      2. Old-age pensions.
      3. Housing subsidies.
      4. Unemployment compensation.
   C. Many of these services came in bits and pieces or did not become effective until the twentieth century.

IV. Social reform came about for many reasons.
   A. Professor Weber mentions "social romanticism," the combination of compassion and guilt that the well-off felt toward the poor.
   B. More people had the right to vote.
      1. By 1914 every male had the right to vote, even in countries that had lagged behind the rest of Europe such as
         a. Italy.
         b. Austria.

      2. Politicians had to mind the interests of a broader section of the population.
- C. The power of the vote should not be exaggerated.
  1. In Germany social reforms came before voting rights.
  2. In France social reforms were slow to appear, although universal suffrage had come fairly early.
  3. In 1914 women had the right to vote in only two European countries:
     a. Finland.
     b. Norway.
- D. Social reform also came from groups who thought they could reorganize production and distribution more efficiently. These "social utilitarians" included
  1. The Saint Simonians (named for the Comte de Saint Simon).
  2. The Comtians (named for the mathematician Auguste Comte).
- E. The Saint Simonians and the Comtians had many concrete achievements to their credit:
  1. The construction of many of Europe's railroads.
  2. The planning of the Suez Canal.
  3. The Eiffel Tower.
  4. The first mass-produced magazines.
  5. The first advertising agency.
- F. These groups, however, did not directly address the problems of the workers.

V. The working class was creating organizations and ideologies of its own.
- A. Karl Marx, for instance, argued that the working class would have to conquer power for itself. Only then would
  1. Liberty and equality reign.
  2. Class oppression end.
  3. Labor and justice exist for all.
- B. Although Marxism did not become influential until the end of the century, many other doctrines made similar arguments about the rights of the working class.

VI. Nationalism was the other great current of unrest.
- A. At the beginning of the nineteenth century many Europeans were ruled by foreign powers:
  1. Greeks.
  2. Poles.
  3. Romanians.
  4. Czechs.
  5. South Slavs.
- B. Other peoples were divided into numerous separate states:
  1. Germans.
  2. Italians.
- C. Romantic ideology and the examples of the eighteenth-century

revolutions stressed that all people had a right to live as free citizens of their own nation, not as the subjects of a foreign ruler.
- D. This attitude inspired
  1. Latin Americans to rise against
     a. Spain.
     b. Portugal.
  2. Greeks to rise against Turks.
  3. Belgians to win independence from Holland.
- E. In the 1860s and 1870s numerous peoples won independence or unity:
  1. Romanians.
  2. Bulgarians.
  3. Serbs.
  4. Italians.
  5. Germans.
- F. Other peoples, like the Poles, suffered defeat but continued their struggle.

VII. National hopes created international instability.
- A. Subject nations were continually conspiring or rebelling:
  1. Czechs.
  2. Slovaks.
  3. Romanians.
  4. South Slavs.
- B. Revolution and national revolt often went hand in hand in the unrest of
  1. 1830.
  2. 1848.
- C. Many European wars were fought over national issues, such as the unification of
  1. Italy.
  2. Germany.
  3. The Balkan countries.

VIII. Throughout the nineteenth century international politics was dominated by the great powers.
- A. The first set of great powers were the nations that conducted the Congress of Vienna:
  1. Britain.
  2. France.
  3. Russia.
  4. Austria (including the Habsburg Empire).
  5. Prussia (including the German Empire after 1871).
- B. In the 1870s a unified Italy joined the group.
- C. The United States was not a member, however.
  1. The United States remained generally aloof from Europe.
  2. The Europeans could not conceive of a great power from outside the continent.

    D. The leading powers were
       1. Britain and France in the first half of the century.
       2. Britain and Germany in the second half of the century.

IX. Whatever their differences, most of the great powers helped one another put down revolutions.
    A. Revolution was a continually recurring problem, especially in the
       1. Early 1820s.
       2. Early 1830s.
       3. 1848–1849.
    B. It was conservative statesmen, however, not revolutionaries, who achieved national unification in
       1. Italy.
       2. Germany.
    C. Such leaders, as well as figures like Napoleon III, tried to defuse radicals by carrying out some of the less radical parts of their programs:
       1. Higher productivity.
       2. Economic improvements.
       3. Moderate reforms.

X. Most European leaders believed that a general war would promote revolution.
    A. Many nineteenth-century wars were marginal, in such places as
       1. The Crimea.
       2. The Balkans.
    B. Other wars were bilateral and did not lead to general warfare:
       1. France against Austria.
       2. Austria against Prussia.
       3. Prussia against France.

XI. Much of the competition between the great powers took place overseas or on the margins of Europe.
    A. Europeans acquired territories in several ways:
       1. Conquest.
       2. Trade and investment.
    B. Between thirty and fifty million Europeans emigrated to countries that were
       1. Already extensions of Europe, such as the Americas.
       2. Were becoming extensions of Europe
          a. Australia.
          b. New Zealand.
          c. North Africa.
          d. South Africa.
    C. Some of these colonies, such as Australia, were
       1. Effectively autonomous in politics.
       2. More prosperous than the homeland.
       3. More open to opportunity, at least for whites.

XII. In some colonies Europeans were a small minority ruling over native peoples.
   A. The British, for instance, effectively ruled Egypt, although the country was nominally independent.
      1. Economic control was profitable.
      2. It cost less than outright conquest.
   B. In other places Europeans thought of themselves as bearing "the white man's burden" by teaching
      1. Christianity.
      2. Hygiene.
      3. Their form of government.
   C. Many of these ideas were self-serving but Europeans
      1. Outlawed the slave trade in Africa.
      2. Used effective medicine.

XIII. Colonial competition was often an outlet for great power rivalries.
   A. By definition a great power needed
      1. Overseas possessions.
      2. A fleet.
   B. Originally, the two powers that were best provided for were
      1. Britain.
      2. France.
   C. Other powers joined the race for colonies late in the game:
      1. Italy.
      2. Germany.
   D. The late entries were often left with the least profitable possessions.

XIV. The competition for colonies dominated international politics in the thirty years before World War I.
   A. The war itself began in what might be described as the last colonial part of Europe, the Balkans.
   B. In 1905 Russia, which had been expanding eastward, suffered a humiliating defeat at the hands of the Japanese.
      1. Revolution broke out in Russia.
      2. Similar revolutions were sparked in Russia's neighbors:
         a. Persia.
         b. China.
         c. The Ottoman Empire.
   C. With Turkey in chaos, its subjects and ex-subjects went to war with one another and with Turkey itself.
   D. War in the Balkans threatened the Austro-Hungarian Empire.
   E. Three archaic empires had interests in the Balkans:
      1. The Austro-Hungarian Empire.
      2. The Russian Empire.
      3. The Ottoman Empire.
   F. The situation was further complicated by the national ambitions of
      1. Serbs.
      2. Croats.

3. Bulgarians.
4. Greeks.
5. Italians.
6. Montenegrins.
7. Albanians.

XV. The crisis began with the assassination of the heir to the Austro-Hungarian throne by a Slav student.
   A. It was believed that Serbia had a hand in the plot.
   B. Austria and its ally, Germany, confronted Serbia.
   C. Serbia, however, was backed by Russia.
   D. The Russians were allied to France and ultimately supported by Britain.
   E. Although none of the powers had probably wanted war, long years of competition had resigned many people to the prospect of a general war.
   F. Within a month nearly all of Europe was at war.

Key to the Images

New cities: During the nineteenth century most of the great European cities were rebuilt. Program 44 shows Les Halles, the great Parisian markets begun by Napoleon and finished in 1862 by Baron Haussmann, as part of his plans for the rebuilding of Paris.

The French satirical artist Honore Daumier (1808–1879) especially loved to portray the quirks and oddities of the new age. In Program 44 we view Daumier's contrasting sketches of first- and third-class railway carriages, in which he implies that the new age has found its own way to make class distinctions.

Political cartoons: The nineteenth century was a great time for political cartoons and, because England was the greatest European power, many of the best cartoons were at its expense. One of the cartoons in Program 44 shows England as "The Devilfish in Egyptian Waters." England was expanding its influence in Egypt at the time and to the rest of the world it often seemed that there was no place where the English were not interfering. Another cartoon shows John Bull, the traditional symbol of England, telling France and Prussia that he is strictly neutral. At the same time, John Bull is trying to conceal a host of his own problems from the rest of the world: India, riots, Fenians, the Alabama affair with the United States.

Focus Questions

1. In what ways had much of the suffering of the early Industrial Revolution been alleviated by the end of the nineteenth century?
2. What were some of the most important movements for social, economic, and political reform that arose in the nineteenth century?

3. By 1914 adult males had the right to vote throughout Europe. In what countries did this extended franchise bring pressure for social legislation? In what countries was electoral pressure less important?
4. In what countries did nationalism become important? In what countries did nationalism lead to wars of independence or movements for national unity?
5. To what extent were the great powers of Europe able to cooperate on international issues during the nineteenth century? What were the greatest areas of agreement? What were the major areas of conflict?
6. What were the motives for imperial expansion during the nineteenth and early twentieth centuries? How did imperialism affect international relations?
7. What were some of the different sorts of European colonies?

ASSIGNMENTS AND ACTIVITIES

IN CONTEXT

Themes and issues that set Unit Twenty-Two in context with other units include the following:

- In Unit Twenty-Two we learn how the desire for colonies and overseas markets created tensions between the great powers of Europe. Look back to the units on the eighteenth century, when England and France fought over colonial possessions in North America and India. In later units we learn how colonial rivalries aggravated the tensions that led to the world wars. In later units we see how the colonial legacy has shaped today's third world.

- Unit Twenty-Two examines the connections between romanticism and the wars of national liberation. Look back to the units on the fifteenth and sixteenth centuries, in which Professor Weber discusses the rise of national consciousness in a few Western European countries. In later units we study the movements for national liberation in the Third World after World War II.

- In Unit Twenty-Two and those that follow, Professor Weber discusses the ways in which the great powers of Europe intervened in various struggles for national liberation. In Unit Twenty-Four we learn that the desire for national independence in the Balkan countries complicated the rivalries between the great empires of Eastern and Central Europe. In Unit Twenty-Five look for ways in which the politics of Third World countries complicate relations between the United States and the Soviet Union.

- Unit Twenty-Two explains how a number of romantic writers were champions of social justice and national independence, both in their own countries and abroad. Look back to Unit Seventeen and Eighteen, to Professor Weber's discussion of the philosophes. In what ways did both groups of writers consider themselves social prophets or social critics? Look for reasons why intellectuals should have assumed this function in the eighteenth century.

Textbook Assignment

Read the following pages in your assigned textbook:

Text: *Western Civilizations* (Eleventh Edition, 1988)
Read: Chapter 24, "Nationalism and Nation-Building (1815–1870)," pp. 795–825; and Chapter 25, "The Progress of International Industrialization and Competition (1870–1914)," pp. 833–860.

Text: *The Western Experience* (Fifth Edition, 1991)
Read: Chapter 24, "The National State and the Middle Class, 1850–1880," pp. 956–1003; and Chapter 25, "The Age of Progress," pp. 1004–1056.

Text: *The Western Heritage* (Fourth Edition, 1991)
Read: Chapter 25, "The Birth of Contemporary European Thought," pp. 885–913; and from Chapter 26, "Imperialism, Alliances, and War," pp. 915–931.

Issues for Clarification

Marxism

Although Marx believed that social and economic justice would come only after the proletariat had triumphed in a violent revolution, Marx was not a working-class Machiavelli. He did not write much about the tactics of revolution. The great majority of his works are sober economic analyses of the capitalist system.

Marx believed that capitalism would destroy itself through a series of ever greater economic crises. That is, capitalism would collapse under its own weight.

The Vote

By 1914 adult males had the right to vote throughout Europe, but it is important to realize that the vote was not always enough to achieve real political power. In Germany, for instance, it was the Kaiser, not parliament that controlled the government. Although cabinet members did have to work with parliament, they were not ultimately responsible to elected officials. Being able to vote in parliamentary elections brought only a limited amount of political power.

Other countries in Europe and abroad devised electoral systems that controlled or limited the popular vote. Throughout most of the nineteenth century, for example, the American House of Representatives was elected by popular vote but the senators were chosen by the legislatures of their states. Although the United States finally began to elect senators by popular vote, many European countries retained their restraints on the popular vote.

Glossary

Positivism: A system of philosophy developed by Auguste Comte based solely on observable, or positive, facts and on their relationships as formulated by scientific laws. Comte rejected speculation about origins.

Rachitic: Afflicted with rickets, a bone disease, chiefly affecting children, resulting from a deficiency of calcium salts and vitamin D. Because the disease is aggravated by lack of sunshine, child laborers were especially prone to it.

Timeline

Place each of the following events on the timeline. In some cases you may have to specify a roughly defined period of time rather than a precise date.

1. Beginning of wars of the French Revolution.
2. First revolution in France after Napoleon.
3. Wordsworth arrives in France during revolution.
4. Publication of *Ivanhoe*.
5. Russia loses war with Japan.
6. Assassination of Archduke Franz Ferdinand.
7. Battle of Waterloo.
8. Russia's first revolution of the twentieth century breaks out.
9. Second revolution in France after Napoleon.
10. Unification of Germany.

1780   1920

Map Exercise

Find the following locations on the map.

1. Country that Byron supported in the revolution against the Turks.
2. Country that became independent from Holland.
3. Country where Franz Ferdinand was killed.
4–5. Two major powers that defeated France at Waterloo.
6. One country where by 1914 women had the right to vote in national elections.
7. Area of the South Slavs.
8. Area of present-day Poland (list the countries that ruled this area).
9. Country from which Brazil won independence.
10. Homeland of Walter Scott.

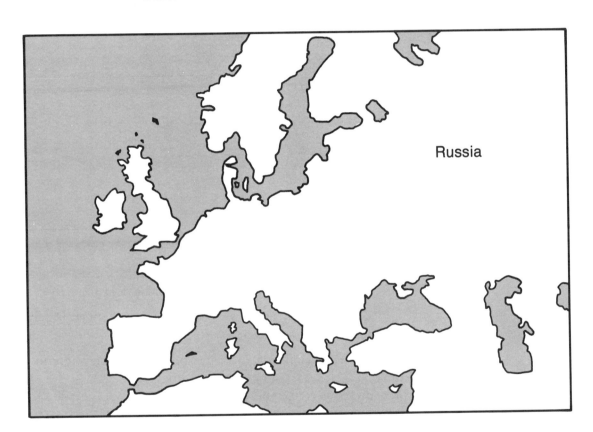

Self-Test

Part I

1. Mark the false choice. In the course of the nineteenth century
   a. Poland won its independence.
   b. Greece won its independence.
   c. Germany achieved national unification.
   d. Italy achieved national unification.

2. Mark the false choice. Among the achievements of the Positivists and Saint Simonians were
   a. the building of the Eiffel Tower.
   b. the construction of the Suez Canal.
   c. the organization of credit institutions.
   d. the organization of mass labor unions.

3. Which of the following countries did *not* experience revolution in the years between 1900 and 1914?
   a. Turkey.
   b. China.
   c. Austria-Hungary.
   d. Persia.

4. Although there was no general European war between 1815 and 1914, France did fight wars with _Russia or Prussia_ (name one country), while Prussia fought with _France+Austria_ (name one country).

5. In 1800 approximately _20_ (percent) of the world's population lived in Europe. All together, perhaps _30_ (percent) of the world's population consisted of Europeans or people of European descent living outside of Europe.

Part II

1. In most countries social legislation was enacted as more and more people received the vote. There were important exceptions to this rule, however. In _France_ universal male suffrage came long before the most important social legislation. In _Germany_ , on the other hand, important social legislation was passed on the government's own initiative.

2. Mark the false choice. According to Professor Weber's interpretation, the Romantics
   a. were forerunners of Marx and Freud.
   b. repudiated such eighteenth-century thinkers as Rousseau.
   c. emphasized the importance of history and the historical imagination.
   d. often supported wars of national liberation.

3. Germany and Italy were late to enter the race to acquire overseas colonies. Germany, however, was able to exert great influence in _Turkey_ , even though that country remained independent. The Italians acquired colonies in some of the less desirable areas of the continent of _Africa_ .

4. Political leaders such as _Napoleon 3_ in France and

Bismark in Germany enacted programs of social legislation as a way of defusing radical demands.

5. Mark the false choice. Marxism
   a. became Europe's most influential doctrine of social reform by the mid-nineteenth century.
   b. claimed that social justice could come only after the working class seized control of the means of production.
   c. was aimed at a society in which people would contribute according to their abilities and be rewarded according to their needs.
   d. claimed that, in the final state of socialism, class differences would be abolished.

Optional Activities

Although the following activities are not required for the course unless assigned by the instructor, students are encouraged to use them as sources of interesting topics for further study.

The Historical Novel

The historical novel brings together many of the trends Professor Weber discusses in his treatment of romanticism. Of all the historical novelists, Sir Walter Scott is perhaps the greatest and the most widely read. Although Scott published many novels, this assignment recommends *Old Mortality* as perhaps the most interesting to read in conjunction with Unit Twenty-Two.

Scott was not a revolutionary. In fact, he was proud of his friendship with the Prince Regent, later King George IV. Nevertheless, Scott was as keenly concerned with social justice and revolutionary movements as any of his more radical contemporaries. *Old Mortality* deals with the insurrection of the Covenanters in seventeenth-century Scotland.

For this assignment, write a paper of 3–5 pages in which you discuss one of the following themes:

• *Revolutionary fanaticism*. Although the Covenanters were religious rather than political revolutionaries, Scott's description of their zeal owes much to the events of the French Revolution. What is Scott's attitude toward religious or social injustice? When does he think that rebellion is justified? When is it not? In what ways is this story of the seventeenth century influenced by the events of Scott's own time? Restrict your analysis to a short section of the novel.

• *Nationalism*. Although *Old Mortality*, like many of his novels, takes place in Scotland, Scott's works were enormously popular throughout Europe and America. How does Scott celebrate his own country? One can understand why the novel was popular in Scotland, but why do you think that people from so many other countries loved Scott's works?

Romantic Poetry

You may wish to read some of the following examples of romantic poetry. They are available in numerous editions, and collections of the poets' works are listed in Further Reading.

Lord Byron
  "The Isles of Greece"
  Childe Harold
  Don Juan

Percy Bysshe Shelley, *Prometheus Unbound*

William Blake, *Songs of Innocence*
  Songs of Experience

Review Questions

1. After the fall of Napoleon, many revolutions or wars of national liberation were fought in Europe and other parts of the world. Name the most important of these struggles. In each case who were the principal opponents of the revolutionaries?
2. Professor Weber speaks of a "revolutionary agenda," or series of beliefs that were shared by many of the revolutionaries. What were the principal articles in this agenda? How had these beliefs arisen from the American and French revolutions?
3. Professor Weber argues that during the eighteenth century European thinkers stressed clarity and precision of thought. The Romantics, on the other hand, were fascinated by the mysterious and incalculable. From your reading and the lectures, how would you define romanticism? Consider the Romantics as writers, artists, and social thinkers. State your reasons for agreeing or disagreeing with Professor Weber's interpretation.
4. During the early stages of the Industrial Revolution, the condition of the poor was so wretched that Benjamin Disraeli, later a Conservative Prime Minister, wrote that England was divided into "two nations between whom there is no intercourse and no sympathy; who are as ignorant of each other's habits, thoughts, and feelings as if they were dwellers in different zones or inhabitants of different planets. The rich and the poor."

    What were some of the most important forms of suffering and exploitation during these years? In the second half of the century, however, some of this suffering was alleviated. What were some of the measures in different countries that lightened the troubles of the poor? How did these measures come about? Through revolution? Through electoral pressure? Through a general rise in the standard of living? These changes followed different patterns in different countries. What were some of the patterns?
5. Many sorts of social reformers appeared in the nineteenth century.

What were the principal similarities between the Positivists and Saint Simonians, on the one hand, and the Marxists on the other? How did each group believe that social or economic change should come about? What classes or social groups were to direct these changes?

6. In the century after Waterloo, Europe was dominated by a group of great powers. What countries originally belonged to this group? What countries joined the group in the course of the century? Although these countries differed from one another in many respects, they did share a number of assumptions about the conduct of European affairs. What was their policy toward revolutions? Although most of the great powers went to war at some time during this period, there was no general European war until 1914. Why?

7. In what parts of the world had the European powers established colonies by the end of the nineteenth century? Some of the colonies enjoyed considerable independence and were even more prosperous than the homeland. Give examples. In other cases countries remained nominally independent but were dominated by one or more European powers. Give examples. In what parts of the world was competition for colonies especially fierce? How did the desire for colonies affect military and naval policies?

Further Reading

Sources

Arnold, Matthew. *Culture and Anarchy.* (1971). Originally published in 1867. Arnold's critique of the England of his time is one of the classics of cultural analysis.

Marx, Karl, and Engels, Friedrich. *The Marx-Engels Reader,* 2nd ed. (1978). A good collection of basic texts.

Weber, Eugen. *The Western Tradition,* 2nd ed. (1965).
"The Reaction," pp. 573–590.
"Romantics and Romanticism," pp. 591–608.

Studies

Avineri, S. *The Social and Political Thought of Karl Marx.* (1968). Especially careful analysis of the relationship among social, political, and economic thought.

Charlton, D. G. *Positivist Thought in France During the Second Empire, 1852–1870.* (1959).

Hauser, Arnold. *Social History of Art.* vols. III–IV. (1958). Suggestive, although interpretations can seem a bit mechanical.

Hayes, C. J. H. *The Historical Evolution of Modern Nationalism,* rev. ed.

(1968). Especially useful for comparisons because nationalism took so many forms across the continent.

Lichtheim, George. *A Short History of Socialism.* (1970). A good, succinct account. Compares Marxist and non-Marxist socialists.

Masur, Gerhard. *Prophets of Yesterday.* (1961). A good analysis of nineteenth-century social thinkers.

Schorske, Carl E. *Fin-de-siecle: Politics and Culture.* (1981). A skillful combination of cultural and political issues.

Taylor, A. J. P. *The Hapsburg Monarchy, 1809–1918,* rev. ed. (1965).
————.*The Struggle for Mastery in Europe, 1848–1918.* (1954). Both texts by Taylor are lively and highly controversial.

Answer Key

Timeline
1. 1792.
2. 1830.
3. 1791.
4. 1819.
5. 1905.
6. 1914.
7. 1815.
8. 1905.
9. 1848.
10. 1871.

Map Exercise
1. Greece.
2. Belgium.
3. Serbia.
4–5. England and Prussia.
6. Norway or Finland.
7. Roughly, the area of modern Yugoslavia.
8. Poland was divided between Prussia, Austria-Hungary, and Russia.
9. Portugal.
10. Scotland.

Self-Test

Part I

1. (a) Poland won its independence.
2. (d) the organization of mass labor unions.
3. (c) Austria-Hungary.
4. Russia or Prussia; Austria or France. (These wars are mentioned in Professor Weber's lectures. Your textbook may supply examples of

other European wars fought by France and Prussia in the nineteenth
century.)
5. 20 percent; 30 percent (these are rough estimates).

Part II
1. France; Germany
2. (b) repudiated such eighteenth-century thinkers as Rousseau.
3. Turkey; Africa.
4. Napoleon III; Bismarck
5. (a) became Europe's most influential doctrine of social reform by the
   mid-nineteenth century.

"Poseuses de la Plage" by Henri de Montaut (1886) By the second half of the nineteenth century, advertising and graphic design were becoming art forms in their own right. This was also a time when beach resorts and accoutrements became popular. Advertising itself is a sign that people have money to spend. By this time, large numbers of people had money and time for leisure. (All rights reserved. The Metropolitan Museum of Art, The Elisha Whittelsey Collection, The Elisha Whittelsey Fund, 1951 [51.624.3].)

UNIT TWENTY-THREE

Program 45: A New Public
Program 46: Fin de Siècle

LEARNING OBJECTIVES

After completing Unit Twenty-Three students should understand the following issues:

- The ways in which the needs of the modern state affected social and economic legislation. Your textbook provides examples of social programs in various states.
- The ways in which the working class and the peasantry began to participate in the mainstream of social and economic life.
- The changing social and economic relations between the cities and the countryside. Use your textbook to examine differing patterns of urbanization.
- The social and political consequences of widespread literacy.
- The development of large-scale organized sports.
- The rise of Social Darwinism. Look especially closely at the influence of Social Darwinism in Germany.
- The relationship between mass culture and the avant-garde.

TV INSTRUCTION

OVERVIEW
PROGRAM 45: A NEW PUBLIC

Many of the social and political developments discussed in earlier units had barely touched the great mass of people in the world. By the middle of the nineteenth century, however, market economies and nation states were affecting all parts of the population. Universal public education appeared in most parts of Europe and mass political movements were rising. Increased production led to higher standards of living and expanded leisure time. The Darwinian theories of evolution were now being applied to social issues.

I. Professor Weber argues that until the nineteenth century most "history" was really the history of small elites.
  A. The great masses of people were invisible or made only sporadic appearances on the stage of history.
  B. Even in a great movement like the French Revolution, the people who were executed and those who gave the orders were ladies and gentlemen, or at least members of the educated classes.
  C. In the early stages even the wonders of the Industrial Revolution were seldom enjoyed by the common people, and hardly ever by common people outside the towns.

II. After the middle of the nineteenth century, however, these patterns began to change.
  A. The standard of living improved. Common people
    1. Ate better.
    2. Dressed better.
    3. Had more regular work.
  B. The middle classes were expanding and diversifying.
    1. The older middle class had included such people as
      a. Industrialists.
      b. Bankers.
      c. Professors.
    2. New sections of the middle classes were appearing.
      a. Shopkeepers.
      b. Shop assistants.
      c. Clerks.
      d. Artisans.
      e. Civil servants.
      f. Salespeople.
      g. Mechanics.
    3. These new members of the middle classes had more
      a. Money.
      b. Leisure time.
      c. Education.

    4. They were becoming a significant force in
      a. Politics.
      b. The economy.

III. Despite these changes, Professor Weber argues that three-quarters of the population remained insignificant and invisible.
  A. The majority of the population was still peasants.
  B. Many workers lived in villages rather than in cities:
    1. Miners.
    2. Weavers.
    3. Potters.
  C. Even by the mid-nineteenth century, these people lived much as their ancestors had.
    1. Because meat was expensive, they ate mostly bread, potatoes, and vegetables.
    2. Many people were barely able to support their children.
    3. Housing was primitive.
      a. Many houses had no windows,
      b. Because the tax on windows and doors made them too expensive.
      c. Sometimes they shared quarters with their animals.
      d. They were not part of a market economy.
  D. For people like these, the nation and national politics meant little.
    1. In some places people spoke local dialects rather than the national language.
    2. They often used local weights and measures, which varied from place to place.
    3. Because they rarely handled cash, even the national currency was largely irrelevant.
  E. From their point of view, the state consisted of intrusive strangers:
    1. Tax collectors.
    2. Customs men.
    3. Soldiers.
    4. Police officers.
  F. In remote areas people often did not realize that they lived in a country such as Italy or France.
  G. Even when they were granted the right to vote, they often followed the instructions of some local notable:
    1. The landlord.
    2. The priest.
    3. The mayor.
    4. The moneylender.

IV. By the middle of the nineteenth century, however, the needs of the nation-state were altering this situation.
  A. According to the theory of the nation-state, all of its subjects
    1. Were citizens.
    2. Were subject to the same laws.

        3. Shared in the national sovereignty.

        4. Had a share in making laws or electing lawmakers.

    B. To meet these requirements, all citizens had to

        1. Understand the laws.

        2. Speak a common language.

    C. Otherwise, the state would have great difficulty making people

        1. Pay taxes.

        2. Serve in the army.

  V. People had to be taught to identify with their nation.

    A. People should think of themselves as French or Italians, rather than as Bretons or Tuscans.

    B. The schools were given this task. Education was now

        1. Public.

        2. Universal.

        3. Compulsory.

        4. Free.

    C. By the 1880s all children, including girls, were being taught to read and write.

    D. By 1900 all young adults within a nation-state had a sense of common identity.

        1. Maps and history lessons in school gave them a clearer sense of their homeland.

        2. Receiving a school certificate became an important rite of passage, like a First Communion or Bar Mitzvah.

  VI. Education gave practical advantages even to humble people.

    A. It was a key to getting a job, especially for new opportunities in the

        1. Railroads.

        2. Police force.

        3. Post office.

    B. In the army noncommissioned officers had to have a school-leaving certificate.

    C. For exceptional young men only a few scholarships for higher education were available.

  VII. Only gradually did the whole population accept the idea of universal education.

    A. Many poor people did not

        1. Understand the point of education.

        2. Want to lose their children's labor or earnings.

    B. The dominant classes, however, favored compulsory education because they felt that

        1. National integration was worth the price.

        2. An industrial society needed a basic level of literacy.

  VIII. Economic changes began to show the value of education even for poor people in the countryside.

    A. In the second half of the nineteenth century, roads and railroads penetrated deep into the countryside.
       1. More goods entered the market.
       2. More salespeople reached the villages.
       3. Peasants now became part of the national economy.
    B. Peasants could not afford to remain illiterate. They needed to be able to
       1. Keep records.
       2. Complete forms.
       3. Fill in shipping manifests.
       4. Use national measures and national currency.
    C. Before long, peasants were glad to have their children go to school to learn
       1. To read and write.
       2. To learn the language one needed to deal with officials.
       3. To keep accounts.
       4. To understand contracts.

  IX. Schooling was becoming a key to social change.
    A. With an education, people, especially women, could leave the villages to find better work in towns.
    B. Schools also taught patriotism and social duties:
       1. Paying taxes.
       2. Performing military service.
    C. Professor Weber argues that the first generations to attend school were more law-abiding and patriotic than any before or since.

   X. Meanwhile, an expanding economy was attracting and accommodating increasing numbers of people.
    A. Conditions in the cities were often miserable, but Professor Weber argues
       1. That conditions in the countryside were often worse.
       2. After all, people continued to migrate to the cities of their own free will.
    B. As people left the countryside, those who remained were often better off.
       1. The problem of under-employment was less severe.
       2. There was less isolation.
    C. The countryside was much better integrated into the national culture and economy.
       1. Country people began to read the newspapers.
       2. The railroads brought new products to the countryside:
          a. Fertilizer.
          b. Better building materials.
          c. Stoves.
          d. Dishes.
          e. Ready-made clothes.
       3. People in the country and cities began to lead increasingly similar lives.

XI. Improvements in the standard of living came from a number of sources.
    A. Organization among the working classes:
        1. Self-help groups.
        2. Unions.
    B. Access to the ballot, which made politicians try to serve the needs of voters with:
        1. Roads.
        2. Water.
        3. Credit.
        4. Jobs.
    C. Greater industrial productivity, which led to
        1. Lower prices.
        2. More accessible goods.
    D. A greater base of consumers.

XII. With a greater volume of production, working conditions improved.
    A. In 1850 a series of English Factory Acts culminated in a regulation limiting the working week for women to sixty hours.
        1. In many factories men worked alongside women.
        2. Therefore, the sixty-hour regulation shortened the week for many men.
    B. The working week now began to end on Saturday at noon. This week was known as *la semaine anglais*, or the English week.
        1. By the beginning of World War I most industrial workers were working these hours.
        2. With a bit more leisure, people became better rested and could enjoy
           a. Dance halls.
           b. Theaters.
           c. Reading.
           d. Eventually, the movies.

XIII. The evolutionary theories of Charles Darwin began to influence social thinking.
    A. In Darwin's *On the Origin of Species by Means of Natural Selection*, published in 1859, he argues that species
        1. Had not originated in a Biblical act of creation.
        2. Had evolved over time as they adapted to their environment.
        3. That failed to adapt became extinct.
    B. In 1871 Darwin published *The Descent of Man*, in which he links human evolution to the higher primates.
    C. Darwin wrote that life is a continuing struggle for existence.
        1. Species that possess or develop useful characteristics survive.
        2. Others become extinct.
    D. Darwin saw no moral or religious pattern in this scheme of evolution.
        1. Some of his followers, however, identified evolution with economic or political progress.

2. These followers sometimes believed that the struggle between nations was simply another form of natural selection.

E. Unfortunately, for such followers industrial and economic surveys demonstrated that the populations of the most advanced
countries were among the least fit.

1. Much of the population was sickly and badly educated.
2. Charity, which was active at this time, demanded that something be done for these people.
3. But the national interest was involved as well. A sickly population could not create a strong nation.

Key to the Images

Country vs. city: For most of European history, peasants and city
dwellers seemed almost to belong to different species. As we view the
images in Program 45, note that some of these differences are beginning to fade. After universal education had spread throughout Europe, even remote villages would contain at least a few educated
people who had traveled to other parts of the country, or even the
world. The mail, the telegraph, and the railroad were also tieing
countries together.

Even the clothing of the countryside began to change. For centuries,
peasants had worn great loose smocks when they were working. By
the end of the century, peasants were wearing work clothes that were
much more like those of industrial workers. Railroad workers, for
instance, had made dungarees and overalls popular. Then, too, mechanical harvesters, threshers, and other sorts of machinery affected
work clothes. Great loose smocks were dangerous to wear around
moving parts.

Popular press: In the second half of the nineteenth century the rotary
press made it possible to produce millions of newspapers and magazines in a single edition. Advertisements would radically alter the
sense of graphic design and create mass markets for new products.

Focus Questions

1. How did the lives of the working class and peasantry change in the
second half of the nineteenth century?
2. In what ways did the European peasantry become integrated into the
political and economic mainstream?
3. In what ways did Europe develop a consumers' economy?
4. What were the political and social consequences of universal compulsory education?
5. What were the political and social assumptions that lay behind the
theory of the modern state?

6. How did Darwin's theory of natural selection come to be taken as a model of social relations?

OVERVIEW
PROGRAM 46: FIN DE SIÈCLE

By the second half of the nineteenth century, even working people had enough time and money to enjoy popular culture, especially sports. As popular culture became stronger and more pervasive, however, members of the older privileged classes felt that their way of life was being challenged. Writers and artists began to mark a sharp separation between popular art, which was enjoyed by the masses, and avant-garde art, which only a select few could appreciate.

  I. Working people had greater amounts of money and leisure.
      A. In England, after the passage of the Bank Holiday Act in 1871, the working-class holiday became a national institution. People enjoyed
         1. Railroad trips.
         2. Steamboat excursions.
         3. Staying in resorts.
      B. Many people wanted to ensure that leisure was put to good use. Organized sports were thought to be especially wholesome because they
         1. Used up energy that might otherwise have exploded in violence or crime.
         2. Could remedy physical degeneration.
      C. In England during the 1870s and 1880s, thousands of teams were founded by
         1. Churches.
         2. Unions.
         3. Factories.
      D. The schools were probably the greatest promoters of sports.
         1. After 1870 all English towns had an educational system.
         2. Schoolboy competitions became popular local events.
      E. Some municipal authorities built sports grounds.

 II. Sports were becoming a profitable business.
      A. With the new widespread literacy, many people read magazines and newspapers devoted to sports.
      B. Sports also sold many commercial spin-offs:
         1. Uniforms.
         2. Equipment.
         3. Medicine.
         4. Food and drink for spectators.
      C. Railroads and streetcars made it possible for spectators to reach distant events.

III. Although the process began in Britain, organized sports were spreading throughout the world.
   A. Soldiers and administrators carried cricket throughout the British Empire.
   B. Sailors, businesspeople, and mechanics carried soccer throughout the world. By the 1890s it was being played in
      1. Austria.
      2. Russia.
      3. Turkey.
      4. Scandinavia.
      5. Latin America.
   C. Rugby, which was played by students, also spread, although not as widely.
      1. French students picked up the game in England.
      2. Eventually, students spread it to
         a. Romania.
         b. Japan.
   D. In the United States the intercollegiate rules for football were formulated in 1873.
      1. By the 1880s the game had evolved into something like its modern form.
      2. It was a violent sport. In the 1905 season, for instance,
         a. Eighteen players died.
         b. There were 159 major injuries.
   E. Baseball was codified as an adult game after the Civil War.
      1. By the 1890s professional organizations were well established.
      2. The game was exported to Cuba and Central America.
   F. In 1891 basketball was invented in Springfield, Massachusetts.
   G. In 1896 the Baron Charles de Coubertin organized the first modern Olympic Games, held in Athens.

IV. The bicycle also revolutionized leisure time.
   A. The machine itself had a long history.
      1. There had been bicyclelike contraptions at the time of the French Revolution.
      2. In the 1880s, however, the velocipede evolved into the modern bicycle.
   B. The bicycle had a complex social history.
      1. Because early bicycles were expensive, the first riders were upper- or middle-class people.
      2. Women also rode bicycles.
         a. The bicycle freed them from chaperones.
         b. Feminists hailed the bicycle as a liberator from oppressive customs and restraining dresses.
   C. A tourist industry grew up around the bicycle.
      1. Cyclists needed better road surfaces.
      2. Hotels and inns catered to these new customers.
   D. Manufacturers organized great races.

       1. Bicycle races were the subject of some of the liveliest art of the nineteenth century.

       2. Bicycle racers were among the first great sports heroes.

   E. A number of bicycle manufacturers had started out manufacturing umbrella spokes and corset stays. The enterprise and ingenuity that turned some of them to the bicycle led others to use similar technology to develop

       1. The automobile.

       2. The airplane.

   F. By the beginning of World War I skilled working people could afford bicycles.

V. Not everyone welcomed new developments.

   A. Many people considered the telephone to be an intrusion on privacy.

   B. Professor Weber argues that many people in the upper classes feared that they were losing their identity in the new mass culture of the 1880s and 1890s.

       1. Everyone seemed to dress alike (although this was not the case).

       2. Their resorts seemed threatened by vulgar crowds.

       3. Higher education and better jobs were becoming available to lower-class people, some of whom had aspirations of equality.

       4. Many people resented the changing status of women. They objected to

         a. New styles.

         b. Contraception.

         c. Working women.

   C. Many politicians catered to the parvenus, even to the working classes.

VI. A politics of resentment was growing.

   A. Many conservatives believed that democracy was necessarily corrupt.

   B. Some believed that the nation needed to be purged of corrupt elements:

       1. Jews.

       2. Freemasons.

       3. Protestants, in Catholic countries.

       4. Catholics, in Protestant countries.

   C. Some wanted to use eugenics to purify their race.

   D. Many wanted to revivify national enthusiasm to

       1. Fight against foreign threats.

       2. To defuse working-class agitation by turning it against enemies abroad.

3. Eventually, Fascists would combine powerful elements of nationalism and socialism.

VII. The national state was going through a rapid evolution.
   A. It was becoming increasingly interventionist in foreign affairs.
   B. At home, the state was becoming the great agency for social change by redistributing wealth.
      1. Although workers continued to talk of internationalism and class warfare, they increasingly relied on the reformist state.
      2. Working-class parties became patriotic.
      3. In 1914 socialist legislators were as quick to vote for war as anyone else.
      4. They believed that workers' interests would be best protected by defending their own countries.

VIII. Professor Weber argues that in art and literature a gap was widening between popular taste and the taste of the avant-garde.
   A. The avant-garde believed that only a small number of initiates could understand great art.
   B. Popular art was corrupt, almost by definition.
   C. In many fields artists experimented by dispensing with familiar features:
      1. Poems were often written without rhyme.
      2. Some novels dispensed with plot.
      3. Paintings often did not have a clearly recognizable subject.
   D. A few people glorified different sorts of nonconformity:
      1. Drug taking.
      2. Homosexuality.
      3. Occultism.
      4. Mysticism.

IX. By the turn of the century, although Europe was prosperous as never before, many people felt that they were living at the end of a world.
   A. Some were frightened by mass politics or popular culture.
   B. Others thought that nonconformity was a sign of degeneration.

Key to the Images

Public parks: During the nineteenth century public parks were laid out in most of the large cities of Europe and North America. In Program 46 we view Winslow Homer's "Skaters in Central Park." Central Park itself was largely the work of Frederick Law Olmsted, one of America's greatest landscape architects.

French painters, especially the Impressionists, loved to paint the world at leisure. In Program 46 we see Manet's "Music in the Tuileries Gardens."

Sports: By the last quarter of the nineteenth century organized sports were spreading throughout the world. As we examine the images of various teams, we should be aware of the different patterns in which sports moved from one country to another. British sports such as cricket and rugby spread throughout the British Empire. They were less popular in areas of the world where the British did not maintain a permanent presence, although rugby did enjoy some popularity among students in Europe and Japan.

A similar pattern holds for baseball, which is most popular in areas where the United States has maintained a long-term presence, such as Central America and Japan. American football has spread even less widely.

The great universal sport is soccer, which was spread by British workers, soldiers, and sailors.

Bicycle: As we look at early images of the bicycle, we should think about how it transformed daily life in Europe and America. As is seen from the prices in some of the early advertisements, the first bicycles were not inexpensive. Even so, they were much less expensive than a horse.

The countryside became more accessible. Once they were away from the train lines, people were no longer faced with the choice of walking or going by horse.

The bicycle, along with public transportation systems, changed the shape of cities as well. It was no longer necessary for people to live within walking distance of their place of work.

Focus Questions

1. How did organized sports become a regular part of European and American life?
2. What were some of the arguments advanced in favor of organized sports? What social and economic factors made them possible?
3. What were the various sports that became popular in different countries? What countries were responsible for spreading sports?
4. What were some of the new forms of transportation developed during this period? What were their social and economic consequences?
5. In what ways did class barriers become more fluid during this period? Who benefited from increased social mobility? Who resented this mixing of classes?
6. What were the reasons for the development of avant-garde art?

―――――― *ASSIGNMENTS AND ACTIVITIES* ――――――

IN CONTEXT

Themes and issues that set Unit Twenty-Three in context with other units include the following:

- Look back to the discussion of athletics in ancient Greece. In what ways did the spectator sports that developed in the nineteenth century differ from those of the ancient world? Look back to the immediately preceding units in which Professor Weber discusses the improvement in the general standard of living that made large-scale sports so popular.

- The nineteenth century was an age of mass politics, although it was not the first period to involve great numbers of people in the political process. Look back to the units on the Roman Republic and Empire. In the first century B.C. the popular party was strong. Why then did Rome eventually become dominated by emperors? Throughout the Middle Ages and afterward Europe saw many examples of self-governing cities, but even in these places only substantial citizens had an important role in government. In later units look for the connection between mass media and mass politics. We learn that in some cases, such as Hitler's Germany, mass politics do not always lead to democracy.

- Earlier units stress intellectual issues of various kinds. Only in the nineteenth century, however, did public education become common throughout Europe. In earlier periods great numbers of people participated in such intellectual movements as the Protestant Reformation, but only in the nineteenth century did a great mass of educated people appear throughout Europe.

Textbook Assignment

Read the following pages in your assigned textbook:

Text: *Western Civilizations* (Eleventh Edition, 1988)
Read: Chapter 26, "The Middle Class Challenged," pp. 861–888.

Text: *The Western Experience* (Fifth Edition, 1991)
Read: Chapter 25, "The Age of Progress," pp. 1004–1056.

Text: *The Western Heritage* (Fourth Edition, 1991)
Read: Chapter 25, "The Birth of Contemporary European Thought," pp. 885–913.

Issues for Clarification

Foundlings

Professor Weber points out that for many poor people the story of Hansel and Gretel was more than a fairy tale. The problem of abandoned children began long before the Industrial Revolution. In the sixteenth and seventeenth centuries, for instance, nearly 20 percent of all homicide cases in England involved mothers who had killed unwanted infants. Nearly all of the women prosecuted were unmarried, but it is likely that murders also took place among the children of married parents, although these killings were usually undetected. The high rates of infant mortality that prevailed everywhere in the world were swelled by a good deal of deliberate killing.

The development of orphanages saved many of these children, although the mortality rate in the orphanages was usually high. In Italy this aspect of social history is recorded in a number of common surnames that were often given to abandoned children by the orphanage. Esposito, for instance, means "exposed"; that is, abandoned. Other abandoned children were given last names like De Sanctis or De Angelis or D'Angelo, meaning that they had come from the saints or the angels.

Natural Selection

Darwin was not the first scientist to claim that modern species were the result of a long evolution over time. His most important contribution to evolutionary theory was his discovery of natural selection: the mechanism that lay behind evolutionary change.

Although natural selection is often described as a struggle for survival, Darwin did not believe that the most successful species were necessarily the most successful predators. The mechanism of natural selection is not so easy to predict.

Darwin believed that individuals of a given species are sometimes born with unusual characteristics that they can pass on to their offspring. Among a species of bears, for instance, some individuals grow heavier, thicker fur. If the bears live in a cold climate, the individuals with heavier fur tend to live longer and to produce more offspring. Over the course of many thousands of years an ever greater proportion of the species is descended from bears with heavy coats, until finally the species as a whole has heavier coats. What began as a characteristic of a few individuals becomes true of the species as a whole.

Such developments, however, do not mean that evolution takes place according to a preordained plan. It is not true, for instance, that mammals in a cold climate will always develop heavier coats. The species might migrate, or adapt to its environment in some other way. And, of course, the species may become extinct.

Because Darwin wrote before the development of modern genetics, he could not say why these individual variations first appeared, nor could he explain how they could be passed on to offspring.

Social Darwinism

During the nineteenth and early twentieth centuries many social theorists tried to use Darwin's ideas to explain differences between races or cultures within human societies. Some of the Social Darwinists were social reformers, who put their ideas to work by improving living conditions, especially in large cities. Many reforms in such matters as sanitation, public water, and the inspection of food were the work of Social Darwinists.

Because most of the Social Darwinists, however, were white Europeans or North Americans, they usually claimed that in evolutionary terms the white race had reached a higher stage of development than other races. Social Darwinism was often used to lay a pseudo-scientific basis for racist theories. Hitler, along with many other anti-Semites, drew many of his ideas from the Social Darwinists.

Glossary

Eugenics: A science that tries to improve species or races by controlling hereditary factors.

Proletariat: The working class. People who had to support themselves by working for wages.

La semaine anglaise: A French phrase meaning "the English week." It refers to the five-and-a-half-day work week that originated in England.

Velocipede: An ancestor of the bicycle.

Timeline

Place each of the following events on the timeline. In some cases you may have to specify a roughly defined period of time rather than a precise date.

1. Free, universal, compulsory schooling becomes common in Europe.
2. English Factory Act establishes the sixty-hour work week for women.
3. Invention of basketball.
4. First modern Olympic Games.
5. Appearance of the modern bicycle.
6. Beginning of World War I.
7. Invention of motion pictures.
8. Publication of Darwin's *On the Origin of Species*.
9. The Bank Holiday Act is passed in England.
10. Beginning of large-scale organized sports.

1850   1920

Map Exercise

Find the following locations on the map.

1. Site of first modern Olympic Games.
2. Country that established *la semaine anglaise*.
3. Homeland of Charles Darwin.
4. Country of greatest importance in spreading soccer.
5–6. Two countries to which soccer had spread by the 1890s.

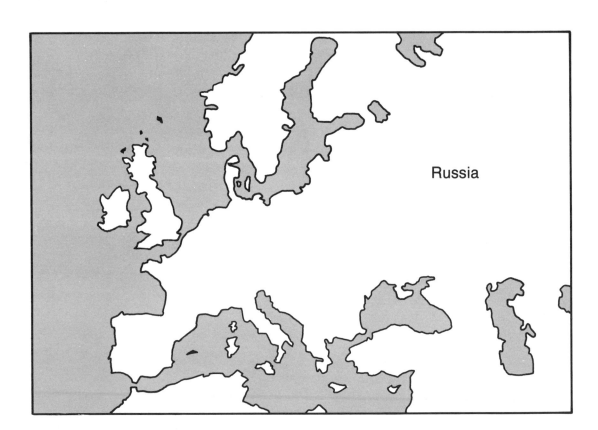

Russia

Self-Test

Part I

1. Mark the false choice. The following industries made important contributions to the development of the first airplane:
   a. The electronics industry.
   b. Umbrella-making.
   c. Bicycle-making.
   d. The automobile industry.

2. The public schools that developed in the last third of the nineteenth century were
   a. open to both males and females.

b. unpopular with the military.

c. too expensive for poor people.

d. unpopular with employers.

3. Mark the false choice. Darwin's theory on the evolution of species by means of natural selection

   a. implies that evolution took place over an enormously long period of time.

   b. argues that evolution proceeds toward a purposeful goal.

   c. argues that species became extinct when they were no longer well adapted to their environment.

   d. argues that useful characteristics arose by chance.

4. Mark the false choice. Social Darwinism

   a. applies Darwin's theories to nations or races rather than to species.

   b. generally argues that the white races are at the height of human evolution.

   c. interprets human history as a series of struggles in which the weak were continually defeated.

   d. was supported by the generally high standards of fitness and health in the industrialized nations.

5. Name two sports that the British spread throughout the world.

   ___Soccer___ and ___rugby___.

Part II

1. Mark the false choice. The theory of the nation-state assumed that

   a. All its citizens should be subject to the same laws.

   b. A country should have a common language.

   c. The Roman Catholic church was the one true religion.

   d. Citizens should be able to elect legislators.

2. Mark the false choice. Initially, many peasants did not want to send their children to school. Eventually, however, peasants became reconciled to compulsory schooling because

   a. literacy was becoming increasingly necessary, even for the work of the peasantry.

   b. literate children were more likely to remain in the countryside to help their parents.

   c. many peasants were being drafted into national armies where literacy was necessary for promotion.

   d. literacy enabled peasants to deal more effectively with officials and outsiders.

3. Mark the false choice. According to Professor Weber, the migration of great numbers of peasants to work in the factories

   a. was a sign that life in the countryside was even more brutal than in the industrial cities.

   b. actually improved the lot of those who stayed behind.

ℯ was slowed by the improvement of education in the countryside.
    d. integrated previously isolated areas into the national culture.

4. Mark the false choice. In the second half of the nineteenth century the increasing amount of leisure time available to the working class
    a. partly resulted from social legislation that limited the work week for women and children.
    b. led to the development of large-scale organized sports.
    c. resulted in an economy that increasingly emphasized consumption.
    d. sharpened the differences between city and countryside.

5. In the last third of the nineteenth century organized sports were
    a. thought to be good for burning up energy that might have been spent in violence or crime.
    b. considered to be good for controlling the lower classes but unsuitable for the middle class or aristocracy.
    c. restricted to England and the United States.
    d. restricted to neighborhoods because transportation was too primitive to permit competition among cities.

Optional Activity

Although the following activity is not required for the course unless assigned by the instructor, students are encouraged to use it as a source of interesting topics for further study.

Manet

The career of Édouard Manet (1832–1883), one of the greatest painters of nineteenth-century France, illustrates many of the themes that appear in Unit Twenty-Three. He loved, for instance, to paint people enjoying the new leisure that Professor Weber discusses. Manet's "Dejeuner sur l'Herbe" was inspired by women he had seen bathing in the Seine.

Manet also painted scenes from current events. On June 19, 1867, the Emperor Maximilian of Mexico was shot before a firing squad along with two of his generals. Manet's various sketches and drawings show the influence of the new means of communication on his painting. In a version of the painting now in the Museum of Fine Arts in Boston, the soldiers in the firing squad are wearing Mexican uniforms and the emperor's face is obscure. Manet was working almost entirely from imagination, for he had only the bare news report to work from.

In August 1867, however, Manet saw from illustrations in the newspaper *Le Figaro* that the soldiers were wearing French-style uniforms. All the later versions of the painting reflect this new piece of information. For the version now in Copenhagen, Manet was able to paint the face of the emperor from a photograph.

Manet's career also illustrates new tendencies in the art world. He wanted to be a popular painter, but his work was rejected by the Salon and for years he was considered shocking. In the end, however, he received official recognition and died a Chevalier of the Legion of Honor.

For this assignment, write a short paper of 3–5 pages in which you analyze one of Manet's paintings. The Penguin Classics of World Art publishes an inexpensive edition of *The Complete Paintings of Manet.* Focus your analysis on one of the following questions:

- In what ways did Manet record new aspects of life that had developed in the nineteenth century?
- In many of the paintings we find Manet alluding to earlier works of art. In what ways did Manet use older forms in a new way?
- Imagine yourself as a nineteenth-century lover of art. What was shocking about these works?

Review Questions

1. What were some of the political, social, and economic changes that began to bring the lower classes into the mainstream of national life? To what extent did the lower classes now begin to play a role in politics?
2. What were the most important effects of free, universal education? What groups of people were especially in favor of it? Why did many people, especially among the peasantry, resist it at first? Why did they gradually come to accept it?
3. What were the principal assumptions that lay behind the ideal of the nation-state? How did these assumptions affect educational policy? How did they affect electoral policy? How did politicians try to create national states in the second half of the nineteenth century? What were their principal obstacles?
4. How did life in the countryside change as great numbers of peasants left rural areas to find work in the cities? How did the relationship change between town and country? What social and economic changes made this great migration possible?
5. What were the motives that lay behind social and economic reforms? What role did religion play in these reforms? To what extent did politicians try to correct abuses simply because they were afraid of revolution? What role did unions and working-class political parties play in these reforms?
6. What countries began to organize sports on a large scale? Which sports were popular in various countries? What classes of people played or watched various sports? What groups promoted organized sports? What were some of their different motives? What social and economic factors promoted organized sports? Which countries were especially important in spreading sports around the world?
7. In what ways was the bicycle more than a popular form of exercise and entertainment? What social changes made it popular? What social changes did it help promote?

8. In what ways did conservative resentment develop against the social changes of the late nineteenth century? Among what groups was the resentment especially strong? What groups were the objects of the resentment? How did the resentment vary from country to country?

Further Reading

Sources

Gosse, Edmund. *Father and Son*. (1963).   One of the greatest Victorian autobiographies. Discusses the impact of Darwin on fundamentalist Christianity.

Webb, Beatrice. *My Apprenticeship*. (1926).   Victorian autobiography that describes how Beatrice Webb became a social reformer after growing up in a comfortable middle-class home.

Weber, Eugen. *The Western Tradition*, 2nd ed. (1965).
"Economic Revolution," pp. 610–642
"Liberalism, Nationalism, and 1848," pp. 643–663
"Nationalism and Imperialism," pp. 746–762.

Studies

Barrows, S. *Distorting Mirrors: Visions of the Crowd in Late Nineteenth-Century France*. (1981).   Discusses crowd psychology and mass culture as sources of social discontent.

Cippola, C. M. *Literacy and Development in the West*. (1969).   Discusses the development of literacy over the past two centuries.

Eiseley, Loren C. *Darwin's Century: Evolution and the Men Who Discovered It*. (1961).   Discusses Darwin in the larger context of nineteenth-century biology and geology.

Poliakov, Leon. *The Aryan Myth: A History of Racist and Nationalist Ideas in Europe*. (1977).   Particularly useful as a link to themes that reappear in later units.

Shattuck, Roger. *The Banquet Years*. (1958).   A study of modern art and literature in France in the years before World War I.

Weber, Eugen. *Peasants into Frenchmen: The Modernization of Rural France, 1880–1914*. (1976).   An exploration of the integration of the countryside into national life.

Williams, Raymond. *The Long Revolution*. (1960).   A study of literacy and popular culture in England.

Answer Key

Timeline

1. 1870s – 1890s.
2. 1850.
3. 1891.
4. 1896.
5. 1880s.
6. 1914.
7. 1895 or 1896.
8. 1859.
9. 1871.
10. 1870s – 1880s.

Map Exercise

1. Athens, Greece.
2. England.
3. England.
4. England.
5–6. The lecture mentions Austria, Russia, Turkey, the Scandinavian countries, and Latin America. Your textbook may supply additional examples.

Self-Test

Part I

1. (a) The electronics industry.
2. (a) open to both males and females.
3. (b) argues that evolution proceeds toward a purposeful goal.
4. (d) was supported by the generally high standards of fitness and health in the industrialized nations.
5. Cricket, soccer, and rugby are mentioned in the lectures. (Your textbook may supply additional examples.)

Part II

1. (c) The Roman Catholic church was the one true religion.
2. (b) literate children were more likely to remain in the countryside to help their parents.
3. (c) was slowed by the improvement of education in the countryside.
4. (d) sharpened the differences between city and countryside.
5. (a) thought to be good for burning up energy that might have been spent in violence or crime.

The United Kingdom, World War II Searching for survivors in the rubble of a bombed-out building. (Courtesy of the Library of Congress.)

UNIT TWENTY-FOUR

Program 47: The First World War and the Rise of Fascism

Program 48: The Second World War

LEARNING OBJECTIVES

After completing Unit Twenty-Four students should understand the following issues:

- The causes that led to war in 1914 and the factors that prevented a lasting peace from being established in 1919. Does your textbook agree with Professor Weber's argument that between 1914 and 1945 Europe was really suffering a new thirty years' war?
- The reasons why Russia, Italy, and Germany developed radically new kinds of states in the years between the wars. Use your textbook to distinguish clearly among these three kinds of government.
- The reasons why England and France were unable to mount a more successful opposition to Germany and Italy.
- The ways in which the United States alternately intervened and stayed aloof from European affairs between 1914 and 1939.
- The ways in which Hitler's allies helped or hindered his ability to wage war. According to your textbook, did the three axis powers operate under a unified command or did they simply have a similar set of enemies?
- The contribution of the United States to the Allied War effort. Does your textbook support Professor Weber on this issue?
- The motives and basic methods of Hitler's policy of genocide.

TV INSTRUCTION

OVERVIEW
PROGRAM 47: THE FIRST WORLD WAR
AND THE RISE OF FASCISM

World War I destroyed four empires and created an unstable collection of national states. As the League of Nations and other forms of international cooperation proved unable to solve Europe's problems, dictators on both the left and right dominated European politics. Although Hitler had clearly embarked on a path of conquest, no one could organize effective opposition to him.

I. Between 1914 and 1918 World War I killed more people than any other European war.
   A. Many people had foreseen such a war.
      1. Winston Churchill had predicted that war would damage the victors as much as the losers.
      2. In 1914 most of the European powers were more afraid of not fighting.
   B. Some countries believed that the balance of power was swinging against them:
      1. Germany.
      2. Austria-Hungary.
   C. In the early days the war was popular.
      1. Both sides expected a quick victory.
      2. Even the socialist parties supported it.

II. Nearly the whole of Europe was involved in the war.
   A. On one side the chief contestants were
      1. Britain.
      2. France.
      3. Russia.
      4. Italy from 1915.
      5. The United States from 1917.
   B. On the other side were
      1. Germany.
      2. Austria-Hungary.
      3. Turkey.
   C. Germany and its allies gained an early advantage.
      1. In 1917 Russia was knocked out of the war.
      2. Finally, Germany and its allies were worn down by their enemies, especially after the United States entered the war in 1917.
      3. Germany accepted stringent armistice terms on November 11, 1918.
   D. Never had a European war been so destructive.
      1. Eight to ten million Europeans died in battle.

2. Germany and France each lost 16 percent of their male populations.

3. Millions more were wounded, many crippled for life.

4. In 1918–1919 a great influenza epidemic swept the world, killing two to three times more people than had died in battle.

III. The Allies were unable to formulate peace terms that would prevent future wars.

  A. Woodrow Wilson, the American president, played a key role at the peace conference because

   1. The United States had supplied crucial material and loans to

    a. Britain.

    b. France.

   2. American troops had helped turn the scale at the end of the war.

  B. Wilson's Fourteen Points were supposed to form the basis of a just peace.

   1. He wanted both large and small nations to enjoy

    a. Independence.

    b. Territorial integrity.

   2. Wilson could not persuade his allies to grant Germany magnanimous terms.

   3. The Treaty of Versailles punished Germany enough to cause enormous resentment but not enough to weaken her permanently.

  C. Wilson pinned his hopes for peace on the League of Nations.

   1. Once back home, however, Wilson collapsed from nervous exhaustion and a stroke.

   2. The United States never joined the League.

   3. The United States determined to remain aloof from European affairs.

IV. After the war the European political structure was in disarray.

  A. Four empires had disintegrated.

   1. The Germany Empire.

   2. The Austro-Hungarian Empire.

   3. The Russian Empire.

   4. The Ottoman Empire.

  B. A series of minor wars broke out across Europe.

   1. Greeks fought Turks.

   2. Hungarians fought Romanians.

   3. Poles fought nearly all their neighbors.

V. In 1917, as the result of two successful risings, the Bolsheviks, led by Vladimir Ilyich Lenin, came to power in Russia.

  A. In 1917 the Russian army was collapsing all along the Eastern front.

   1. The Bolsheviks came to power by promising

    a. Land to the peasants.

          b. Better conditions to the workers.

          c. Peace at all costs.

      2. In the city of Brest-Litovsk the Russians ceded large parts of western Russia to Germany.

  B. After several years of war at home and abroad the Bolsheviks were firmly in control.

  C. The Bolsheviks established power through

      1. An extensive bureaucracy.

      2. The secret police.

  D. In the late 1920s and early 1930s Joseph Stalin collectivized Russian agriculture.

      1. Family farms were prohibited.

      2. Perhaps ten million people were killed outright or died in the resulting famine.

      3. Millions more were transported or exiled from their homes.

  VI. Right-wing dictatorships were coming to power in other parts of Europe.

  A. In 1922 Benito Mussolini came to power in Italy.

      1. Italy had been on the victorious side but had gained little in the war.

      2. The country suffered from economic anarchy and social disorder.

      3. Mussolini carried out many impressive operations.

          a. He improved the railroads.

          b. He built a large aircraft industry.

          c. He drained the Pontine Marshes outside Rome.

      4. Mussolini and the Fascists failed to solve Italy's basic problems.

  B. In Germany the Nazi party under Adolf Hitler was gaining strength.

      1. In the early 1920s inflation had crippled the middle classes.

      2. Although Germany recovered somewhat in the late 1920s, the Depression hit Germany especially hard.

      3. Extremist parties gained strength on both the right and left.

          a. In 1932 the Nazis were the second largest party in the Reichstag.

          b. The Communists were the third largest.

      4. In January 1933 the Nazis came to power at the head of a conservative coalition.

          a. Hitler began to rearm the country.

          b. By 1936 Germany was the only industrial country to have returned to full employment.

  VII. The other powers could not organize effective resistance to Germany, Italy, or other Fascist powers.

  A. The United States remained isolationist.

  B. Britain and France drifted into a policy of appeasement.

      1. Both countries were afraid to risk another war.

        a. France had lost 16 percent of its male population in World War I.

        b. England was suffering from economic depression and the problems of maintaining its empire.

    2. The intellectual elite rejected war.

  C. In Spain, General Francisco Franco led right-wing rebels against a left-wing government.

    1. Franco was helped by

        a. Italy.

        b. Germany.

    2. The government was supported by

        a. France.

        b. Russia.

  D. Italian and German aid finally proved more effective.

    1. In April 1937, the German air force bombed the town of Guernica.

        a. Europe's fear of mass bombing was enormously heightened.

        b. Pablo Picasso's "Guernica" became one of the great anti-war paintings.

    2. In 1939 Franco finally defeated the republic.

VIII. Neither France nor England would take action against Hitler.

  A. Hitler reoccupied the demilitarized Rhineland.

  B. He illegally annexed Austria.

  C. In September 1938, he demanded part of Czechoslovakia.

    1. It seemed that Europe was about to go to war again.

    2. British Prime Minister Neville Chamberlain negotiated a deal in which the Czechs surrendered their western borders, a vital part of their defenses.

    3. Chamberlain hoped that he had established peace in his time.

    4. War came the next year.

Key to the Images

Cheering masses: Program 47 shows crowds cheering as war was declared or as troops left for the front. The popularity of the war in its first days surprised leaders in every country. Many people believed that the international socialist movement would cripple any attempt to declare war, and that workers would refuse to fight their comrades from other countries. This opposition to war did not materialize, however. The war was popular at first partly because both sides expected victory within a few months.

Trench warfare: Notice that many of the battle scenes from World War I in Program 47 are hazy. This is not just the result of bad lighting. During a battle the smoke from artillery and small arms often reduced visibility to a few yards, and commanders directing hundreds of thousands of men had no clear idea of the shape a battle was taking. Radio was in use by this time but the walkie-talkie had not appeared, and advancing troops had to communicate with head-quarters by messengers. Troops who had settled into a fixed position could communicate over landlines, although these could be cut by artillery fire. Some of the largest battles in world history were directed with communications systems that at times were not much better than those of Alexander the Great.

Nazi pageantry: The Nazis were imagemakers. In Program 47 note the clips of their great processions, especially the opening sequence where torch-bearers are marching in the formation of a giant swastika. Leni Riefenstahl's film, *Triumph of the Will* is one of the most impressive pieces of this sort of German propaganda. The Nazis were continually trying to make public demonstrations of their unity, organization, and overwhelming strength. If we look closely, however, we can see that they were not always successful. One sequence shows the police force at the edge of the frame trying to beat back spectators who are jeering at a Nazi parade. Before coming to power, the Nazis often staged marches through hostile parts of cities, where the Communists and Socialists, their strongest opponents, were strong.

Focus Questions

1. How did the political map of Europe change after World War I? How great was the slaughter caused by the war?
2. What factors shaped the peace treaties at the end of the war?
3. How did Russia's defeat in World War I affect the Communist revolutionaries as they tried to form a new society?
4. What were the sources of Hitler's and Mussolini's power in their countries?
5. Why were France and England so slow, or so reluctant, to prepare for World War II?
6. What were the most prominent signs in the 1930s that another war was coming?

OVERVIEW
PROGRAM 48: THE SECOND WORLD WAR

The tactics and strategies of World War II were different from those of the First World War. The civilian population now became important targets on both sides of the war. Along with his plans for conquest, Hitler also carried out a policy of genocide against Jews and other groups he considered enemies of the Third Reich. By the end of the war social and political patterns had been destroyed all over Europe. A new arrangement of powers would have to be made.

I. Both militarily and politically, World War II followed a very different pattern from World War I.

    A. In August 1939, Hitler and Stalin signed a non-aggression pact.

        1. They divided up

            a. Poland.

            b. Other parts of Eastern Europe.

        2. Hitler could go to war in the West without fear of being attacked by the Soviet Union.

    B. On the military side, the attrition of trench warfare was avoided.

        1. There were long periods of relative inaction.

        2. At intervals, however, there were sharp thrusts of great power.

    C. Until the spring of 1940, the French and English sat tight, taking relatively little action.

        1. Hitler then launched a blitzkrieg attack through Belgium and northern France.

        2. He bypassed the French Maginot line.

        3. Paris fell within seven weeks and the French were knocked out of the war.

        4. The British army hastily evacuated from Dunkirk.

        5. In 1940 the Germans won the quick victory they had hoped for in 1914.

II. At the height of Hitler's power, however, Germany suffered a few setbacks.

    A. The British, led by Winston Churchill, resolved to go on fighting.

    B. In June 1940, Italy blundered into the war.

        1. Mussolini wanted to share the spoils of victory.

        2. Hitler had to divert troops to help his inept ally.

    C. Japan, Germany's ally in the Far East, was alarming the United States through its actions in

        1. China.

        2. Southeast Asia.

        3. The Pacific.

    D. Nevertheless, these need not have been fatal problems.

        1. By June 1941, the Germans had forced the British to the gates of Cairo.

        2. Hitler might have driven on to

            a. Oil-rich Persia.

            b. India.

III. In 1941, however, Hitler and his allies made a series of fatal decisions.

    A. In June 1941, Germany attacked Russia.

        1. Hitler wanted *lebensraum* in the East.

        2. He believed that a quick victory in the East would persuade the British to come to terms.

    B. At first the Germans won a series of great victories in Russia.

        1. The Soviet Union lost 2.5 million men in only four months.

    2. The German army reached the gates of
      1. Leningrad.
      2. Moscow.
  C. Finally, the Soviets held firm. Soon the German army was being worn down in a war of attrition.
  D. On December 7, 1941, the Japanese attacked Pearl Harbor and brought the United States into the war.
    1. The American economy turned to the war effort.
    2. Within a year, American military production equaled the combined output of
      a. Germany.
      b. Italy.
      c. Japan.

  IV. Nevertheless, the war lasted another three and a half years.
    A. The Allies won a series of victories in
      1. North Africa.
      2. Italy.
      3. Normandy on D-Day, June 6, 1944.
      4. The Battle of the Bulge.
    B. In May 1945, the Third Reich surrendered.
    C. In August 1945, after the dropping of two atom bombs, the Japanese surrendered as well.

  V. The air war was responsible for much of the devastation.
    A. For a long time after 1940 the British believed that one of the best ways to strike back was the indiscriminate bombing of German cities.
      1. The idea was to destroy German morale.
      2. Ultimately, six hundred thousand Germans died in the raids.
    B. The Germans carried out raids of their own.
    C. Both sides devastated great cities:
      1. London.
      2. Coventry.
      3. Lubeck.
      4. Hamburg.
      5. Dresden.
        a. In February 1945, British and American bombers attacked, on the insistence of the Russians.
        b. 135 thousand Germans died.
      6. Berlin.
    D. Both the Allies and the Axis had made deliberate targets of their enemies' civilian population.
      1. Civilian morale, however, did not collapse on either side.
      2. If anything, bombing stiffened civilian determination.

  VI. German genocide began once the war was underway.
    A. On the day Hitler invaded Poland, orders went out to exterminate
      1. The incurably ill.
      2. The chronically insane.

    B. The Germans killed seventy thousand of their own people.
        1. Intervention by the German churches brought this experiment to an end.
        2. The Germans, however, had learned much about genocide that they would soon put to use.
    C. Hitler had picked up some of his anti-Semitism from the example of Karl Lueger, a mayor of imperial Vienna.
        1. Lueger had given Vienna
          a. A fine transportation system.
          b. Better schools.
          c. Improved police.
          d. Higher employment.
        2. Lueger also had exploited hatred against the Jews.
    D. Anti-Semitism was more than a political tactic for Hitler.
        1. He believed that a nation's strength lay in its racial purity.
        2. He argued that Jews corrupted Germany spiritually and morally, as well as physically.
        3. According to him, Jews were responsible for
          a. The humiliating peace of World War I.
          b. Russian communism.
          c. The Great Depression.

  VII. Hitler decided to exterminate the Jews, as well as to persecute or destroy a long list of other enemies.
    A. In addition to the Jews, Hitler hated
        1. Slavs.
        2. People of color.
        3. Mixed races.
        4. Gypsies.
        5. Homosexuals.
        6. Jehovah's Witnesses.
        7. Communists.
        8. The mentally impaired.
    B. In 1942 mass gassing techniques were introduced.
        1. By 1945 the Germans had killed six million Jews.
        2. There were probably about eleven million victims of the Holocaust altogether.
    C. The Holocaust had been so central to Hitler's plans that he even diverted transport and supplies to the extermination camps at a time when the German army was suffering desperate shortages.

 VIII. The Germans also used great quantities of slave or forced labor.
    A. The Germans, under General Ludendorff, had forced four hundred thousand Belgians to work in German factories during World War II.
    B. By August 1944, 7.5 million foreigners were working in German industry, including
        1. Two million prisoners of war.
        2. Five million forced laborers from a dozen countries.

IX. After the end of the war, millions of people were displaced.
- A. There were huge transfers of populations in
  1. Russia.
  2. Eastern Europe.
  3. East and West Germany.
- B. Millions of other people lived in territories that were transferred from the sovereignty of one country to another.
- C. In earlier wars rulers had acquired or lost great numbers of subjects, but Professor Weber argues that the lives of most people did not change much under their new rulers.
- D. In the twentieth century, however, such transfers could lead to deeper changes in
  1. Language.
  2. Administration.
  3. The economic system.
- E. People could lose
  1. Personal liberty.
  2. Property.
  3. Life itself.

X. Europe was now divided into two spheres of influence:
- A. The Soviet Union.
- B. The Western Allies.

Key to the Images

Mobility: In several of the battle scenes in Program 48 we see tanks advancing in great numbers, supported by masses of infantry. This tactic was one of the key innovations that allowed World War II armies to break out of the stalemate that had characterized World War I.

Infantry and armor had to work together because tanks are vulnerable to attack from behind and infantry can be easily pinned down by machine-gun fire. Although the Germans first perfected these tactics, both sides soon made them standard practice.

Witnesses to genocide: If we look carefully at the films showing the liberation of concentration camps, we can note, at several points, lines of civilians, many of them women, dressed in ordinary street clothes. Since these people are obviously neither prisoners nor soldiers, what are they doing in places like Dachau? The answer is quite complex.

The allied armies who opened the camps had been horrified by what they found, but they were afraid that if they took photographs before burying the bodies, Germans would be able to claim that the evidence had been doctored for the sake of propaganda. To make certain that no one could make such claims, the allied forces took large numbers of German civilians from nearby towns and forced them to see what had gone on in the camps so close to their homes.

Propaganda as history: The Germans were masters of the propaganda film. To make the scenes we see in Program 48 of the conquest of Paris, the German army imported the best camerapeople and producers it could find. Many of the images are very strong, especially the ones of German troops marching through Arc de Triomphe or against the backdrop of the Eiffel Tower. Notice that the streets are deserted in many of the scenes. This was a problem that especially bothered the filmmakers because triumphal parades do not look impressive while marching past empty sidewalks. To make the films more imposing, the German army rounded up French civilians and forced them to watch the parade, if only for the sake of the camera.

Focus Questions

1. What were some of the unexpected developments that took place just before the outbreak of fighting in 1939? How did these developments affect the course of the war?
2. There were great international alliances on both sides of the conflict. How did these alliances help or hurt Hitler?
3. What were some of the ways in which war was waged directly against civilians?
4. In some sense, both Hitler and Stalin waged war against their own countrymen, even in the midst of the fighting. Why would they turn so much of their energy in this direction, when it would seem that their most immediate tasks were to fight the armies with which they were at war?
5. What were the most important ways in which the balance of power in Europe had shifted by 1945?

ASSIGNMENTS AND ACTIVITIES

IN CONTEXT

Themes and issues that set Unit Twenty-Four in context with other units include the following:

• Unit Twenty-Four concentrates on the ways in which Germany destroyed the peace of Europe. Remember that the German Empire, established in 1871, was the youngest of the great powers. Look for ways in which the German Empire tried to expand its influence both in Europe and in the colonial world.

- Throughout Central and Eastern Europe various subject peoples of the great empires were struggling to attain national sovereignty. Unit Twenty-Two on romanticism and nationalism traces the growth of European nationalism in the years after the Napoleonic wars. In later units look carefully at the fate of the national aspirations in the years after World War II.

- In many respects Hitler's racism was a reaction shared by many Germans, who felt surrounded by a hostile Europe. Look back to earlier units, especially those on the end of the nineteenth century. Why should so many Germans have felt isolated in the midst of a hostile continent?

- In many ways World Wars I and II created the world we live in today. In later units look for ways in which the balance of power in Europe was shaped by the victory of 1945.

- For the past forty years Europe has been dominated by two superpowers. At the same time Europe has been considerably more stable than in the years from 1900–1945. Examine earlier units for sources of instability in the earlier period. In later units look for signs of stability or weakness in the current balance of power.

Textbook Assignment

Read the following pages in your assigned textbook:

Text: *Western Civilizations* (Eleventh Edition, 1988)
Read: Chapter 28, "The First World War," pp. 923–952; Chapter 29, "The West Between the Wars," pp. 953–990; and Chapter 30, "The Second World War," pp. 991–1009.

Text: *The Western Experience* (Fifth Edition, 1991)
Read: From Chapter 26, "Imperialism and the Great War, 1870–1920," pp. 1071–1118; Chapter 28, "Totalitarianism Triumphant and World War II, 1924–1941," pp. 1160–1217; and from Chapter 29, "World War II and the Survival of Europe," pp. 1218–1249.

Text: *The Western Heritage* (Fourth Edition, 1991)
Read: From Chapter 26, "Imperialism, Alliances, and War," pp. 931–959; Chapter 27, "Political Experiments of the 1920s," pp. 961–991; Chapter 28, "Europe and the Depression of the 1930s," pp. 993–1023; and Chapter 29, "World War II," pp. 1027–1067.

Issues for Clarification

Fascism

Although the Fascist regimes shared many traits, especially their anti-communism, militarism, and extreme nationalism, remember that they also differed from one another on important points. Anti-Semitism was central to Nazism, for instance, but racism was not so important to Italian or Spanish fascism. Italy passed its anti-Semitic laws only under pressure from the Germans, and Franco's Spain actually allowed some Jewish refugees to pass through the country on their way to refuge.

Inflation

Keep in mind that Germany's inflation of the early 1920s had different effects on different classes of people. Members of unions, for instance, were able to make at least some attempt to bring their wages into line with the rate of inflation. People living on pensions and other sorts of fixed incomes were devastated. Some people actually benefited. All savings were wiped out but all indebtedness vanished as well.

Marxism-Leninism

Remember that Marx's most important work was an economic analysis of the causes that he believed would lead to the inevitable destruction of capitalism. Marx did believe that the working classes should organize themselves, but he had little to say about revolutionary parties or about the nature of the new Communist society. It was Lenin and the Bolsheviks who emphasized the need for a disciplined Communist party that would exercise a monopoly of power in the new society.

Glossary

Allies: The victors in World War I. The leading members were England, France, Belgium, the British Commonwealth, and the United States. Russia had also been a member of the alliance but made a separate peace with Germany early in 1918.

Allies (World War II): The powers allied against Japan and Nazi Germany. The leading members were Great Britain, the United States, the Soviet Union, and the Free French.

Auschwitz: The most notorious of Hitler's extermination camps, located in what is now Poland.

Axis: The alliance of powers led by Nazi Germany. The most important members were Germany, Italy, and Japan.

Central powers: The alliance in World War I led by Germany, Austria-Hungary, and Turkey.

Cheka: The first name given to the Soviet secret police.

Dresden: A major city in what is now East Germany. In February 1945, the British and Americans bombed it in a raid that was probably even more devastating than the raids on Hiroshima and Nagasaki.

Dunkirk: The port city in northern France from which the British army evacuated in the spring of 1940.

Genocide: A systematic attempt to annihilate an entire people. The word was first used to describe Hitler's attempt to exterminate the Jews.

Gestapo: The German secret state police under Hitler. Eventually, the leader of the Gestapo, Heinrich Himmler, came to control all of the German police organizations.

Nonaggression Pact: The pact signed by Germany and the Soviet Union in August 1939. The two countries divided up Poland between them and Hitler was assured that he could go to war without being attacked by Russia.

Versailles: Palace near Paris. Site of the conference that negotiated the terms for major peace settlements after World War I.

Timeline

Place each of the following events on the timeline. In some cases you may have a roughly defined period of time rather than a precise date.

1. Germany invades Russia in World War II.
2. Hitler achieves power in Germany.
3. Outbreak of Spanish Civil War.
4. Normandy Invasion.
5. Invasion of Poland.
6. First fighting of World War I.
7. Bolshevik Revolution.
8. Fall of France.
9. German-Soviet Nonaggression Pact.
10. Bombing of Pearl Harbor.

1900   1950

Map Exercise

Find the following locations on the map.

1. Serbia.
2. Austria-Hungary.
3. Germany.
4. Czechoslovakia.
5. Normandy.
6. Sicily.
7. Rhineland.
8. Poland.
9. Sudetenland.
10. Spain.

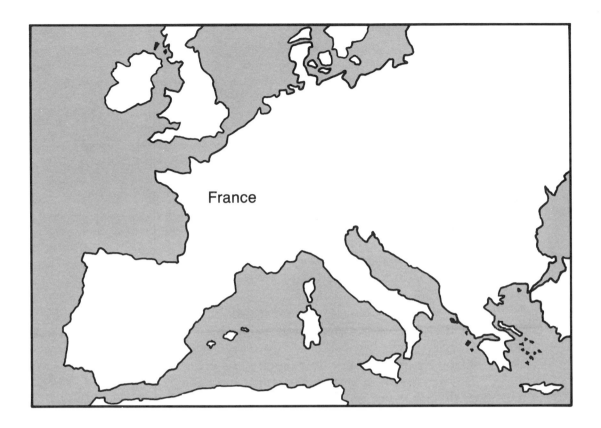

France

Self-Test

Part I

1. Which of the following countries fought on the side of the victors in World War I?
   a. Turkey.
   b. Italy.
   c. Germany.
   d. Spain.

2. Mark the false choice. In 1917 Lenin and the Bolshevik party were winning popular support by promising
   a. to take Russia out of World War I.
   b. to improve industrial conditions for the working classes.
   c. to honor Czarist war debts.
   d. to distribute land to the peasants.

3. Mark the correct completion. The League of Nations
   a. halted the Spanish Civil War.
   b. was able to halt Italian aggression in Ethiopia.
   c. was principally conceived by an American statesman.
   d. expelled Hitler's Germany.

4. In 1939 England and France went to war over Germany's invasion of
   a. The Rhineland.

   b. Czechoslovakia.
   c. Poland.
   d. Russia.

5. Mark the correct choice. Fighting did not begin on the Western front
   until the spring of 1940
   a. because Hitler's initial campaigns soon bogged down.
   b. because Germany had to go to the aid of its Italian ally.
   c. but England and France were still unprepared for Hitler's armor
      attack.
   d. so to give the Japanese time to attack the United States.

Part II

1. Mark the correct choice. In the early 1920s the savings of the German
   middle classes were wiped out by
   a. inflation.
   b. the abolition of private property in agriculture.
   c. a massive rearmament program.
   d. the burden of trying to regain Germany's lost territories.

2. Mark the correct choice. Once war had broken out in 1939, Hitler
   a. abandoned his plans for genocide so to concentrate on victory.
   b. gave orders for the extermination of the terminally ill and chroni-
      cally insane.
   c. kept his allies from entangling him in further conflicts.
   d. was careful to limit his war aims.

3. Mark the correct choice. Hitler's racial theories were
   a. largely the result of religious anti-Semitism.
   b. an attempt to protect the weaker members of his own race.
   c. aimed exclusively at the Jews.
   d. based on the idea that the weaker ought to be destroyed in the
      struggle for life.

4. Mark the correct choice. Germany was finally defeated by
   a. the overwhelming numbers of allied manpower and material.
   b. mutiny in the army and navy.
   c. internal revolution.
   d. the collapse of civilian morale.

5. Mark the false choice. Hitler enjoyed striking early successes in the
   a. counterattack against the allied invasion of Normandy.
   b. invasion of Russia.
   c. attack on France.
   d. invasion of Poland.

Optional Activities

Although the following activities are not required for the course unless assigned by the instructor, students are encouraged to use them as sources of interesting topics for further study.

Firsthand Accounts

One of the great advantages of studying this period of history is that we do not have to depend entirely on documentary sources. Each of us probably knows a number of people who lived through at least some of the events studied in this unit.

Conduct interviews, on tape if possible, in which you use your own knowledge of the period to ask questions that encourage your sources to describe their experiences as fully as possible. Instead of simply transcribing your tape, however, try to construct as clear a narrative as possible.

You might examine Studs Terkel's *The Good War* to find out more about the kinds of stories that you can construct from your interviews. If you interview members of your family, you may find yourself compiling a kind of family archive. If this assignment works well, consider doing more interviews about matters outside the scope of this unit.

Art History

Professor Weber writes, "the art of the time reflects the madness going around: absurd, discordant, sometimes incomprehensible."

Think about some of the different ways in which art can be a witness to history. Some artists clearly had a social purpose in mind. Others, however, denied that their work made any kind of straightforward comment. Even Picasso, who thought of himself as a socially committed artist, did not create works that lend themselves to any simple interpretation.

Here is a list of artists who in some sense might be considered witnesses of these times:

Pablo Picasso   Salvador Dali
Georg Grosz   Paul Klee
Max Beckmann   Egon Schiele
Fernand Leger   Oskar Kokoschka
Joan Miro   Arshile Gorki

This is a purposely varied list. If you find any of your favorite artists on it, look at some of their paintings from the period 1914–1945 and ask yourself if it makes sense to think of them as witnesses to their times.

Films

You may also wish to view some of the following films, which deal with matters discussed in this unit.

- *Grand Illusion,* directed by Jean Renoir, is about allied fliers taken prisoner by the Germans in World War I — one of the greatest movies ever made on the subject. Produced shortly before World War II, it also implies an enormous amount about its own time.
- *The Sorrow and the Pity,* directed by Marcel Ophuls, is a long investigation of the German occupation of France. Both its documentary footage and its extensive interviews make an important historical contribution to understanding this period.
- *Triumph of the Will,* directed by Leni Riefenstahl, is a propaganda film made for one of Hitler's great rallies. Try to decipher what kind of appeal the Nazis were trying to make through their propaganda.
- *Lacombe, Lucien,* directed by Louis Malle, tells the story of a French boy who collaborates with the Germans. A good complement to *The Sorrow and the Pity*.
- *Open City,* directed by Roberto Rossellini, was made in Italy almost immediately after the fighting ended. Although some of Italy's best actors appear in it, many early audiences looked at the movie almost as a documentary.
- *Berlin, Alexanderplatz,* directed by Rainer Werner Fassbinder, is a television series of Alfred Doblin's great novel.
- *Adolf Hitler: The Last Ten Days,* starring Alec Guiness, portrays Hitler at the end of World War II. Much of the film, however, contains his reminiscences of the period.

Review Questions

1. At first sight it appears that in 1919 the allies could have dictated any peace terms they wanted. Why didn't they create a lasting peace? How is their failure here related to their failure to take effective action against Hitler in the 1930s?
2. What contributions did the United States make to the allied victory in 1918? What were our principal contributions to the victory in 1945? Why then did the United States not play a more effective role in the 1930s?
3. The police state is not a twentieth-century invention, yet three of the new governments that rose to power between the wars — in Russia, Italy, and Germany — were police states of a kind that had never been seen before. Unit Twenty-Four emphasizes that each of these three governments was responding in different ways to the problems of severe losses in world war. But why should three such different countries choose to solve their problems in this way? Why should they all feel it necessary to destroy all internal opposition to their rule?
4. In some respects Hitler was hurt as much by his allies as by his enemies. Discuss some of the ways in which Hitler's allies may have hurt his chances of winning the war.

5. Although civilians suffered enormously during World War I, most military operations had been aimed primarily at military targets. In World War II, on the other hand, both sides made a systematic policy of attacking civilians. How can you explain this difference?

6. Compare and contrast Hitler's genocide to Stalin's displacement of millions of his own countrymen. Both leaders were responsible for the deliberate killing of huge numbers of people. What do these policies reveal about the similarities and differences of the two regimes?

7. At the end of his discussion of World War II, Professor Weber states that at the end of earlier wars a country's leader or flag might change but that most people's lives were relatively unaffected. In our times, however, a defeat in war can mean a change of economic and administrative practices, of lessons learned in school, of permissible behavior. Even a country's language may change. Drawing from your knowledge of the two wars, why do you think defeat in war carries such drastic consequences in the twentieth century?

Further Reading

Sources

Reed, John. *Ten Days that Shook the World.* An American journalist's account of the first days of the Russian Revolution.

Weber, Eugen. *The Western Tradition,* 2nd ed. (1965).
"War and Revolution," pp. 763–769.
"Russia," pp. 770–795.
"Mussolini and Italian Fascism," pp. 799–811.
"National Socialism," pp. 812–824.
"The Second World War," pp. 853–878.

Studies

Bullock, Alan. *Hitler: A Study in Tyranny.* (1971).

Dawidowicz, Lucy S. *The War Against the Jews, 1933–1945.* (1976).

Falls, Cyril B. *The Great War.* (1961). A clear military account.

Fay, Sidney B. *The Origins of the World War.* 2 vols. (1938).

Feis, Herbert. *Churchill, Roosevelt, Stalin: The War They Fought and the Peace They Sought.* (1957).

Smith, Denis Mack. *Mussolini's Roman Empire.* (1976).

Ulam, Adam B. *Lenin and the Bolsheviks.* (1969).

Answer Key

Timeline
1. 1941.
2. 1933.
3. 1936.
4. 1944.
5. 1939.
6. 1914.
7. 1917.
8. 1940.
9. 1939.
10. 1941.

Self-Test

Part I

1. (b) Italy.
2. (c) to honor Czarist war debts.
3. (c) was principally conceived by an American statesman.
4. (c) Poland.
5. (c) but England and France were still unprepared for Hitler's armor attack.

Part II

1. (a) inflation.
2. (b) gave orders for the extermination of the terminally ill and chronically insane.
3. (d) based on the idea that the weaker ought to be destroyed in the struggle for life.
4. (a) the overwhelming numbers of allied manpower and material.
5. (a) counterattack against the allied invasion of Normandy.

A promotion picture for American aid to Europe after World War II. A Greek
woman is wearing an apron made from a flour sack, which had been part of an
American relief shipment. (Courtesy of the Library of Congress.)

Program 49: The Cold War

Program 50: Europe and the Third World

LEARNING OBJECTIVES

After completing Unit Twenty-Five students should understand the following issues:

- The division of Europe into Soviet and Western spheres of influence. Your textbook discusses how the various countries of Eastern Europe became part of the Soviet sphere of influence.
- The ways in which Europe was affected by the changing relationship between the United States and the Soviet Union.
- The relationships among military, political, and economic power in Europe and the Third World. Use your textbook to supplement or rebut Professor Weber's arguments about the dependency of the Third World.
- The distribution of wealth between the Third World and the industrial nations. Use your textbook to determine how this distribution of wealth has changed since the Second World War.
- The legacy of colonial imperialism in the Third World.
- The success or failure of economic development in different parts of the Third World. Which parts of the Third World have made the most economic progress? Which have lagged the farthest behind?

─────────── *TV INSTRUCTION* ───────────

OVERVIEW
PROGRAM 49: THE COLD WAR

Since 1945 Europe has been dominated by two superpowers: the United States and the Soviet Union. Although numerous wars have been fought throughout the world, the superpowers have so far not confronted one another directly, probably deterred by the enormous destructive force of atomic weapons. Western Europe has known greater material prosperity than at any other time in history. Organizations like the Common Market have promoted a greater degree of economic interdependence.

I. After World War II, the Allies created a new international organization: the United Nations.
   A. The United Nations was supposed to balance the interests of the great powers against those of the weaker nations.
   B. It is meant to be an improvement on the League of Nations, which was discredited as an ineffectual talking shop.
      1. The United Nations has often suffered from this fault.
      2. Nevertheless, some of the talking may have prevented the spread of war.
      3. Part of the problem is that 159 different countries are represented.

II. Professor Weber argues that global war has been avoided through "the balance of terror."
   A. Both the United States and the Soviet Union possess nuclear weapons.
      1. The United States since 1945.
      2. The Soviet Union since 1949.
      3. The missile that launched the first Soviet satellite in 1957 could also be used to deliver atomic weapons.
   B. Both sides possess the means to annihilate one another.
      1. Nations that possess such weapons tend to treat one another with caution.
      2. Although there have been many wars since 1945, none of the atomic powers has gone to war with each other.

III. In 1945, however, this "balance of terror" had not yet been worked out.
   A. In the West many feared that the Soviet Union would continue its conquests into
      1. Central Europe.
      2. Western Europe.
      3. The Mediterranean area.
   B. By the end of 1945 the Soviet Union had already annexed
      1. Parts of Poland.

    2. Parts of Germany.

    3. Latvia.

    4. Lithuania.

    5. Estonia.

C. The Soviet Union had also set up a series of vassal states from Poland to the Balkans.

D. Professor Weber argues that the area outside Soviet control generally follows the borders of western Christendom.

E. After the war Germany became a main target for Soviet probes.

    1. The country was divided into

        a. An eastern zone dominated by the Soviet Union.

        b. A western zone combined from the areas of Germany occupied by France, Germany, and the United States.

    2. During 1948–1949 the Soviet Union tried to blockade access to sections of Berlin occupied by the Allies.

    3. A successful airlift, however, kept West Berlin supplied with food and other necessities.

IV. The continuing tensions between the United States and the Soviet Union became known as the Cold War.

A. In 1947 the United States began helping two countries that were under strong pressure from the Communists:

    1. Greece.

    2. Turkey.

B. In March 1947, President Truman enunciated the Truman Doctrine: "It must be the policy of the United States to support free peoples who are resisting attempted subjugation by armed minorities or by outside pressures."

C. The Truman Doctrine did not prevent a coup by Czech Communists in 1948.

D. To defend Western Europe, the North Atlantic Treaty Organization (NATO) was formed, consisting of

    1. Britain.

    2. France.

    3. Belgium.

    4. The Netherlands.

    5. Luxembourg.

V. The great confrontation between East and West took place in Korea, not in Europe.

A. In 1950 Russian-trained North Korean troops invaded South Korea.

B. The United States and UN troops fought to keep the South independent.

C. The Chinese Communists entered the war on the side of the North.

    1. General MacArthur advocated invading China.

    2. He was recalled from duty, however, perhaps in fear that a third world war would result.

        D. The war lasted until 1953.
           1. There were three million casualties.
           2. One hundred forty thousand casualties were Americans.
        E. As a result of the Korean War, the NATO Allies decided to rearm Germany. In 1955 Germany became a member of the alliance.

   VI. American planners believed that the Communists were most successful in areas of social and economic dislocation.
        A. In June 1947, U.S. Secretary of State George C. Marshall announced a new policy.
           1. The United States would help revive the western European economy.
           2. Further, the aid would not be distributed haphazardly but administered by Europeans themselves.
        B. By 1951 the European economy had regained prewar levels.
        C. The Soviets responded:
           1. The coup in Czechoslovakia in 1948.
           2. As West Germany was given increased responsibility, East Germany was also given sovereignty.

  VII. Europeans began to coordinate economic development.
        A. To restrain and control German economic development, the European Coal and Steel Community was formed, consisting of
           1. Belgium.
           2. Holland.
           3. Luxembourg.
           4. France.
           5. Germany.
        B. In 1957 the European Economic Community was formed to establish
           1. Common tariffs.
           2. Free movement of
              a. Capital.
              b. Labor.
              c. Goods.
           3. Common social and economic policies.
        C. By 1960 consumption, productivity, and the standard of living were double what they had been before World War II. Western Europe possessed
           1. Three percent of the world's land.
           2. Ten percent of its population.
           3. Twenty percent of its food.
           4. Twenty-five percent of its total output.
           5. Forty percent of world trade.
         D. Professor Weber argues that prosperity created stability in that most people now had something to lose in a war.

 VIII. Professor Weber argues that western Europeans preferred to leave much of the burden of their defense in the hands of the United States.

  A. This makes economic sense.

    1. Europeans could devote resources to investment instead of to defense.

    2. In the nineteenth century the American economy had grown so rapidly partly because the United States had only a small army and navy.

  B. Two of the world's great economic powers spent little on defense:

    1. West Germany.

    2. Japan.

  C. The United States was left with much of the military burden.

    1. The United States increasingly relied on atomic weapons.

    2. Conventional forces are much more expensive.

IX. Political systems have rapidly changed in both Eastern and Western Europe.

  A. The capitalist countries have adopted a number of socialist or social welfare policies:

    1. Nationalization of such industries as

      a. Railroads.

      b. Mines.

      c. Public transportation.

      d. Utilities.

      e. Banks.

      f. Insurance.

      g. Heavy industry.

      h. Radio and television.

    2. Economic planning to

      a. Redistribute wealth.

      b. Create social security.

  B. The Soviet world retains many features of the old dictatorial regimes that it claimed to replace:

    1. Police control.

    2. Intellectual control.

    3. Militarism.

    4. Nationalism.

Key to the Images

Marshall Plan: As we view the images of great shipments of food and supplies being shipped to Europe, we must be careful not to misunderstand the great triumph of the Marshall Plan. The United States did not simply pour wealth into the European economy. In fact, the United States had already supplied somewhat more aid than the Marshall Plan would finally provide.

The genius of the Marshall Plan was that European governments themselves played a major role in planning and distributing aid. In general, the aid usually went where it could do the most good.

Since that time American aid programs have often been less successful. Perhaps projects like the Marshall Plan work best with countries that already have an economic foundation on which to build. Developing countries may need different sorts of aid.

Berlin airlift: Even though the former German capital lay in the middle of the Russian zone of occupation, it was decided that Berlin itself would be occupied by all four Allies.

In July 1948, after disagreements over economic and currency reforms being made in the areas of Germany occupied by the Allies, the Soviet Union cut off all traffic to the city by roads and rail lines running through the eastern zone.

For more than a year, until the end of September 1949, the Allies supplied West Berlin entirely by air.

Conventional warfare: In several images in Program 49 we see tanks and other conventional weapons guarding the countries of Western Europe. Although the United States maintains a considerable presence in Europe, we must realize that the conventional forces of the Soviet Union and its Allies heavily outnumber the forces of NATO Allies. To avoid the huge cost of maintaining an army in Europe equal in strength to those of the Eastern bloc countries, the United States and its Allies depend on nuclear weapons to act as a deterrent against attack by conventional forces.

Focus Questions

1. In what ways have the United States and the Soviet Union created a balance of military forces between one another?
2. Which parts of Europe have become part of the Soviet or the Western spheres of influence?
3. What were the principles of American foreign policy that were established in the second half of the 1940s?
4. How did the United States perceive the connection between Soviet influence and economic unrest?
5. What were the most important stages in Europe's economic recovery?
6. What are some of the trade-offs between defense spending and economic growth?

OVERVIEW
PROGRAM 50: EUROPE AND THE THIRD WORLD

Since World War II the gap has widened between the living standards of the developed nations and those of the Third World. The western nations were able to develop slowly over the course of centuries; the developing countries now find themselves trying to catch up in a few decades. The rush to develop often makes Third World countries even more dependent on the technology and financial assistance of the West.

I. The European colonial empires transformed the societies they touched.
   A. In some places, western nations educated the leaders who eventually expelled them.
   B. As world markets grew more interdependent, industrialized nations became more likely to interfere in the affairs of weaker nations to ensure
      1. Markets in the colonies.
      2. Colonial products.

II. The need to modernize has led to many different political strategies.
   A. Many countries had to allow foreign meddling in their affairs so to acquire the capital and skills of the West:
      1. Turkey.
      2. China.
      3. Peru.
      4. Egypt.
   B. Some poor countries, however, were able to limit the influence of foreign investors:
      1. Algeria.
      2. Brazil.
   C. There were many ways to develop without surrendering control to foreigners:
      1. The Japanese adapted western skills to their own special needs.
      2. Some countries simply expropriated foreign capital:
         a. The Soviet Union.
         b. Mexico in the 1920s.
      3. Some countries assimilated capital by going bankrupt and not paying their debts.
      4. Communist China tried to develop with little foreign capital.
      5. Israel relies heavily on foreign capital, but has retained control of its own affairs.

III. Western practices and ideas have dissolved traditional ways of life in many places.
   A. The western notion of land as private property has broken up older forms of land tenure based on

        1. Tribes.
        2. Communities.
    B. As a result traditional societies are often broken up.
        1. Older methods of production disappear.
        2. Older forms of labor organization are replaced.
        3. Economic life is transformed with the introduction of
            a. Money wages.
            b. Open markets.
            c. Regular hours.
        4. Money replaces barter or subsistence.
        5. Exchange replaces self-sufficiency.
    C. The West went through these changes over the course of centuries. Developing countries try to do so in a few decades.
    D. Professor Weber argues that as people in the Third World suffered the insecurities of change, they often took refuge in
        1. Migration.
        2. Religions that provide an excuse for evading the modern world.
        3. Politics as a substitute for hope.

IV. Professor Weber argues that developing countries are living through an accelerated version of western history.
    A. Contract is replacing tradition.
    B. Individualism replaces loyalties to
        1. Family.
        2. Tribe.
    C. The uncertainties of democracy are replacing the stable hierarchies of status and birth.
    D. Technological developments are turning heaps of provinces into countries.
    E. Modern means have replaced older methods of exploitation and oppression.

V. The economic gap between rich and poor nations is widening.
    A. There is a huge disparity in longevity. In the mid-twentieth century life expectancy was
        1. 67 years in Canada.
        2. 70 years in Holland.
        3. 58 years in Japan.
        4. 44 years in Egypt.
        5. 32 years in India.
    B. The most advanced countries are advancing most rapidly. Europe and North America
        1. Possess less than 30 percent of the world's population.
        2. Produce 80 percent of the world's income.
    C. Other parts of the world suffer great economic disadvantages.
        1. Asia, Africa, and Latin America are also advancing but not nearly as fast.
        2. Most of the world's trade occurs between advanced nations.

3. Poorer countries no longer make as much money by selling raw materials.
   a. In 1964 Ghana produced more cocoa than in 1954 but earned only half as much money.
   b. The oil crisis has intensified the problems of the developing world.
D. Nonindustrial countries were once backward but self-sufficient. Now they are backward and heavily dependent on the rest of the world.
   1. Many developing countries are heavily dependent on a single product.
      a. Sugar accounts for 99 percent of Mauritius's exports.
      b. Tin accounts for 97 percent of Bolivia's exports.
      c. Liberia depends on rubber for 95 percent of its exports.
   2. Fluctuations on world commodities markets are disastrous for such countries.
   3. Caught between the demand for modern goods and insufficient supply, poor countries often suffer disastrous inflation.

VI. Modern medicine and sanitation have radically altered the economic structure of poor countries.
   A. Populations are growing much faster than production.
   B. The growth is often fastest in places that are least able to bear the burden.
      1. Asia has 50 percent of the world's population but only 11 percent of its revenues.
      2. In 1950 the population of Ceylon was growing at nearly six times the rate it had in 1900.
   C. It took all of human history for world population to reach five billion. That figure may double in the next forty years.

VII. Productivity is often lowest in countries that need it most.
   A. In terms of agricultural efficiency,
      1. An American farmer can feed forty-four people.
      2. A French farmer can feed twelve people.
      3. A farmer in a poor country is lucky if he can feed himself and one other person.
      4. One American cow gives as much milk as fifteen Indian cows.
      5. A rice paddy in Australia produces seven times as much rice as a paddy in Vietnam.
   B. The pattern is often self-defeating.
      1. When agriculture is inefficient, fewer resources can be invested for growth.
      2. When growth is low, the gap between resources and needs increases.
   C. However, there are signs of hope.
      1. Throughout the 1950s and 1960s Israel raised food production by 9 percent a year.

2. The area of cultivated land can be expanded.

3. Better diets might even cut down population growth in that protein-rich diets are believed to decrease fertility.

4. Japan has managed to decrease its birthrate to compensate for a lower death rate.

VIII. The industrialized countries have contributed great amounts in gifts and loans to developing countries.

A. Between 1950 and 1963, the Organization for Economic Development and Cooperation contributed $50 billion to developing countries.

B. Between 1970 and 1985, Africa received $60 billion.

C. Nevertheless, many developing countries are even poorer than before.

1. Africa now imports 20 percent of its food supply.

2. A huge proportion of resources goes to armaments rather than to development.

IX. Professor Weber argues that in the West many developments of the past one hundred years are now being reversed.

A. Literacy is seeping away in some areas.

B. Law and order are under increasing strain.

C. Cultural uniformity is declining.

1. Even linguistic unity is being challenged in

a. Belgium.

b. Canada.

c. Wales.

d. Catalonia.

e. Yugoslavia.

2. Cultural unity is declining in countries like the United States.

Key to the Images

Third World development: As we view the images in Program 50 of economic activity in the Third World, you may be struck by strange incongruities, such as tractors plowing fields being irrigated by methods hundreds or thousands of years old. This sort of uneven development often characterizes economies that are being forced to modernize at rates much greater than anything the West ever experienced.

In some places women are still spinning yarn by hand. These inefficient forms of production put Third World countries at a severe disadvantage. Handmade goods are usually too expensive to compete on the international market.

Armaments: Note that although the economies of the Third World are generally depressed, their weapons are surprisingly modern. Because resources that are spent on weapons cannot be used for investment, a top-heavy military establishment can retard economic growth. This is a problem in all parts of the world. When such costs, however, are imposed on economies that produce little or no surplus, the results are devastating.

Commodity prices: In Program 50 we see Third World countries exporting great quantities of local products. This is the way they earn the revenues needed to expand their economies and raise their standards of living.

Many Third World countries, however, are forced to concentrate most of their export production in only a few areas: cocoa, tin, and oil are only a few of the products on which Third World countries may depend for earnings.

When world commodity prices for such products are high, the country prospers. The problem, however, is that commodity prices may fluctuate greatly. When a country depends on only a few products for most of its export earnings, a drop in the price of only one commodity can be disastrous for the country's economy.

Focus Questions

1. What are the most important patterns of population growth in the developing world?
2. To what extent are the problems of the Third World a result of colonialism? To what extent do these problems result from more recent developments?
3. What are some of the principal economic relationships between the Third World and the industrialized nations?
4. What social, political, or economic obstacles have hindered economic growth in the Third World?
5. How have the economics of development disrupted traditional social patterns in the Third World?
6. In what ways have achievements of the nineteenth century been eroded in the West?

—————— ASSIGNMENTS AND ACTIVITIES——————

IN CONTEXT

Themes and issues that set Unit Twenty-Five in context with other units include the following:

• Ever since World War II the United States and the Soviet Union have dominated European politics. Look back to earlier units for other examples of rivalry on the continent: look at the wars between Spain and France in the sixteenth and seventeenth centuries, and at the competition between England and France in the eighteenth century.

• As we study in Unit Twenty-Five the problems of economic development in the Third World, look back to the units on the early years of the Industrial Revolution. For example, although England faced many of the same problems that now afflict the countries of the Third World, we must keep important differences in mind. During England's period of development, it was already the leading naval and commercial nation in the world. How do military and political weaknesses contribute to the economic problems of the Third World?

• Earlier units discuss nineteenth-century colonialism. The political traditions of many Third World countries have developed from that colonial legacy. Many countries of sub-Saharan Africa, for instance, are still strongly tied to France. Most of the former colonies of the British Empire are still strongly marked by British institutions and traditions.

• In Unit Twenty-Five Professor Weber discusses the enormous economic burden of defense spending. Look back to earlier units to find other examples of the high cost of warfare. In Unit Two of Semester I, on the transition from bronze to iron, Professor Weber argues that iron "democratized" warfare, in that iron weapons were less expensive to produce than weapons made of bronze. In Unit Ten of Semester I, on the Middle Ages, we learn how feudal relationships were affected by the high cost of providing knight-service. In later periods we learn that the use of gunpowder and firearms make warfare so expensive that military strength comes to depend on the ability to collect great sums in taxes.

Textbook Assignment

Read the following pages in your assigned textbook:

Text: *Western Civilizations* (Eleventh Edition, 1988)
Read: Chapter 31, "New Power Relationships," pp. 1015–1040.

Text: *The Western Experience* (Fifth Edition, 1991)
Read: From Chapter 29, "World War II and the Survival of Europe, 1941–1958," pp. 1249–1265; and from Chapter 30, "The Present in Historical Perspective," pp. 1266–1285.

Text: *The Western Heritage* (Fourth Edition, 1991)
Read: Chapter 30, "The Era of Cold War and Superpower Confrontation," pp. 1069–1109.

Issues for Clarification

Division Between Eastern and Western Europe

As Professor Weber points out, most of the Eastern bloc nations lie outside the boundaries of the old Roman Empire. Keep in mind, however, that nations like Czechoslovakia, Poland, and Hungary were converted to Christianity by Rome, not by Moscow or Constantinople. Czech and Polish writers such as Milan Kundera and Czeslaw Milosz have insisted that their countries have always been a part of Western European culture.

Nuclear Deterrence

The strategy of nuclear deterrence assumes that a nuclear war would cause such devastating destruction that no country could gain from launching a first strike. This theory of mutually assured destruction (MAD), however, requires an enormous buildup of weapons on both sides. It is not enough, for instance, for the United States to possess sufficient weapons to cripple the Soviet Union. For the strategy to work, the United States needs to have enough weapons to retaliate effectively, even if the Soviet Union were to launch a first strike that destroyed most of the American arsenal. The same assumptions hold true for any nuclear power. Each side needs to have so many weapons that it could retaliate even if the greater part of its arsenal had been destroyed.

Glossary

First strike: The initial attack in a nuclear exchange. Most strategists assume that a first strike would be launched against an enemy's nuclear arsenal.

Mutually Assured Destruction (MAD):   A fundamental principle in the strategy of nuclear deterrence.

Timeline

Place each of the following events on the timeline. In some cases you may have to specify a roughly defined period of time rather than a precise date.

1. The Soviet Union explodes its first atomic bomb.
2. Enunciation of the Truman Doctrine.
3. Bernard Baruch's Cold War speech.
4. The Soviet Union launches Sputnik.
5. Years of the Berlin Airlift.
6. Creation of the European Economic Community.
7. The United States explodes the first atomic bomb.
8. Communist coup in Czechoslovakia.

616-582-3989

250   **UNIT TWENTY-FIVE**

    9. Years of the Korean War.
  10. Launching of the Marshall Plan.

1940   1960

Map Exercise

Find the following locations on the map.

1–2. Two countries that were annexed by the Soviet Union.

3. Last country in Eastern Europe to lose its independence to the Soviet Union.

4–5. First two countries to receive aid under the Truman Doctrine.

6–7. Two European countries that were originally part of NATO.

8. Algeria.

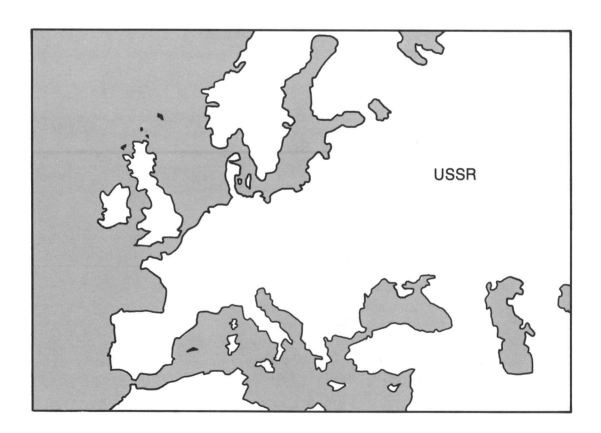

Self-Test

Part I

1. The European Coal and Steel Community, which included
   ___*Germany*___ and ___*France*___ (name two
   countries), was a forerunner of ___*European Economic Community*___, which established a common market in Western Europe.

2. Europe and North America account for ___*30*___ (percent) of the world's population but produce ___*80*___
   (percent) of its income.

3. Mark the false choice. Among the economic problems faced by developing nations,
   (a.) is that the greatest amount of trading takes place between industrial
       nations and developing nations.
   b. is that their economies are becoming increasingly dependent on
       world trade.
   c. is that many developing nations can export only small variety of
       goods.
   d. is that fluctuations on the world commodity markets can drastically
       reduce national income.

4. At the end of World War II, ___*Germany*___ and
   ___*Korea*___ were two countries divided between Commu-
   nist and non-Communist regimes.

5. Which of the following was *not* part of United States strategy to consol-
   idate or protect its power in Europe?
   a. The Marshall Plan.
   b. The Berlin Airlift.
   c. Guarantees of protection to Greece and Turkey.
   (d.) Guarantees of protection to Hungary and Czechoslovakia.

Part II

1. Mark the false choice. The Truman Doctrine
   a. pledged United States aid to countries resisting "subjugation by
       armed minorities or by outside pressures."
   (b.) developed plans for the economic recovery of Western Europe.
   c. was first formulated to deal with problems in Greece and Turkey.
   d. was a key element behind United States involvement in the Korean
       War.

2. Mark the false choice. To preserve their strength in Western Europe,
   the United States and its Allies
   (a.) have insisted that Germany remain unarmed.

b. have used their nuclear arsenal to counterbalance the superior conventional forces of the Soviet Union and its Allies.

c. have formulated plans for the economic recovery of Western Europe.

d. have created NATO.

3. According to Professor Weber, many of the achievements of the nineteenth century are now in serious danger. Which of the following is *not* one of the contemporary trends that Professor Weber sees in the Western World?

a. High rates of literacy are becoming difficult to maintain.

b. Minority cultures are vanishing.

c. Law and order are declining.

d. Standards of rational discourse are being challenged.

4. Population growth in the Third World

a. owes little to medicine and public health measures.

b. is slowest in the poorest countries.

c. is occurring at the same rates that Europe experienced in its most rapid periods of expansion.

d. has not been matched by a proportionate increase in agricultural productivity.

5. According to Professor Weber, the massive buildup of armaments after World War II

a. has been evenly distributed throughout the Western World.

b. has stimulated economic growth.

c. has created a balance of terror between the Soviet Union and the United States.

d. has left the NATO Allies and the Soviet bloc countries evenly balanced in both conventional and nuclear weapons.

Optional Activity

Although the following activity is not required for the course unless assigned by the instructor, students are encouraged to use it as a source of interesting topics for further study.

Eastern European Writing

Choose one of the following works:

Czeslaw Milosz, *The Captive Mind* (1953). Milosz writes of the different ways that Polish intellectuals accommodated themselves to the Communist domination of their country. The book was published only a few years after Milosz left Poland, where he had served in the diplomatic corps.

Kazimierz Brandys, *A Warsaw Diary: 1978–1981* (1983). Brandys's is a more recent account of Polish history, written during the rise of the Solidarity movement. It is particularly important in that Brandys not only chronicles events from day to day but also looks far back into Polish history for the roots of present-day troubles.

Write a paper of 3–5 pages in which you discuss one of the following questions on the basis of the book you have chosen.

- In what ways has it been possible or impossible to reform the governments of Communist Poland?
- To what extent do the troubles of Poland result from factors other than Soviet domination?
- What is the attitude of the author toward the West?

Review Questions

1. Although the Soviet Union and the United States have considered each other enemies since the late 1940s, the two countries have not gone to war. Among other reasons, Professor Weber argues that peace has been preserved through the balance of terror and through the fact that most people in Europe and North America would have little to gain by war. State your reasons for agreeing or disagreeing. In what ways have the United States and the Soviet Union strengthened themselves against one another? What have been some of the sharpest points of conflict? In your opinion, why did these incidents not develop into total war?

2. Which European countries were absorbed, completely or in part, by the Soviet Union? Which countries, although nominally retaining their independence, became part of the Soviet sphere of influence? Other countries in which there was a strong Soviet influence remained neutral or even became part of NATO. How would you outline the division between Soviet and Western spheres of influence? What factors forced countries into one sphere or the other?

3. What role did the Marshall Plan and the Truman Doctrine play in American foreign policy? What were the immediate circumstances that lay behind them? What were the long-range goals of each policy? What were some of the first steps that the United States took to carry them out? What have been the long-term results of these policies?

4. What were some of the most important ways in which the European economy reorganized itself after World War II? In what ways do Europe and North America exert economic influence over the rest of the world?

5. According to Professor Weber, to what extent is the burden of defense evenly shared by the Western Allies? Which country or countries have assumed the greatest expenses? How has the economic development of different countries been affected by the burden of defense?

6. What are some of the obstacles to economic progress in the Third World? Which obstacles are the result of relationships between the industrial powers and the developing countries? Which obstacles are the result of indigenous problems? Discuss two countries as examples.

7. What are some of the developing countries that have been able to attract foreign investors without losing control of their own economic policies? Discuss two countries. How have they been able to limit the influence of foreign economic powers?

8. Professor Weber argues that many nations in the Third World are living through an accelerated version of European history. State your reasons for agreeing or disagreeing. Discuss this issue with reference to two countries.

Further Reading

Sources

Kennan, George F. *Memoirs, 1925–1950*. (1967).   Kennan is one of the most important shapers of American foreign policy toward the Soviet Union.

Weber, Eugen. *The Western Tradition*, 2nd ed. (1965). "Another Postwar World," pp. 880–901.

Studies

Dyson, Freeman. *Weapons and Hope*. (1985).   Discusses the history of the arms race between the United States and the Soviet Union.

Emerson, R. *From Empire to Nation: The Rise to Self-Assertion of African and Asian Peoples*. (1960).   A good study of decolonization.

Fanon, Frantz. *The Wretched of the Earth*. (1968).   A social and psychological study of European dominance in the Third World.

Fejto, François. *A History of the People's Democracies: Eastern Europe Since Stalin*. (1971).

Laqueur, Walter. *Europe Since Hitler*, rev. ed. (1982).   One of the best general surveys.

Myrdal, Gunnar. *Asian Drama: An Inquiry into the Poverty of Nations*. 3 vols. (1968).   A classic study that can be studied in sections.

Postan, M. M. *An Economic History of Western Europe, 1945–1964*. (1967).

Ulam, Adam B. *The Rivals: America and Russia Since World War II*. (1972).

Answer Key

Timeline
1. 1949.
2. 1947.
3. 1947.

4. 1957.
5. 1948–1949.
6. 1957.
7. 1945.
8. 1948.
9. 1950–1953.
10. 1947.

Map Exercise

1–2. Latvia, Lithuania, and Estonia were completely annexed. The Soviet Union also annexed large sections of Finland, Poland, Germany, and Romania.
   3. Czechoslovakia.
4–5. Turkey and Greece.
6–7. Britain, France, Belgium, the Netherlands, and Luxembourg are mentioned in the lectures.

Self-Test

Part I

1. Belgium, Holland, Luxembourg, Germany, and France were all members of the European Coal and Steel Community. The answer to the last section is the European Economic Community.
2. Less than 30 percent; 80 percent
3. (a) is that the greatest amount of trading takes place between industrial nations and developing nations.
4. Germany; Korea
5. (d) Guarantees of protection to Hungary and Czechoslovakia.

Part II

1. (b) developed plans for the economic recovery of Western Europe.
2. (a) have insisted that Germany remain unarmed.
3. (b) Minority cultures are vanishing.
4. (d) has not been matched by a proportionate increase in agricultural productivity.
5. (c) has created a balance of terror between the Soviet Union and the United States.

Louis Bleriot's Flight Across the English Channel as Seen from a Ship Bleriot, who had no navigational gear, found his way to England by following the ships that sailed from France to Dover. In this picture he has almost reached the white cliffs on the English coast. (Courtesy of the Library of Congress.)

UNIT TWENTY-SIX

Program 51: The Technological Revolution

Program 52: Toward the Future

LEARNING OBJECTIVES

After completing Unit Twenty-Six students should understand the following issues:

- The most important developments in medicine during this period. Your textbook supplements Professor Weber's discussion by providing examples of other medical advances.
- The development of atomic weapons. Use your textbook to determine how and why weapons research increased during World War II and the Cold War.
- The interplay of inventions in transportation and communications.
- Improvements in the quality of daily life. Use your textbook to understand how these improvements are related to larger social and scientific issues.
- Progress and setbacks in the emancipation of women. Use your textbook to compare the status of women in various parts of Europe and North America.

TV INSTRUCTION

OVERVIEW
PROGRAM 51: THE TECHNOLOGICAL REVOLUTION

As a result of technology, the quality of daily life has probably changed more rapidly in the twentieth century than in any earlier period. The airplane, automobile, and radio have transformed the grand patterns of life. Other developments, such as modern stoves, dishwashers, and vacuum cleaners, have transformed domestic routines.

I. The airplane was invented within living memory by the Wright brothers in 1903.
   A. The balloon had been invented in the eighteenth century but had remained largely a curiosity.
   B. The airplane, however, immediately underwent rapid development.
      1. In 1908 Louis Bleriot flew across the English Channel.
      2. In 1909 airplanes were used to take photographs of military installations at Mourmelon in France.
      3. In 1911 the Italians used airplanes against the Turks to scout out positions and drop handheld bombs.
      4. Within a few years British units were being supplied with antiaircraft guns.

II. After World War I airplanes became widely used for commercial purposes.
   A. Former war pilots began to carry
      1. Passengers.
      2. Mail.
   B. By the 1930s regular routes had been set up around the world for
      1. Passengers.
      2. Freight.
   C. After World War II air travel ceased to be the prerogative of the wealthy.
      1. In 1952 BOAC introduced passenger planes powered by jet engines, which had originally been designed for
         a. Fighter planes.
         b. The German V–1, or vengeance plane.
      2. By the 1960s wide-bodied jets could carry hundreds of passengers.
      3. In 1976 the British and French Concorde carried passengers across the Atlantic in less than three hours.

III. The bicycle also revolutionized transportation.
   A. In 1889 the unwieldy velocipede was transformed into the bicycle, a result of the invention of the rubber tire by
      1. John Boyd Dunlop.
      2. The Michelin brothers.

B. There was now an alternative to the costly horse.
C. Women welcomed the bicycle as a liberator from
  1. Voluminous skirts.
  2. Corsets.
  3. Chaperones.
D. By 1900 bicycles were becoming less expensive. Within a few decades, even people of modest means could afford them.

IV. By the turn of the century automobiles and other forms of motorized transport were appearing.
  A. The technology used in making automobiles was similar to that used for
    1. Bicycles.
    2. Airplanes.
  B. In Europe low-priced cars for the middle classes did not appear until the 1930s.
    1. In France, Andre Citroen adopted Henry Ford's assembly-line methods.
    2. In 1938, Ferdinand Porsche introduced the German "people's car," or Volkswagen.
    3. After World War II other cars appeared that most people could afford:
      a. The Morris Minor.
      b. The Citroen 2CV.
  C. Automobile ownership varied widely in degree throughout the world.
    1. By 1960 there was one private car for every thirty-one people in the world.
    2. In the United States: one car for every three people.
    3. In Europe: one car for every twenty-two people.
    4. By 1983 three out of four families owned a car in France.
  D. Some of the early freeways were built in Fascist countries:
    1. Germany.
    2. Italy.

V. Some of the most familiar features of daily life are no older than the century.
  A. The inexpensive box camera appeared in 1900.
  B. Vacuum cleaners were available in 1901.
  C. Gramophone records also appeared in 1901, and by 1913 Decca was selling a portable gramophone.
  D. One of the most sweeping inventions of the time was the radio.
    1. In 1901 the Italian Guglielmo Marconi sent the first wireless message across the Atlantic.
    2. In 1920 Marconi opened the first British broadcast station near Chelmsford, Essex.
    3. Radio became a political tool exploited by
      a. Franklin Roosevelt.
      b. Stanley Baldwin.

        c. Winston Churchill.

        d. Hitler.

    E. In 1926 television first appeared.

VI. The world seemed to become a smaller place.

    A. In the fourteenth century the Black Plague had taken many months to spread throughout Europe.

    B. In 1918 the influenza epidemic spread within a few weeks.

    C. Mass communications can create a vague sense of doom in that people can be immediately informed of disasters occurring anywhere in the world.

    D. Professor Weber argues that mass communications are important not only for their explicit message but for the sense of possibilities and other ways of life they create.

    E. Advertising created a whole new set of aspirations.

        1. The advertising boom had begun in the nineteenth century with

            a. Posters.

            b. Displays.

        2. Technology soon turned to advertising.

            a. In 1910 the first neon tube was demonstrated in Paris.

            b. In 1912, two years later, the first neon advertisements appeared, promoting Cinzano.

VII. Many of the greatest changes affected ordinary, daily life.

    A. Until after World War I, the following were considered exceptional luxuries.

        1. Sidewalks.

        2. Sewers.

        3. Streetlights.

        4. Paving.

        5. Bathrooms.

        6. Toilets.

        7. Hot and cold running water.

        8. Gas and electric ranges.

    B. Bakelite was invented in Belgium in 1907, but plastic objects did not become common until the 1930s and 1940s.

    C. It was a long time before many domestic conveniences became common in Europe.

        1. The first electric refrigerator for the home went on sale in Chicago in 1913.

        2. Many European homes still lacked them well into the 1950s and 1960s.

    D. Labor-saving devices were especially important.

        1. Detergents were first produced in 1917.

        2. Instant and dehydrated foods appeared (Nescafe came on the market in 1938).

        3. New fibers were simpler to wash and press.

VIII. Many of these developments lightened the drudgery of household

work, made clothing more comfortable, and made birth control possible.
  A. Women's clothing became more convenient and comfortable.
    1. In 1905 elastic rubber replaced whalebone and lacing in foundation garments.
    2. Bras shortened the corset in 1914.
    3. Skirts were of lightweight fabric and hemlines rose in 1917.
    4. In 1915 lipstick became available in metal cartridges.
    5. Artificial silk appeared in 1910.
    6. Nylon stockings appeared in 1939.
  B. In 1956 the first oral contraceptive was marketed.

Key to the Images

Technological integration: As we view the images in Program 51 of aviation, we should remember that the airplane, beginning with the most primitive models that appear in the program, is only eighty-five years old. The airplane has seen remarkably rapid growth, especially when compared to the development of the balloon, which was invented in the eighteenth century but remained no more than a curiosity throughout the nineteenth century.

Part of the reason for the rapid development of the airplane is the convergence and integration of technologies. Without the internal combustion engine, developed in the last half of the nineteenth century, the airplane would never have progressed beyond the glider stage.

Labor-saving devices: As we view the images of early washing machines, vacuum cleaners, and other labor-saving devices, it is easy to underestimate how much they have changed modern society. Professor Weber emphasizes their role in freeing homemakers from some of the burden of household work, as well as their effect on class structure.

Today only the well-to-do can usually afford to employ full-time domestics. Up until quite recently, however, even people of the lower middle classes hired domestics. The burden of household work was often too great for one homemaker, especially if there were no children at home to help.

The domestics, many of them immigrants, were paid low wages, sometimes no more than room and board and a small amount of spending money.

Affordable automobiles: In the United States, Henry Ford pioneered the production of affordable automobiles. Ford did not invent the assembly-line or the use of interchangeable parts, but he applied these techniques to make the automobile more than a luxury for the well-to-do.

As we view Program 51's images of automobiles from the first half of the twentieth century, we should try to determine the kinds of people likely to buy them. Are the images of luxury cars or of cars for the mass market?

In Europe mass production of automobiles did not begin until the 1930s, and was then interrupted by World War II. As you view Program 51, try to determine at what time the automobile began to transform the economy as well as the landscape.

Focus Questions

1. What were the most important inventions in communications and transportation during the early twentieth century?
2. What inventions or new forms of technology were important for the development of the airplane and the automobile?
3. What were the principal stages in the development of aviation?
4. How did the inventions of the twentieth century create "a revolution of aspirations"?
5. What were some of the improvements in the quality of daily life made during this period?
6. How did the inventions of the twentieth century aid or hinder the emancipation of women?

OVERVIEW
PROGRAM 52: TOWARD THE FUTURE

Modern medicine has conquered diseases that once killed millions. At the same time, atomic energy has raised the specter of complete annihilation. Discoveries in physics have altered the most elementary assumptions about matter, energy, and time.

I. Many of the most important discoveries of the twentieth century have been made in medicine and the related sciences.
   A. In 1901 the first Nobel Prizes were awarded.
      1. Wilhelm Roentgen received the Nobel Prize in physics for his work on X-rays.
      2. Emil von Behring was awarded the Nobel Prize in medicine for his work on diphtheria.
   B. Modern medicine has conquered such fatal diseases as:
      1. Tuberculosis.
      2. Smallpox.
         a. Two hundred years ago 90 percent of all Europeans contracted smallpox.
         b. Fifteen percent died.
         c. Most of the survivors were badly scarred.

    3. Cholera.
    4. Whooping cough.
    5. Diphtheria.
    6. Polio, since 1954.
C. Modern diseases tend to be those associated with stress and longer life expectancy:
    1. Cancer.
    2. Heart disease.
D. Even after the mechanisms of disease were discovered, it was often difficult to wipe out the causes.
    1. In 1909 it was discovered that lice transmitted cholera to human beings.
    2. Nevertheless, during World War I more Serbian soldiers died of cholera than of wounds.
    3. Between 1917 and 1921, cholera struck twenty-five million people in the Soviet Union, of whom three million died.
E. Nevertheless, the death rate declined rapidly because of
    1. Better access to medical care.
    2. Development of new or improved
        a. Drugs.
        b. Serums.
        c. Antibiotics.
F. Because people were living longer as a result of advances in medicine, the population rapidly increased.
    1. In some places agricultural productivity could partly compensate for increased population, a result of synthetic nitrogen fertilizers developed in Germany in 1910.
    2. Poorer countries were hit hardest by population growth.

II. The development of atomic power proceeded rapidly through the first half of the twentieth century.
A. By 1911 the instability of the atom in radioactive substances had been discovered by
    1. The Curies in France.
    2. Rutherford in England.
B. Important discoveries in quantum mechanics were made in
    1. Germany.
    2. Denmark.
    3. Switzerland.
    4. Italy.
C. Albert Einstein was among the greatest scientists involved in the new physics.
    1. In 1905 his theory of special relativity suggested that neither time nor space was absolute.
    2. By 1915 his general theory of relativity presented matter itself as only one form of energy.
D. Scientists soon realized that matter could be converted into energy by bombarding atoms with smaller, subatomic particles.

1. In 1932 the first cyclotron was built to accelerate this bombardment.
2. It was discovered that, in certain elements such as uranium, this disintegration sets off a chain reaction, emitting great amounts of energy that could be
   a. Harnessed in a nuclear reactor.
   b. Used to make a nuclear bomb.
3. On August 6, 1945, the first atomic bomb used in warfare was dropped on the Japanese city of Hiroshima.

III. The deciphering of the DNA molecule has revolutionized biology and medicine.
   A. In 1953, at Cambridge University in England, Francis Crick and James Watson discovered the molecule's double-helix configuration.
      1. DNA acts as a kind of biological computer that instructs cells to make certain proteins.
      2. It therefore controls the structure and function of all living things.
   B. By 1972 scientists had learned to split and recombine DNA for new purposes.

IV. Professor Weber argues that many of the greatest scientific achievements of the twentieth century have undermined our confidence in ourselves and in our most basic ideas about the world.
   A. The Danish physicist Niels Bohr commented that human beings now know that they do not live at the center of the universe.
   B. The French philosopher Jean-Paul Sartre tried to formulate a way out of this dilemma.
      1. The world no longer gives people sure norms or faith.
      2. Therefore people must choose between
         a. Despair.
         b. The decision to create one's own destiny.
      3. Although Sartre's philosophy, known as existentialism, is no longer as highly regarded as it once was, it does stress the necessity of making choices in the midst of uncertainty.

V. Computers have revolutionized the processing of information.
   A. During World War II, the British built the first computer to break enemy codes.
   B. The first civilian computer was unveiled in the United States in 1946.
      1. It weighed thirty tons.
      2. It contained eighteen thousand vacuum tubes.
      3. Today an inexpensive home computer can outperform machines that cost $500 thousand twenty years ago.

VI. The Western Tradition is actually made of many traditions.
   A. Throughout its history, the Western Tradition has contrasted such issues as:
      1. Authoritarianism and individualism.

2. Personal initiative and centralization.
3. Obedience and revolt.
4. Faith and skepticism.
5. Inertia and enterprise.
6. Conflict and reconciliation.
B. Professor Weber argues that perhaps the two most important drives in western history have been
1. Curiosity.
2. Ambition.
C. The Western Tradition has been a kind of *yellow pages* of human behavior.

Key to the Images

Inoculations: In Program 52 we view several scenes of people in Third World countries, lining up to receive inoculations. Part of the reason for explosive population growth in the Third World is that modern medicine makes it possible for people to live far longer than in earlier times.

As we view these scenes, we should realize that medicine involves more than the analysis of disease. One of the triumphs of modern medicine has been to find cheap methods of prevention, such as inoculation, which can be made available to millions of people.

Antibiotics like penicillin have saved millions of lives from infection. Insulin has lengthened the lives of people who suffer from diabetes. Penicillin and insulin would have done little good, however, if they had remained enormously expensive to produce.

Public health: In Program 52's images of the Third World, look for signs of public health measures. For instance, we see people spraying stagnant water to kill mosquitoes that spread such diseases as malaria. One of the greatest public health measures is a supply of clean water. Public sewers are equally important in that many diseases can be spread by human waste.

Focus Questions

1. What are some of the most important discoveries in medicine made during the twentieth century?
2. What diseases has modern medicine eliminated or at least greatly curbed?
3. What diseases or disorders have been especially resistant to modern medicine?
4. How has research on the structure of DNA contributed to modern medicine and biology?
5. What were the principal stages in the development of atomic energy and atomic weapons?

ASSIGNMENTS AND ACTIVITIES

IN CONTEXT

Themes and issues that set Unit Twenty-Six in context with other units include the following:

- The first atomic weapons were used only at the end of World War II. Look back to earlier units for other dramatic leaps in the technology of warfare. Gunpowder, for instance, was developed in China in the thirteenth century but was not widely used in Europe until the fifteenth century. Dynamite was not invented until the nineteenth century. Keep in mind that our most terrifying weapons were developed within our own time.

- In Unit Twenty-Six Professor Weber discusses the advances made by twentieth-century medicine. Look back to earlier units — especially those on the Middle Ages — to determine the degree of devastation caused by infectious diseases. In the units on the nineteenth century, we learn that public health measures, especially in the great cities, saved many lives even before the diseases themselves were understood.

- Less than a hundred years have passed since the flight of the first airplane. The first atomic bomb was exploded less than fifty years ago. To understand such rapid developments in science and technology, look back to the units on the twentieth century, especially those on World Wars I and II. Your textbook explains further how these technologies advanced under the pressure of military necessity.

- In Unit Twenty-Six, Professor Weber discusses many material improvements in the quality of daily life. Look back to earlier units for examples of other periods that witnessed such improvements. In the Dark Ages, for instance, Europeans learned to harness draft animals more effectively and to build various kinds of mills (Semester I). Similarly, many of the developments discussed in Unit Twenty-Six are continuations of trends that began during the Industrial Revolution.

Textbook Assignment

Read the following pages in your assigned textbook:

Text: *Western Civilizations* (Eleventh Edition, 1988)
Read: Chapter 32, "Problems of World Civilization," pp. 1041–1068.

Text: *The Western Experience* (Fifth Edition, 1991)
Read: Chapter 30, "The Present in Historical Perspective," pp. 1266–1331.

Text: *The Western Heritage* (Fourth Edition, 1991)
Read: Chapter 31, "Toward a New Europe," pp. 1111–1157.

Issue for Clarification

Modern Medicine

Well into the nineteenth century, most doctors believed that diseases were caused by imbalances in the body's fluids, or "humours." To restore proper balance, doctors induced vomiting, administered purges, or drew blood, sometimes more than a pint at a time. These techniques killed many more patients than they cured.

In the second quarter of the nineteenth century, a series of experiments tested the techniques of traditional medicine. Groups of people with the same disease were divided into two groups. One group received the traditional treatment of purges, vomiting, and bleeding. The second group received no treatment at all, although the patients were made as comfortable as possible.

The results were appalling. People in the groups that received no treatment were more likely to recover than those who received the standard course of treatment. Up until this time, most doctors had believed that persons suffering from a disease would inevitably die of the disease unless treated by a doctor. However, it now became clear that the human body could cure itself.

Much of the most valuable medical research of the nineteenth century concentrated on tracing the symptoms and development of various diseases. Until Pasteur's work on microorganisms, however, little was known about the causes or transmission of disease.

It was known that many diseases were spread by contaminated food and water, even before the precise agents of transmission were discovered, and great progress was made in public health throughout the nineteenth century. Further, doctors learned the value of sterilization. Infection, one of the most important causes of infant mortality and death in childbirth, could now be combated.

Only in the 1920s, however, was progress made in the development of antibiotics. As a result of these drugs, many diseases have almost vanished in the West, although they are still deadly in parts of the world where medical care is insufficient.

As we look back at the history of disease in earlier units, remember that many of the greatest discoveries in medicine were made within our own time. Throughout much of human history, medical care was often more dangerous than the disease itself.

Glossary

Antibiotics: Drugs that stop or destroy the growth of bacteria. Penicillin and sulfa drugs were among the earliest antibiotics.

Cholera: A group name for a number of intestinal diseases. Some forms are spread by contaminated food.

Detergents: Detergents were originally introduced by the Germans during World War I as a substitute for soap.

Influenza: An acute, contagious disease caused by viruses. The influenza epidemic of 1918–1919 claimed more lives than did World War I.

Smallpox: An acute, infectious disease. Smallpox once attacked the majority of Europeans. It was one of the first diseases for which an effective inoculation was developed.

Typhus: An acute, infectious disease spread by fleas and lice.

Velocipede: A forerunner of the bicycle.

Timeline

Place each of the following events on the timeline. In some cases you may have to specify a roughly defined period of time rather than a precise date.

1. First airplane flight across the English Channel.
2. First use of airplanes in war.
3. First transatlantic radio communication.
4. First marketing of birth-control pills.
5. First airplane flight.
6. Discovery of the double-helix structure of DNA.
7. First marketing of inexpensive box cameras.
8. First widely used polio vaccine.
9. Dates of the great Russian typhus epidemic.
10. Einstein formulates his theory of special relativity.

1900   1956

Map Exercise

Find the following locations on the map.

1. First country to use the airplane in war.
2. Country in which the Curies did most of their research.
3. Homeland of Jean-Paul Sartre.
4. First country to introduce passenger jet service.
5. Site of Watson and Crick's research on DNA.
6. Homeland of Niels Bohr.
7. Country to build the first electronic computer.

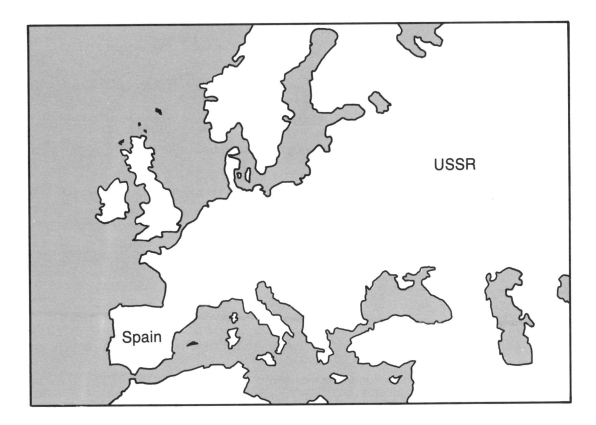

Self-Test

Part I

1. Mark the false choice. In the history of aviation
   a. the Wright brothers made their first airplane flight in 1903.
   b. the first flight across the English Channel was made in 1909.
   c. the Germans made the first military use of airplanes.
   d. passenger and freight services had been established around the world by the 1930s.

2. Mark the false choice. Each of the following men pioneered the production of low-priced cars in his country.
   a. Henry Ford in the United States.
   b. Andre Citroen in France.
   c. Ferdinand Porsche in Germany.
   d. William Morris in England.

3. Guglielmo Marconi was responsible for all but one of the following achievements.
   a. the invention of the phonograph.
   b. the invention of the wireless telegraph.
   c. the transmission of the first wireless signal across the Atlantic.
   d. the establishment of the first British broadcasting station.

4. Mark the correct choice.
   a. By the mid-1950s an effective vaccine had been developed against polio.
   b. Typhus was quickly controlled as soon as researchers discovered that the disease was transmitted by lice.
   c. The first inoculations against smallpox were administered shortly after World War I.
   d. effective vaccines prevented the spread of influenza during and after World War I.

5. All but one of the following made important contributions toward the unleashing of atomic energy.
   a. Einstein.
   b. The Curies.
   c. Rutherford.
   d. Watson and Crick.

Part II

1. Mark the false choice. The twentieth century has seen great progress in the control of disease
   a. through improved sanitation.
   b. because health care is available to greater numbers of people.
   c. through the development of antibiotics.
   d. through improved transportation, which can halt the spread of disease.

2. All but one of the following politicians used the radio as an effective political tool.
   a. Woodrow Wilson.
   b. Hitler.
   c. Roosevelt.
   d. Churchill.

3. According to Professor Weber, all but one of the following were considered exceptional luxuries in Western Europe until after World War I.
   a. Bathrooms and water closets.
   b. Regular postal service.
   c. Gas and electric ranges.
   d. Streetlights and paving.

4. According to Professor Weber, all but one of the following are important signs of the emancipation of women in the twentieth century.
   a. Birth control devices, which allow women to plan pregnancies.
   b. Labor-saving devices, which have eliminated much household drudgery.
   c. The fact that women now earn as much per capita as men.
   d. The fact that women have the vote throughout Europe.

5. According to Professor Weber, all but one of the following develop-

ments have created anxieties among the general public about the dangers of scientific investigation.

a. The dropping of the atomic bomb.
b. The use of sulfa drugs.
c. The discovery of the double-helix configuration of DNA.
d. Techniques for splitting and recombining DNA.

Optional Activity

Although the following activity is not required for the course unless assigned by the instructor, students are encouraged to use it as a source of interesting topics for further study.

The Twentieth Century Novel

Novels are especially good at portraying change. Many of the greatest novels of the twentieth century concern the passing away of a world and the creation of another. For this assignment, read one of the following novels:

- Max Frisch, *Sketchbook, 1966 – 1971* is a fascinating blend of fiction and reportage.
- Lars Gustafsson, *Funeral Music for Freemasons,* is written by one of Sweden's best novelists and poets. The book traces the connections of the lives of a poet, a singer, and a nuclear physicist from the 1950s to the 1980s.
- John Dos Passos, *The 42nd Parallel* is the first novel in the *U.S.A.* trilogy on life in the United States during the years before and after World War I.
- William Carlos Williams, *White Mule* is the first volume of a trilogy in which Williams treats the costs of success in America.

Write a paper of 3 – 5 pages in which you discuss one of the following issues. Confine your discussion to one short section of the novel you've chosen.

- All of these works are likely to seem fragmented to you. Why has the author chosen to tell the story in this manner? How does the subject matter lend itself to this type of treatment?
- What is the greatest source of fear or danger in the novel? Do the characters understand their situation or do they act blindly? What do these issues reveal about the world the author describes?

Review Questions

1. The balloon was invented in the 1780s, but for the most part remained not much more than a curiosity. The airplane, on the other hand, reached its present stage of development in less than a hundred years.

What were the most important stages in the history of aviation? Why did the technology of aviation develop so rapidly?

2. What were the most important discoveries in medicine during the twentieth century? What were the key discoveries in the treatment of infectious diseases? Why have cancer and heart diseases been more resistant to treatment?

3. What were the most important developments in mass communications? How was radio exploited by various politicians during this period? In what ways was the impact of radio different from that of the popular press?

4. Discuss the greatest developments in the technology of warfare during the twentieth century. Some historians have argued that the discoveries discussed in Unit Twenty-Six are really the results of war. The development of atomic energy seems to be an obvious example, as does the progress of aviation. Even the development of antibiotics was greatly spurred by the needs of World War II. State your reasons for agreeing or disagreeing with this argument.

5. Professor Weber argues that "the world probably changed no more between the birth of Jesus and 1900 than it has changed from 1900 to the present." State your reasons for agreeing or disagreeing. Instead of discussing the whole of world history, however, confine your discussion to an issue covered in Unit Twenty-Six.

Further Reading

Sources

Kaufmann, Walter, ed. *Existentialism from Dostoevsky to Sartre.* (1956). An excellent collection of writings. A much better introduction to existentialism than most other treatises.

Wagar, W., ed. *Science, Faith, and Man: European Thought Since 1914.* (1968). An excellent collection of documents with good introductions.

Weber, Eugen. *The Western Tradition,* 2nd ed. (1965). "Science and Social Change," pp. 903–938.

Studies

Barber, B. *Science and the Social Order.* (1958). On the interplay of science and social institutions.

Ellul, Jacques. *The Technological Society.* (1964). An attack on the social effects of technology.

Galbraith, John Kenneth. *The New Industrial State.* (1967). Discusses the changes in capitalism under the impact of advanced technology and centralized management.

Heilbronner, Robert G. *An Enquiry into the Human Prospect.* (1974).

Stromberg, Ronald M. *After Everything: Western Intellectual History Since 1945.* (1975).   A sardonic treatment of intellectual fashions.

Answer Key

Timeline
1. 1908.
2. 1911.
3. 1901.
4. 1956.
5. 1903.
6. 1953.
7. 1900.
8. 1954.
9. 1917–1921.
10. 1905.

Map Exercise
1. Italy.
2. France.
3. France.
4. England.
5. Cambridge, England.
6. Denmark.
7. England.

Self-Test

Part I
1. (c) the Germans made the first military use of airplanes.
2. (d) William Morris in England.
3. (a) The invention of the phonograph.
4. (a) By the mid-1950s an effective vaccine had been developed against polio.
5. (d) Watson and Crick.

Part II
1. (d) through improved transportation, which can halt the spread of disease.
2. (a) Woodrow Wilson.
3. (b) Regular postal service.
4. (c) The fact that women now earn as much per capita as men.
5. (b) The use of sulfa drugs.